Author's Note

In the spirit of reconciliation, I acknowledge the traditional custodians of country throughout Australia and their connections to land, sea and community. I pay my respects to their Elders past and present, and extend that respect to all Aboriginal and Torres Strait Islander peoples today.

My Life in Crime

John McKechnie AO KC

Born in Perth in 1950 and educated at Scotch College and UWA, John McKechnie AO KC has spent his adult life in the law – as King's Counsel, Director of Public Prosecutions for seven years, a Supreme Court judge for 16 years, and Corruption and Crime Commissioner 2015–2025.

John has authored legal textbooks and taught legal and judicial practice. He has served on various non-profit boards over the years.

John is a member of the Uniting Church of Australia. An avid sailor, he is an Australian Sailing Race Officer. John is a fellow of the Australian Academy of Law.

In 2024 he was appointed an Officer of the Order of Australia.

John McKechnie AO KC

My Life in Crime

UPSWELL

First published in Australia in 2025
by Upswell Publishing
Perth, Western Australia
upswellpublishing.com

Upswell operates in the city of Perth, on ancient country of the Whadjuk
people of the Noongar nation who remain the spiritual and cultural
custodians of this beautiful land. We acknowledge their continuing
connection to country and express gratitude to elders past and present for
their strength and creativity…Always was, always will be, Aboriginal land.

ISBN: 978-1-7637331-5-2

 A catalogue record for this
book is available from the
National Library of Australia

Cover image: Shot by Thom
Cover design by Chil3, Fremantle
Typeset in Foundry Origin by Lasertype
Printed by McPherson's Printing Group

Upswell Publishing is assisted by the State of Western Australia
through its funding program for arts and culture.

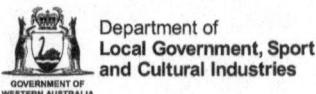 Department of
**Local Government, Sport
and Cultural Industries**

Introduction

Over the years, people have often said to me, 'You should write a book.' In fact, I have. For twenty years I have been a co-author of *Criminal Law in Queensland and Western Australia*, now in its tenth edition. It is a textbook for law students and a steady, though hardly best, seller.

They didn't mean that sort of book, however.

During a social occasion many years ago, Gordon Staples, a well-respected Master of the Supreme Court of Western Australia, mentioned the High Court case of *Presley v Geraghty* (1921) 29 CLR 154. I was fascinated by it, not because it had any great legal significance but because of the unusual facts. In the 1980s I wrote an article about the case for the Law Society of Western Australia's magazine, *Brief*.

Presley v Geraghty remained in my mind over the ensuing decades, and I eventually rewrote the case for a more general audience. It became 'The Tale of the Bootleg Brewer'. Doing this aroused my curiosity, and I began to look for quirky cases from Australia, New Zealand and (latterly) Papua New Guinea. Again, my interest was piqued not by the legal merit or importance of a case but by the interesting situations I discovered.

Reported cases are a rich, though undeveloped source of social history, and the examples I chose to explore offered a glimpse of times past. My research into the background of the cases shone a light on societies that were developing in a hostile environment, often bringing the manners and etiquette of the old countries to a new world. I began to feel that the quirky cases—which I had written up chiefly for my own amusement, and for that of members of the Law Society, as they were being published in *Brief*—might be of interest to a wider audience.

Most cases contained in old law reports are not very interesting today. They are replete with cases about debts, paid and unpaid, company reorganisations, and disputes over property and wills. But in among those mundane accounts of life gone by are tiny gems. My plan was to publish my quirky cases as a collection.

My friend Mario D'Orazio was unconvinced that a book on quirky cases alone was sufficient. He invited me to dinner each month for a home-cooked Italian meal and a bottle of red wine. Each time he would suggest why I needed to explain my choice of cases, and why I could not avoid giving some account of my own experiences in the law. Each time I would push back.

Our biggest battles were over criminal cases I had been engaged in. I did not want to refer to them. Some had been fought in the glare of media attention and so there was already a public record. Many others had never been reported but were of great importance to the participants. What's more, I had stayed away from crime when selecting my quirky cases, feeling that there was little of amusement in the misery of lives upended.

Mario's invitations to dinner kept coming and the red wine kept flowing. Finally, I succumbed. As you read on, therefore, you will find I have led a life in crime. It has been, overall, a fascinating way to observe the human condition in all its rich array. It has brought me face to face with premiers and paupers, with the hopeless and the hapless, with the evil and the angelic. Often stories behind the cases are of violence and heartbreak, betrayal, and lives lost or wasted.

I was a lawyer in Crown service for twenty-three years.[1] As a government lawyer specialising in litigation, I regularly conducted

---

1 In 2003 the West Australian parliament removed reference to 'the Crown' from many statutes, replacing it with 'the State of Western Australia'. This was a development with which I fully agreed. However, as my whole professional life as a lawyer occurred before the change, I have kept references to 'the Crown'. Barristers and lawyers who appear in court are referred to as 'counsel', a term I shall use throughout.

civil trials and appeals and acted as the prosecutor in criminal cases. I have never kept score, but in one capacity or another I must have been involved in hundreds of criminal pleas of guilty, trials before judge and jury, and appeals. I have been counsel or judge in dozens of civil cases.

A prosecutor has a special responsibility as a minister of justice. It is not the role of a prosecutor to press for a conviction at all costs, but to present the case fairly and firmly. A prosecutor neither wins nor loses. Justice is served by the appropriate verdict.

Defence counsel have a more harrowing job. The 'cab rank principle' means that a lawyer practising in criminal law has little option to refuse a client, no matter how heinous the offence or how apparently hopeless the defence. Counsel must do their best and put their own feelings to one side. A criminal defence counsel is sometimes criticised for representing a repellent accused. However, the rule of law depends on the presumption of innocence: the onus is on the prosecution to prove its case. That case must be tested, and doing so is the duty of defence counsel. Unless there are competent counsel on both sides, the scales of justice will tip into injustice.

Criminal lawyers, both prosecutor and defence, learn quickly to set aside their own feelings. All counsel can do is make submissions. The court has no interest in the views of counsel or what counsel believes about the case. Any counsel who says 'I believe ...' to a jury is likely to be reprimanded from the bench. The only opinion that matters is that of the tribunal, whether a magistrate, judge or jury. Lawyers should always be wary of causes. Ron Cannon, an old friend and formidable adversary who was a leading criminal counsel in his day, used to tell clients: 'I fight cases, not causes.'

Somewhat cynically, one of my influential mentors, Paul Seaman, occasionally advised me: 'Only ever believe 10 per cent of what your opponent tells you—and 5 per cent of what your client tells you.' His point was that an advocate should be objective and detached from the cause if they are to give good advice and counsel to their client.

In Part One of this book, I outline my journey to becoming a lawyer and judge. Part Two is a brief introduction to the sources of law in Australia. In Part Three I explain how some cases led to a fundamental change in the criminal law. Part Four, 'A Tapestry of Cases', is a selection of interesting cases, while Part Five is the collection of quirky cases that led to this book. My hope is that the reader will come away enlightened and entertained.

PART ONE
WHY LAW?

My Early Life

I am a second-generation West Australian, born in Perth in 1950. My dad, Alan, an electrical engineer, served in the Royal Australian Electrical and Mechanical Engineers during World War II, rising to the rank of colonel, and was re-establishing himself in civilian life when I came along—the second of two boys. My brother, Ranald, was nine years older, but we were nevertheless close. A few months before I was born, North Korea had invaded South Korea and Australia had joined the war. There was every possibility that my dad, although aged 50, would be recalled to service.

When I was born, the family lived in what is now the fashionable suburb of Wembley, while my father more or less single-handedly built the family home in the leafier suburb of Dalkeith. We moved into the new home in 1952.

Because there were still significant shortages of building supplies, the house's basic structure was limited. Many homes had jerry-built sleepouts over the verandah, often open to the elements. Our sleepout was enclosed with glass louvres, making it more habitable. My brother and I shared the sleepout for many years, sleeping in a bunk bed Dad had made. Naturally, the older brother got the top bunk. Of course, the younger brother was jealous.

The sleeping arrangements changed for a time when I was four. Ranald and a group of friends spent a week of the holidays camping on nearby Garden Island. One day, while exploring the reef off Bauche Beach, Ranald received a sting from a blue-ringed octopus. Within a short time he was having trouble breathing and his muscles were weakening. He was evacuated to the mainland, and I have a memory of standing with Dad as Ranald was wheeled past on a gurney and into an ambulance. He was paralysed for six weeks, confined to the lower bunk. In time he made a complete recovery.

Milk was delivered early each morning by horse and cart. This was more efficient than it sounds, because the horse knew the route and would gently move forward, stopping at the next house while the milkman collected bottles from the cart and kept a running delivery up paths and bypassing thorny rose bushes. Our carbohydrates were delivered each day when a young woman would appear at the back door carrying a wicker basket full of freshly baked bread and rolls. Once a week, a fishmonger steering a Morris Minor with an ice box on the back would drive slowly up and down the street waiting to be hailed.

Dalkeith was and is a village, and from an early age I would roam or ride my bike around its streets, getting up before school to explore. We had an unusual alarm to wake us. A Carmelite monastery was nearby, and every day at 6 am the Angelus bell would sound.

Like thousands of children in the pre-television age, I grew up with fabulous stories. Dad would sit beside my bed each night and either read to me or tell me tales he would invent, which of course featured me as the boy hero. An early and avid reader, I would sometimes wake at 4 am to read the latest Biggles book or the adventures of the Secret Seven. Sometimes I was allowed to stay up until 8 pm to listen to a radio play or serial. Hop Harrigan was a favourite, and for a time I had dreams of becoming a pilot.

I attended Dalkeith Primary School from 1956. Our Year One teacher, Mrs Hicks, would finish lessons most days by reading a chapter from one of Enid Blyton's *Noddy* books. I would work closely with law enforcement in the future, but the first officer I encountered was Mr Plod the policeman.

In those far-off days, there seemed to be few Australian books for young readers. We learned to read from books imported from Britain, the 'Happy Venture' stories of Dick and Dora, dog Nip and cat Fluff.

While reading about their adventures catching the train to Cornwall was of some interest, it had very little relevance to Aussie kids.

We sometimes had visitors to school. Charlie Skehan was a police officer and a famous Perth Football Club member helping to win the 1955 Grand Final. I have always grudgingly admired the unmatched ability of most police forces in managing their public image and reputation. Bad news or criticism are often followed by a good news story that swamps the earlier one. I now realise that choosing Constable Skehan to deliver us a message on bike safety was a masterstroke. All the boys knew him and hung off his every word. He was perhaps an inspiration for one of my classmates, who would go on to be one of the all-time great footballers: VFL champion and Brownlow medallist Graham Moss.

Occasionally a group of fresh-faced, enthusiastic Americans employed by Coca-Cola would arrive to show us how to do tricks with a yo-yo. Didn't help me. My attempts at 'rocking the cradle' always ended in an unmanageable tangle. There was also a woman who would appear once a year to give performances with her trained and costumed poodles. It seemed odd even then.

The one visitor not appreciated was the health caravan. The 1950s was a time of polio. The young were especially vulnerable—until Dr Jonas Salk created a vaccine, which had to be administered in three doses. We would arrive at school in the morning to see the looming presence of the caravan. One by one, classes would be called up. The playground transformed into a line of apprehensive children snaking up the stairs into the darkened interior. Opposite this line was another line of children emerging, rubbing their arms and often crying.

As you entered the darkness of the van, a hefty nurse would grab you, spin you around and hold your arm for the threatened jab. When it was done, you were unceremoniously shoved out the door, arm aching and generally traumatised. A Covid vaccination is nothing in comparison.

Thanks to Dr Salk, our generation was vaccinated, and the scourge of polio removed.

At high school in 1963, we were told one day that we would be vaccinated against polio. Our pleas that we were already vaccinated fell on deaf ears, and we made our way to the quad in dread. But there was no caravan. Instead, a gentle nurse handed out sugar cubes covered in a pink liquid. This was it? No needle? Score. Thank you, Dr Albert Sabin, not only for your polio vaccine but also for the manner of delivery.

*

My childhood was carefree and happy. I learned to swim in the Swan River, which bisects Perth, at a spot known as the Nedlands Baths, now home to an upscale eatery. We holidayed on Rottnest Island, just seventeen kilometres from the coast, then and now a favourite for families. Although Rottnest is horrendously expensive these days, it is still home to the subject of millions of selfies: the quokka, a marsupial that looks like a very small kangaroo.

Later, my family would journey for holidays to the south coast, Nornalup and Walpole, or fight the bluebottle stingers at Siesta Park in Busselton, the gateway to our fabulous wine region, Margaret River. Dad would insist that we set off from home at 4.30 am. Usually, by 7.30 am we would be stuck by the side of the road with a flat tyre or an overheating engine.

My dad and brother had built a dinghy—one of three boats they constructed in our living room, to my patient mother's resignation. We would tow the dinghy when off on holidays and spend hours fishing for herring, whiting and tailor.

My parents worshipped at St Aiden's Presbyterian Church, in the inner-city suburb of Claremont, but this was no deeply reflective religious choice. My father had been born in the Coromandel Valley, South Australia, and grew up in Australia's only palindrome—Glenelg. His father was strong in the Christian Endeavour movement, whose leader was an American, Dr Francis Clark. My grandfather was so enmeshed that he named his second son Alan Francis Clark McKechnie—a cruel trick, one might think, to play on an infant.

My mother, Erica, came from German stock and attended St John's Lutheran Church in Aberdeen Street, Northbridge. She and my father were married there in 1940, one hour after her sister Edna had married Leo Ulbricht, a farmer from Brookton. My father was best man and my mother bridesmaid, then they all swapped places for my parents' wedding. A selfie opportunity verily captured by Uncle Bob's box brownie.

By 1952, St John's was full of my mother's somewhat bossy sisters, so when my father had finished building our house in Dalkeith, they moved churches for a bit of peace. As a result, I made many friends in the busy Sunday school as we confronted existential questions from an early age. Many of which, sixty years on, continue to perplex.

In 1959, Mum went on a slow boat to China—the SS *Anshun*. Many years later, the ship would become famous to lawyers as a leading case on estoppel. While Mum was exploring the wide world for the first time, Dad, Ranald and I drove east.

The bitumen on the Eyre Highway ended one mile out of Norseman and recommenced five miles out of Ceduna. The road, as it still does, traverses the Nullarbor Plain—the Latin name means 'no trees'. It has scenic views as it travels along the escarpment, dips down to the coastal plain at Madura before climbing up again, hundreds of kilometres later, at Eucla. There were also a lot of boring bits for a nine-year-old prone to car sickness. Air conditioning for cars was unknown, at least in my family. There were gates to open and close again.

Dad had a Rover 75, made for the upper classes in England. The back doors opened from the front, not back, to allow easier exit for the chauffeured gentry. But such a configuration was lethal if the door latch failed, as the door immediately blew wide open. The Rover was suitable for English roads and climate but the journey across the harsh Australian desert proved too much, despite our regular stops to boil a billy and replenish the water in the radiator without cracking it. On these frequent occasions I would be sent to walk ahead to cure my car sickness until the Rover, newly hydrated, came steaming into view.

There was a telegraph station at Eucla, built before Federation. Messages would come from Adelaide and be decoded, then be passed to the West Australian side for transmission through Albany. My great-uncle Peter McKechnie was stationed there for some years. After Federation, the telegraph station was no longer necessary; its remains can still be seen today. In Ceduna I met relatives I did not know I had, Uncle Colin and his wife, Lottie. Their two sons were of an age with me.

We stayed with Auntie Beth in Frewville, Adelaide, and Auntie Kath in Russell Lea, Sydney. I met a multitude of second cousins I have never seen again. Among other things during our journey, we drove to the top of Mount Kosciuszko, Australia's highest mountain. Yes, you could do that then.

The return journey was eventful and a portent of things to come on Australia's great connector, the Eyre Highway. Mum had flown to Adelaide to join us, so there were now four in the increasingly frail Rover. Out from Norseman, it finally gave up the ghost and Dad arranged for workers at his firm to tow us the 720 kilometres home to Perth. So our big adventure ended with us sitting in the back of a Holden Ute for two days.

We arrived back in Perth the night the Leaving Certificate results were published in the *West Australian* newspaper. The first edition came hot off the press just after midnight, and there was a long queue in front of Newspaper House in St Georges Terrace. Ranald waited patiently in line and read the results. He had passed only three subjects and therefore failed to matriculate. The journey home was made in silence.

Back in Perth there were long games involving many kids down by the Swan River running through the bamboo groves from the hot pool to Nedlands Yacht Club. I joined the Cub Scouts, and then the Sea Scouts at Pelican Point, where my love of sailing began. I also learned discipline, eventually becoming Troop Leader, Starboard Watch. Pelican Point was and is an ideal position for aquatic activity. During World War II, Catalinas would leave Pelican Point for the 'double sunrise' flight to Ceylon. When I joined the Scouts you could still see traces of the base.

The Swan River is a resting point for migratory birds. Their habitats are now protected. One was a small lagoon at the end of the point. My good friend Perran Ross, now a distinguished marine scientist, would submerge himself and breathe through a straw to get close to the birdlife while I waited on the shore.

Every year, our Scout group would set off at 10 am on Boxing Day, sail down the Swan River, wait for the morning easterly wind and sail to Careening Bay, Garden Island, where we would camp for the week. The theory was sound, the practice different. In all my years, the easterly never developed. Instead, we would battle a stiff south-westerly, tacking endlessly in our ketches to reach the camp, which was ten nautical miles directly upwind of us. Once there, with tents pitched, we passed the week in bliss—swimming, fishing, sailing and collecting abalone from the reefs off Bauche Beach. We took extra care to avoid any blue-ringed octopus.

The first white settlers in Western Australia had wintered on Garden Island, and traces of their occupation could be found near Twiss Jetty, or when snorkelling beneath the ancient pier. It is all gone now. What was once our camp is now part of the naval base HMAS *Stirling*.

My brother, who was always cheerful, soon overcame his disappointment at the exam results. Our neighbour Roland Boyle was a stockbroker with JB Were & Co., and with his help Ranald became a trainee stockbroker. In November 1962, Ranald moved to Melbourne to further his career. Six months later, he was killed when a car travelling at high speed ran into the back of his small Austin 10 in Geelong. He was twenty-two. When the school chaplain came to tell me, I already knew. For years, joy was gone from our home. I still grieve for him.

*

By 1963, when I was to start secondary school, the Presbyterian school in the parish of St Aiden's, Scotch College, was my parents' choice. My five years there were unremarkable. I played hockey, if not very well, and rugby a little better: I was a passable breakaway, gaining my colours. In my final year, 1967, the Scotch College rugby team was undefeated. This was partly due to our fitness.

Scotch was dominated by Aussie rules football, to the extent that no space could be found for a rugby field. Twice a week we would run two miles to Cottesloe rugby field, next to the Sea View golf course. The route took us along the railway line in Curtin Avenue and past a flour mill. The air would be thick with wheat dust and our throats and lungs would clog up for the rest of the run. After training for an hour or more, we would then run back to school. Today, no doubt, this assault on respiratory organs would spark decades of litigation. We were just happy to win games.

I rowed indifferently, preferring to be driven along by the wind than by physical effort—which, some might argue, is an aversion I continue to harbour.

Scotch College had a strong cadet contingent—Navy, Army, Air Force. In Year Ten I joined the Army Cadets, and was promoted in Year 12 to Cadet Underofficer. It was only twenty years since the end of World War II, and less since the Korean War, so some form of military training was prudent. The army was engaged in the Vietnam conflict and some of our instructors had been deployed there. This made our training realistic.

The Army taught its cadets discipline, resilience and self-reliance, especially in the bush. One cadet took the message to heart and ate a snake. We attended camp at Northam and bivouacs at Dwellingup and Collie, learning the rudiments of jungle warfare. Firing live practice mortars was always fraught. The advice given to us—'If the shell lands close by, hit the deck'—seemed somewhat inadequate.

We trained with several weapons of the World War II variety. All cadets were issued a Lee–Enfield .303 rifle, which had a kick like a mule. As I love poetry, I once gave my platoon a lesson on the Lee–Enfield rifle based on Henry Reed's poem 'Naming of Parts'. My target practice using the rifle can be charitably described in one word: woeful. The Bren light machine gun and the Owen machine carbine were easier, and more fun. For all that, I have not fired a weapon since I was twenty.

At Scotch, I tried to overcome my natural shyness by enrolling in public speaking and debating. I would arrive by myself to compete in public speaking competitions, often the sole male. The girls from Iona Presentation College would be surrounded by nuns. Despite this blatant appeal to the Almighty, I nevertheless held my own, winning some prizes. Our debating team was occasionally brilliant, but erratic. Bit by bit, I overcame my constant attack of nerves and gained confidence. It was good training for my later career.

Scotch had a wonderful library. An old Oxonian teacher recommended we read the work of an obscure professor whose fantasy trilogy had been published the decade before. This was my introduction to *The Hobbit* and *The Lord of the Rings*. I was inspired by J.R.R. Tolkien and other writers such as Dylan Thomas, and the library enriched my love of tales. I entered short-story competitions and was published in the school magazine.

It was expected that every boy in my class would go to university. I entertained vague thoughts of medicine or law, but with little idea what was entailed, apart from qualifying for an ambulance badge at Scouts. Dad had the mistaken notion that a career in medicine or law required matriculation in Latin and French, so I spent five years conjugating verbs and trying to remember whether a table was masculine or feminine and why that mattered.

I had no real knowledge of lawyers or what they did when I was growing up. Dad's wide circle of acquaintances did not include many lawyers. Mum was more influential in that regard. She had been a legal secretary at Darbyshire & Gillett, solicitors, in the 1930s and would sometimes tell stories of sharpening pencils for Mr Eric Gillett before his court appearances, always a tense time in the office. Copy documents were created using a letter press to imprint the original on treated paper. Wills were finalised using Mr Darbyshire's signet ring, impressed on red wax as proof of authenticity, and then were locked into a large iron safe.

As a young woman in her twenties, Mum often caught the tram to the Nedlands Park Hotel before walking a mile with her friends to the hot pool situated under the Claremont Old Men's home (later Sunset Hospital). While the girls swam in the pool, young men would sail their skiffs to the adjacent jetty and join the girls or take them out for a jaunt on the river. It was there that Mum met a young law clerk named Colville Parslow, whose story is recounted in 'The Tale of the Lawyer Who Leaped'.

My senior class sat the Leaving Certificate exams in November 1967. By that time, I had been selected for a Rotary Exchange scholarship and was destined to sail by ship to the United States in early January 1968—but only if I had passed my exams. It was a nailbiting time.

The results were published in the *West Australian* in early January. My friends and I got our results together. Remembering my brother's experience and the disappointment that followed, I was too scared to look until one friend, David Rees, took the paper from me, went to 'M' and said, 'There, you have passed.' I had indeed. All seven subjects.

That was a surprise. I had expected to fail Latin, having struggled for five years. My teacher, John Blair, wrote in my final report: 'John tries hard but is a marginal prospect, I fear.' I rarely studied the night before an exam. Usually, I played canasta with my parents. An exception was made that year for Latin. Deeply depressed, I revised by translating the famous opening of Julius Caesar's *Gallic War*: 'All Gaul is divided into three parts ...'

The next day, Dad dropped me off at Winthrop Hall, part of the University of Western Australia, for my final school exam. At 8.50 am the invigilator intoned, 'You may turn over your question paper. You have ten minutes to read through.'

I looked at Question 1: 'Translate into English "*Gallia est omnis divisa in partes tres* ..."' Thank you, God. I passed with a respectable C+ and received a congratulatory note from Mr Blair.

*

In 1968, only the rich travelled by aeroplane; jumbo jets were not yet on the scene. We exchange students, eleven of us, set sail on the SS *Himalaya*, via Durban and Cape Town, to London's Tilbury Docks. After a fortnight in London, we caught the train to Southampton and embarked on the *Queen Elizabeth* for an Atlantic winter crossing to New York. Arriving on a snowy afternoon, I caught the train to Utica, thence with my host family to West Winfield, a small rural community on the Cherry Valley Turnpike in upstate New York.

I went to school across the road in what is now Mt Markham School. Being unworried by exams, I studied different subjects, including the basics of animal husbandry—I milked a cow—and, for some even stranger reason, Latin. During the lengthy summer vacation, I spent six weeks at a Scouts camp in the Adirondack Mountains at Camp Russell, where I taught sailing in lateen-rig canoes on White Lake—a different experience from the sixteen-foot ketches I was used to.

I lived for a time with an attorney, and may have gained from him a rosier notion of being a lawyer than was the reality. Tony Cosentino would leave work by 4.30 pm and play eighteen holes of golf before dinner. This was in summer. In winter, he and his wife, Millie, would become snowbirds and head for Florida to play golf all day long. This was my introduction to a lawyer's life.

Nineteen sixty-eight was an eventful year in the United States. Lyndon Johnson announced that he would not seek a second term as president. First Martin Luther King and then Robert F. Kennedy was assassinated. The Democratic Convention in Chicago was disrupted, and out of the protests came the trial of the Chicago Seven, seen even then as a travesty. I read and admired the exploits of one of the trial counsel, William Kunstler.

The musical *Hair* was first performed that year, and a friend and I caught the bus to New York City to see it off Broadway. He did not return with me. The son of the local Methodist minister, he had no desire to be drafted to Vietnam and so fled to Canada. Many others did likewise. There were riots on campuses protesting the Vietnam War, and barricades at Columbia University and San Francisco State. I went behind the police lines at each.

In September 1968 I took my leave from the Rotary Club at West Winfield and spent three months travelling by Greyhound bus throughout the United States: from Boston to New Orleans, up through New Mexico to Wyoming, across to Salt Lake City and the Grand Canyon, finishing in San Francisco.

In Los Angeles, my Rotarian host family invited me to dinner with General Curtis LeMay, the independent presidential candidate George Wallace's running mate. They came third in a tight race in which the Republican, Richard Nixon, narrowly prevailed over the Democrat, Vice President Hubert Humphrey.

Meeting with the Australian contingent of returning exchange students, we set sail on the RMS *Orsova* in December 1968, arriving in Sydney just before the new year. It was time to decide my future.

Learning the Law

On my return to Perth, with first term rapidly approaching, I settled on law over medicine.

I had developed confidence in public speaking, giving many speeches to Rotary Clubs, schools and community groups. The stories that unfold in a trial are part of the law's attraction. I found the prospect of listening to stories more appealing than memorising the scientific names for the parts of a body. An English County Court judge, Henry Leon, writing under the pen name Henry Cecil, put these words into the mouth of a King's Counsel who left his junior barrister to conduct the trial: 'Tell them the tale, dear boy, just tell them the tale.'

I had won a prize for a short story and enjoyed writing, so I decided to play to my strengths, such as they were. I am clumsy, which was another good reason to avoid medicine. No doubt hundreds of potential patients have lived full lives happily ignorant of what might have been foisted upon them.

There was only one university teaching law—the University of Western Australia. In 1969, its Law School had recently moved into a new building at Crawley that had won an architectural prize. When I later taught there for two years in 1985–86, I became aware of its flaws, but when opened it was an exciting change from the Nissen huts in Pier Street. Under the dean, Professor Douglas Payne, the school had only recently foregone the wearing of robes by undergraduates. The more successful students spent their time in the library between lectures. The rest of us haunted the common room.

The undergraduate degree took four years to complete. It was expected that half the first-year cohort would fail. We did not disappoint. The Australian Army was engaged in the Vietnam War, and a draft conscription, based on birthdays drawn by lottery every six months, was in operation. Deferment depended on satisfactory progress at university. My birthdate was not drawn. I scraped through my first year with four Cs, a pattern repeated annually until my fourth year, when I somehow managed two Bs.

One of the first-year subjects was the law of contract. I was immediately attracted to the stories that lay behind the turgid prose of the judgments. The seminal case known to law students throughout the common law world is the story of Louisa Carlill and her attempts to avoid influenza: the famous case of *Carlill v Carbolic Smoke Ball Co.*

Louisa, who had the good sense to marry a solicitor, purchased one of the company's products. This was a squeeze bladder with a long tube that was inserted into the nose three times a day. The user would then spray phenyl up each nostril. (Sounds disgusting.) The company was so sure of its product that it offered £100 to anyone who caught influenza after using the smoke ball. Fairly brave of what we would now call their marketing department.

After two months, Louisa contracted influenza and, on recovery, sought the £100 reward she said the company was contractually bound to provide. The company's defence was that it was not a bona fide offer, and that anyone could see it was just a bit of puff. In due course, after a legal battle, she recovered her winnings. Louisa Carlill lived another forty years, passing away in 1942 at the age of ninety-six. A cause of her death was influenza.

In tort, the equally famous case of *Donoghue v Stevenson* told of a young lady of impoverished circumstances who, on taking afternoon tea with a friend in the Scottish town of Paisley, allegedly discovered a decomposing snail in her bottle of ginger beer. This was enough to cause her illness. The case is famous because the House of Lords—then Britain's final Court of Appeal—stated the principle of duty of care, now accepted throughout the common law world. A little-known fact, except in Queensland, is that the leading judgment was delivered by Lord Atkin, who was born in Brisbane in 1867.

Even criminal law had its moments. Two sailors, Dudley and Stephens, survived the sinking of the yacht *Mignonette*, in part by killing and eating the cabin boy, poor Richard Parker. (Richard Parker makes a comeback of sorts in Yann Martel's novel *Life of Pi*.) The law had to grapple with the morality of necessity—can a person take a life to save their own?

My fascination with the stories behind the cases has remained with me throughout my legal career.

Our class graduated in 1972. At the end of that year, a federal election was held. The Liberal Party had been in office continually since 1949 and now change was in the air. The Labor Party ran on the slogan 'It's Time' and a promise to withdraw from the war in Vietnam. A lot of my fellow students had been drafted, but their service had been deferred until they had finished their degree. Many highly conservative lawyers of today voted Labor for the only time in their life in 1972. As a leading politician once remarked, in any horse race, always back the horse named 'self-interest'. It is the only one trying hard.

Labor won office and Gough Whitlam became prime minister. Nobody knew it then, but the era of big federal government had begun. The next twenty years would see bitter battles in the High Court as the Commonwealth sought to expand its power and the states fought to oppose it.

Despite an indifferent law degree, I obtained articles at a leading law firm, Jackson, McDonald. A degree of Bachelor of Laws was a prerequisite to practice, but more training was needed. A prospective lawyer was required to spend two years as a legal apprentice known as an articled law clerk. I was bound in articles to David Charters, then a partner of the firm, later a distinguished District Court judge. It was the custom to spend about six months on rotation in different divisions of the firm.

I fell under the gaze of the first and most influential of my many mentors, Paul Seaman. At the time he was preparing to go to the bar and practise solely as a barrister. I think it amused him to have a callow youth to whom he might pass on his knowledge and craft—and, it must be said, an audience for his brilliance. I did only one rotation through the commercial and conveyancing division. Realising perhaps that the young articled clerk was not well suited to the intricacies of conveyancing, Paul encouraged me to be an advocate. It suited my interest in people and the human condition. As Ron Cannon, then a partner, remarked, 'Conveyancers have ice water in their veins.'

Despite the terror I felt at working for him, Paul and I became friends. He indeed did go to the bar and became a Queen's Counsel. In a landmark case in the Court of Disputed Returns, *Bridge v Ridge*, Paul led a future premier, Peter Dowding, in a successful action before Justice Smith on behalf of Ernie Bridge, who had lost an election for the district of Kimberley. Bridge was later elected and served the electorate for twenty years, also becoming Australia's first Aboriginal minister. He became a client of mine, too, as will be seen.

Paul Seaman QC became Master of the Supreme Court and then a judge. When he died at eighty, I gave the eulogy. He was the first of many wise and patient mentors and leaders, without whom, perhaps, I would have remained in a small back room drafting leases.

*

After completing two years as an articled law clerk, in December 1974 I took the oath of office and was admitted as a barrister, solicitor and proctor of the Supreme Court of Western Australia. A proctor was an attorney who gave advice in the admiralty and ecclesiastical courts. It was an ancient profession. In 1875, the *Judicature Act* of Great Britain effectively abolished the office of proctor, folding its duties and title into that of solicitor. One hundred years later, Western Australia was still to receive the memo.

With the ink of my signature on the roll of legal practitioners still drying, I appeared in my first case in early January 1975. My client was charged with being a peeping tom. We were before Magistrate J.B. Anton, an irascible Scot sitting in the Midland Court of Petty Sessions.

As was the custom for one appearing before a judicial officer for the first time, I arranged to see His Worship in chambers a few minutes before court commenced for the morning. I introduced myself, and he spent the next minutes complaining about the lack of repairs to his courthouse and why there seemed to be a plot in Crown Law Department against refurbishment. Since I was not from the Crown Law Department, I took our meeting as an ill omen. So it proved to be. My client was convicted.

Nor did my next defence prove any better. My client was charged with obstructing police by placing a warning sign in front of a speed camera. Driving past the camera repeatedly and grinning at the lens, it must be said, did not help the defence case. Mr Anton—him again—gave my arguments short shrift, convicted my client and gaoled him for three months. It was a monstrous sentence, way out of proportion for the offence.

Jackson, McDonald acted for the Royal Automobile Club (RAC) and many insurance companies. RAC members could obtain free legal advice to do with driving, and representation if they chose to plead guilty or defend a traffic charge. I spent the next eighteen months advising and defending club members who had transgressed the traffic code and appearing in the local court to deal with 'crash bangs', or minor road accidents.

Workers' compensation claims were another source of advocacy. In this way, my contemporaries and I began to learn our craft. Sadly, penalty infringement notices, restrictions on lawyers appearing in some tribunals and the general cost of litigation have greatly reduced opportunities for new advocates to do this today.

Workers' compensation and personal injury cases were occasionally enlivened by the efforts of private investigators. A plaintiff, believed to be malingering, would be discreetly observed and often filmed. An interesting time could be had when, after the plaintiff had given evidence of their significant disability, a film would be shown of the same plaintiff playing tennis with ease and agility. The chair of the Workers' Compensation Board, Newton Mews, did not like these films much and often contrived ways around the evidence. I can't altogether bring myself to say he was wrong. While there were undoubtedly some malingerers, many plaintiffs did genuinely have pain.

Private investigators also made their money with delinquent spouses. Until the reform of matrimonial law, proof of the other party's adultery was often obtained through intrusive means. Some private investigators would observe for hours before catching and photographing a couple caught *in flagrante delicto*—in blazing offence. Leading such evidence in a court felt grubby.

Jackson, McDonald had a big matrimonial practice, and I occasionally appeared for a client who had to prove one of the causes of marital breakdown. The *Matrimonial Causes Act* required proof of one of several possible wrongs: adultery, constructive desertion and cruelty, to name some.

A successful party would obtain an order nisi. This was a provisional order, so as to give an opportunity for reconciliation. After three months the order nisi became absolute—a final order. Only then were the parties divorced. Both parties had to behave themselves, with no hanky-panky for the three-month period, or else the order might be rescinded and they would remain in wedlock.

If a party seeking dissolution of marriage on the grounds of adultery had themselves committed adultery, they would have to file a 'discretion' statement. This was not disclosed to the other side, but at some point during the proceedings the judge would be directed to the sealed envelope on the court file and would read the contents silently. Much consternation ensued on the other side, especially if the statement ran to several pages! If adultery had been proved but the petitioning party had committed adultery as well, then the granting of an order nisi for dissolution was not automatic but depended on the judge exercising a discretion to grant the petition—hence the name. Fortunately, the *Family Law Act* of 1975, the brainchild of federal Attorney-General Lionel Murphy QC, simplified and dignified the process, doing away with the need to prove grounds, other than the irretrievable breakdown of marriage over more than twelve months.

Matrimonial causes were in the Supreme Court's jurisdiction until the Family Court was established. I often attended judge's chambers on interim custody orders, always supported by affidavits of the party seeking custody. Sometimes these would be listed before Justice Virtue.

Sir John Evenden Virtue had been a judge since 1951, had heard it all and was frankly terrifying. He knew my mother but that was no help. A friend of mine, Malcolm Whitely, who had worked as the judge's associate—a form of court secretary—gave me a tip. Always know the names and ages of the children. If you don't, the judge would be very tough on you as he would consider you were not well prepared. Thus armed, I could confidently reply when, inevitably, the judge would murmur, 'What age is the little girl?' Other young lawyers were less fortunate, and I listened while the judge, perhaps to enliven a boring day, relentlessly pursued counsel for all manner of facts or law.

Guided by patient and wise partners of the firm, and by my scary and rewarding relationship with Paul Seaman, I began to understand the importance of facts in a lawsuit. The right facts are far more important than the right law. Paul also introduced me to the red pen. I would submit a draft document to him for approval. Its return would be covered in amendments and comments, always in red pen. I have continued the custom, returning work with suggested emendations in red. My schoolteacher daughter tells me that red is now regarded as too confronting and she makes comments to students in pencil.

Paul Seaman led me as counsel in an industrial accident case in the Full Court (where we won), then in the High Court (where we lost). It involved a tie-down on a truck. Trucks were also the subject of a long trial, recounted later, where we opposed each other. His last trial as a judge took place in Bunbury. Gail Archer and I appeared for the prosecution against Andrew Hodge and Tim Whittingham in a case of alleged sexual assault relying on memories said to have been repressed.

After retirement, Paul continued to edit the 'red book'—the bible of Supreme Court practice and procedure. He lived in the country and would come to Perth once a month to work in the law library and update the red book. He and I would catch up over lunch at a Japanese restaurant, where he would entertain me with the latest cases on practice and procedure—important but dull.

After a year in practice at Jackson, McDonald, I received a brief to defend a youth accused, with his friend, of manslaughter. At that time, I was responsible for the RAC work in the firm. The youth arrived with his parents for a consultation. He chose to put faith in me to defend the charge in the Supreme Court.

There are times when a chance event changes the course of one's life. This was my event. Although unaware at the time, I was about to embark on a life of crime.

My First Supreme Court Trial

The two accused young men were only seventeen. Driving their own cars, they were alleged to be drag racing each other on a winding road in Serpentine on Boxing Day 1975. Eventually one of the two— not my client—lost control of his vehicle on a bend and in the ensuing rollover, one of his young passengers was killed. He was charged with manslaughter. Because it was alleged they were racing, my client was also charged with manslaughter, it being contended by the prosecution that the reckless racing had contributed to the death of the passenger.

The other driver was defended by Brian Singleton, then at the beginning of a long and successful career as a criminal defence lawyer. Brian was a complicated man. He had been charged with conspiracy to defraud as a young lawyer and been acquitted.[2]

The trial took place in 1976 in the Supreme Court No. 2, a courtroom which in due course became my second home as counsel and later as judge.

Court No. 2 dates from the beginning of the twentieth century and is largely unchanged. Intended to be an imposing structure that demonstrates the majesty and power of the law, it is a large and

---

2 Years later, he would be charged again with conspiracy—this time by me. I had to indict him for dealings involving the businessman Laurie Connell. He was again acquitted. Despite that, we remained friends. When starting his address to the jury, before attempting to shred my prosecution case—sometimes with success, it must be said—he would say in respect of me, 'my learned friend, and my good friend too'.

forbidding space, lined with jarrah panelling and brass railings. A judge sits beneath the imperial crest in a position of elevated majesty.

The witness box is also elevated so the jury can see the witness clearly. The dock is reached by an accused person climbing a steep flight of stairs from the cells below. The public is permitted to watch the proceedings from an upper gallery.

The front bar table runs nearly the width of the well of the court. The prosecutor sits closest to the jury, who are crammed together in the jury box along one side wall. Defence counsel sit at the other end of the bar table. There is a second table behind counsel's table where instructing solicitors sit. The tops of the tables are red. They are narrow and can hardly hold the documents and exhibits generated in every case.

The seats resemble ancient school seats of cast iron and red leather, anchored to the floor. This leads to problems for lawyers who, like me, are not tall. I could not reach the bar table to rest my brief and take notes, instead having to hold a pad on my knees. I soon found it easier to memorise the evidence than take notes.

All in all, Court No. 2 was and is a formidable place, best avoided if possible.

The trial was conducted before a judge, Sir John Lavan, and a jury. Sir John was the senior puisne judge, highly respected, gentle of tone. Like Brian Singleton, he was a devout Catholic. He knew my mum.

At 10 am the court orderly rapped three times on the door and the judge, dressed in red robes with a black stole and wearing a horsehair wig, entered the court and took his seat. All in the court, who had risen at the judge's entrance, now resumed their seats. The two accused climbed the long stairs from the cells and looked nervously around. They seemed very young. We had suggested they wear suits, and they had taken the advice. The collars to their white shirts were too large. They could not see members of their family, who were seated upstairs in the gallery.

They were not the only nervous ones. My first Supreme Court jury trial was before a venerable judge and against one of the most formidable prosecutors in Australia, Ron Davies, widely regarded as the best jury advocate of his generation.

There was not much to work with. The two had been racing. Still, a conviction for manslaughter required a jury to be satisfied that the driving was not simply negligent, but so grossly negligent as to amount to a crime against the state. There was an alternative charge of dangerous driving causing death. Was the driving a breach of the proper standards of road users and objectively dangerous to any person? This offence had recently been added to the *Road Traffic Act* and carried a lesser penalty.

The clerk of arraigns—effectively the judge's court secretary—read the indictment. 'How do you plead: guilty or not guilty?'

'Not guilty,' replied each young man.

Next, Ron Davies, quietly spoken and a deadly cross-examiner, announced that he represented the Crown. Brian and I announced that each of us appeared for an accused.

It was time to empanel a jury. Counsel had a list of jurors and their occupations. Each counsel had six challenges. What sort of jury did we want?

There are many myths about the 'right sort of jury'. Some counsel used all their challenges. Ron Cannon, whom I first met when he was a partner at Jackson, McDonald, specialised in crime. He never challenged anyone. On one occasion, Ron Cannon reversed a challenge to a juror made by the accused, who was subsequently convicted. The High Court overturned the conviction, holding that there had been a miscarriage of justice. (The accused was convicted on retrial.) Ron's success rate was as good as that of any defence counsel who routinely used all their challenges.

The jury was selected and the trial began. Ron Davies opened the case for the prosecution by telling them what it was all about. A lectern was available for counsel but Ron did not use it. I took heed. The lectern can be a barrier to communicating directly with the jury, and Ron had the gift of telling his story in a way that was attractive to a jury.

The two cars were allegedly racing on country roads near Serpentine, south of Perth. Someone in the front car threw a bucket of water over the second car, distracting the driver. After some formal evidence, Ron called the other lads who had been in the cars. During the cross-examination of one of the passengers, I suggested that the witness had said something different to his present testimony when giving evidence-in-chief for the prosecution.

Ron Davies objected: 'That's not what the witness said.'

Knees knocking, I stuck to my guns. Justice Lavan sided with the prosecutor and upheld the objection. Brian Singleton said quietly that I was right.

Hours later, the printed transcript arrived: I was correct. Still quaking, I raised the matter with the judge. He brusquely told me to continue my cross-examination and never apologised, but thereafter treated me with more respect. I learned a valuable lesson: don't back down.

After the evidence was given and the witnesses examined and cross-examined under oath, counsel for each side addressed the jury, highlighting the arguments for or against conviction or acquittal. I went first. My client was not driving the fatal car. He had not caused the death. Brian summed up his client's case. He had the knack of speaking with juries in a way that rivalled Ron Davies, who followed, and left no stone unturned.

Justice Lavan summed up the case for the prosecution and defence and directed the jury on the law. He was very fair to everyone. What facts were to be considered proven beyond reasonable doubt were matters for the jury alone, not the judge, who told the jury that. Finally, the jury retired. They were led by the sheriff's officer along a passage to a flight of stairs to the first floor above Court No. 2. This was where they would deliberate on the verdict for as long as necessary.

The Criminal Code once specified that the jury had to be supplied with light and fire because some judges were in the habit of depriving them of such things to hasten a verdict. These days, juries are given all the time they need in comfortable surroundings and supplied with food as necessary.

The judge left the court. The rest of us sat around for what could be a long time. We were joined by a little man with a painted moustache, whom I later got to know well. He was a court watcher, one of a band of folk who attended court because of their interest in watching trials. In time I learned that if he liked a lawyer, he would offer to share one of his cough lozenges. He claimed to be able to tell what the verdict would be. He predicted my client would be convicted. He told us that, in all his years, he had only been wrong once.[3]

Finally, the word was passed around—the jury had reached a verdict. The moment of verdict is always a very tense time for everyone concerned, except possibly the judge. The court is always very quiet, everyone hanging on the foreperson's answers to a series of questions.

The lawyers reassembled, putting their robes and wigs back on. Ron Davies looked relaxed. Brian Singleton was still. He was staring at the door where the jury would enter, trying to discern from their faces what the verdict might be. It was said that if the jury looked at the accused, they were likely to acquit. If they refused to look, they would convict.[4]

The accused were brought up from the cells. Interested members of the public and the family of the victim returned to the gallery. When all was ready, the judge entered and took his seat. The accused were ushered into the dock and remained standing to hear the verdict.

There was complete silence. The jury returned. They looked grim. The clerk of arraigns asked the foreperson of the jury a series of questions in respect of the first accused:

'Members of the jury, are you agreed on your verdict?'

'We are.'

'How say you—is the accused guilty or not guilty of the crime of manslaughter?'

'Not guilty.'

'Is that the verdict of you all?'

---

3 Later, after a few trials where I witnessed his getting the verdict wrong, I still heard him say to counsel and spectators that he had only been wrong once.

4 In my experience of hundreds of jury trials, there was no truth in this.

'Yes.'

A loud sigh came from the gallery, but the proceedings had not yet concluded. There was the alternative charge.

'As to the crime of dangerous driving causing death—is the accused guilty or not guilty?'

'Guilty.'

'Is that the verdict of you all?'

'It is.'

This was repeated for the other accused, with the same answers.

The judge thanked the jury, who made their way from the court. Some stayed to hear what would happen next. The judgment of conviction was entered. Brian and I made a plea in mitigation, an address to the judge of matters to be considered in deciding the proper sentence. My client was 'the accused' no longer. He was now referred to as 'the prisoner'.

We highlighted, for our respective clients, their youth, remorse, prospects and family support.

Justice Lavan was merciful. Easter was approaching, and perhaps he felt the burden that a prison sentence would have on these two young lives. Each was placed on probation for four years, with a similar licence suspension.

I took off my wig, packed up my papers and left the court. My first jury trial was over. I survived: my client was not gaoled. I was exhilarated. I had chosen the right career. There would be many more trials to come, with successes and disappointments.

A lot has changed since 1976. Judges no longer wear red robes but a single black robe. Wigs for judge and counsel have gone. The prosecutor no longer has the last word to the jury. Majority verdicts of ten or more are now available in certain circumstances. Juries are no longer confined together until a verdict is reached but can return home at night.

Despite these changes, Supreme Court No. 2 remains as it has for over a century. And the hush of fear and expectation when the jury returns is still as keen today.

Three weeks after the trial, I received a phone call from Ron Davies inviting me to apply for a job with the Crown Solicitor's Office (now known as the State Solicitor).

Ron was a hugely competent and effective advocate. He and I would work as colleagues for the next twenty years. When the Rothwells conspiracy trial commenced, there was no better choice than Ron Davies QC as lead prosecutor. When I was sitting as judge with a jury he appeared before me prosecuting a drug importation trial on behalf of the Commonwealth. The years had done nothing to dim his photographic attention to detail or his quiet, persuasive manner. It felt strange that the person who had helped change the course of my life, and who had led me in many complex trials, would nevertheless bow and show deference to his former junior counsel. Such is the way of the law.

I was perfectly happy at Jackson, McDonald, but Paul Seaman advised me there would be greater chances for advocacy at the Crown. Moreover, the Crown was offering $2500 more in annual salary—a lot of money for a recently married young solicitor.

On the morning of my job interview, I was sent by a partner of Jackson, McDonald to adjourn by consent a matter in the Mining Warden's Court. This was my introduction to mining law, and I had to ask directions, then take a bus down the Terrace to Mineral House. The actual appearance took thirty seconds.

During my interview that afternoon, one of the panel, Kevin Parker, asked me if I was familiar with mining law. I responded nonchalantly and truthfully that I knew where the Warden's Court was. I later found out that the panel took this as a modest response concealing a deep knowledge of the subject. I was duly hired as a young solicitor, and in time was sent all over the state to appear in Wardens' Courts in matters in which the government had an interest. It even led to an intervention in the High Court.

On one occasion, when acting for the National Parks Authority, I found myself in Marble Bar, reputedly one of the hottest places in Australia. The court adjourned for lunch, and my witness and instructor, Dr Tony Start, suggested we get something to eat from the old general store and then visit the actual marble bar—a colourful jasper outcrop in the middle of the Coongan River. I bought a pie and opened the fridge to select a soft drink. The fridge was full of bottles of methylated spirits. Paying for my lunch, I remarked to the cashier that the bottles must be in the fridge to prevent them exploding in the heat.

She looked at me strangely and said no, that wasn't the reason. 'You wouldn't want to drink them warm, would you?'

The Crown Solicitor's office was divided between solicitors, who advised government departments and did not usually argue cases themselves, and counsel, who did the court work. At an early stage I joined the counsel stream.

Shortly after starting, I gave advice on some minor matter. A few weeks later, I was called in by the Crown Solicitor, Clyde Langoulant, and asked to justify my opinion. I did so, and later found that he had adopted my advice, which was contrary to some government desire. Although politically unpopular, Mr Langoulant's advice was accepted. From this I learned that the boss would stand by his staff.

The incident had another effect. I decided that if I was going to advise government, it was best that I have no political leanings so I could give frank and fearless advice. In fact, this was the credo of the whole of the Crown Solicitor's office.

Constitutional Law and the High Court

I had received an A for a compulsory essay in constitutional law at university. The topic of the essay was 'Does Australia need a bill of rights?'. One night, I'd been in a group having a few drinks with the constitutional law lecturer, during which he had mentioned many reasons why he thought Australia should not have a bill of rights. I duly repeated his arguments in the essay. No wonder he thought it was excellent.

In 1979, Ron Wilson QC was appointed to the High Court after a storied legal career. He was the first West Australian on the court. His appointment left a vacancy as Solicitor General, and in due course the Crown Counsel, Kevin Parker QC, was selected for the role. He had been Ron's constitutional junior counsel, arguing many cases with him on behalf of the state. Kevin's knowledge of constitutional law was profound, aided, as Ron's was, by very knowledgeable professional assistants, all of whom went on to great things in the law.

Ron had a direct way about him. Shortly before his appointment, I received a phone call from him one evening. 'John, Geoffrey Kennedy is retiring from the council of St Columba's University College (now Trinity). We need a lawyer to replace him. That is you.'

I had been junioring Kevin from time to time in the Full Court and High Court, especially in criminal matters, but never considered I would be asked to appear in an important constitutional case. The nearest I had come to a constitutional case, *Payne v Young*, was more about pleadings. The dispute was about inspection fees payable by an abattoir to the government and never got to full trial.

I was working at my desk one day in June 1982 when I was summoned to a conference with the Solicitor General. I arrived to find that the meeting had been going awhile with representatives from Treasury and the Premier's office, and with Kevin's ferociously intelligent associate Mary Ann Yeats, who had been Ron Wilson's associate.

The state of Victoria, seeking to cash in on recent discoveries of oil in Bass Strait, imposed a tax on a pipeline owned by Hematite Petroleum Pty Ltd. It did not purport to tax the oil flowing through the pipeline. That would have been an excise, which states could not impose. The scheme was the brainchild of the Solicitor General for Victoria, Daryl Dawson QC. Hematite sued Victoria in the High Court, claiming the tax was an excise and thus forbidden under Section 90 of the Constitution. By the time the matter was argued in September 1982, Dawson had been appointed to the High Court and therefore recused himself.

Back to the meeting. Mary Ann was in the middle of a detailed exposition of previous cases and why Western Australia should join the action on the side of Victoria. I was completely flummoxed, having no idea what she was talking about, but I was in a room full of important and influential people who obviously did. Kevin noticed my stricken expression because he quietly passed over a copy of the Constitution with his finger pointing out Section 90, which forbids states from raising an excise. He had recognised the limits of my knowledge of constitutional law.

In due course, despite Dawson's ingeniousness, the states lost. The tax was an excise. Intervening on behalf of a state in the 1980s, one became used to losing.

With his profound knowledge of the law and its practical application, Kevin was an enormous influence on my career. When a case required delicate handling, he would often send for me. He was Solicitor-General for fifteen years and a Supreme Court judge for nine, during which time I became a colleague on the bench. Appointed at short notice as a judge of the International Criminal Tribunal for the

Former Yugoslavia, he served for eight years before retiring. He was awarded a Companion of the Order of Australia for his service to law and the Anglican Church.

I continued happily to be junior counsel to Kevin. We argued constitutional cases, criminal appeals and other matters in which the state had an interest.

In the days before videoconferencing allowed counsel to appear remotely, we made many trips to the High Court before and after its move to permanent quarters in Canberra. When in Canberra, preparation for the next day's appearance would somehow always finish in a small upstairs pub in Kingston, where a glass or two of red wine would make even the most tenuous argument seem appealing.

I was the useful idiot. In conferences I would often take a contrary stance to the argument we were considering. Kevin would then try to destroy my argument. If he couldn't, we would realise we had a problem. Constitutional work—indeed, work in the High Court generally—is intense. The landscape is quite likely to change during argument. Principles that had seemed immutable become permeable.

It is a given that all the judges have formidable intellects and deep knowledge. Preparation for a High Court appearance might involve hours or even days discussing the case, trying to find the persuasive argument on behalf of the state. Often, a constitutional case would involve parties outside Western Australia. The *Judiciary Act* allows attorneys-general of the Commonwealth or any state to intervene in any court on a matter that involves the Constitution or its interpretation. During the 1970s and 1980s, there was a judicial expansion of federal power and a corresponding diminution of state power, so we were busy intervening in cases. Often, although we decided not to intervene, this decision was made only after long discussion and argument as to the possible ramifications.

As an example of the range of cases, in 1984 I led Christine Wheeler in a case about abattoirs and slaughterhouses, *Gosford Meats Pty Ltd v New South Wales*. At issue was whether a licence fee imposed by New South Wales was an excise. By majority, the court held that it was an excise, and so was impermissible under section 90 of the Constitution.

Ms Christine Wheeler had been Ron Wilson's professional assistant before heading to London for further study. On her return she did articles at the Crown Solicitor's office and became one of Kevin Parker's trusted constitutional advisers. Quietly spoken, she was incredibly clever. In due course Chris went to the bar and became Queen's Counsel—the first West Australian woman to do so. She completed her public service as a judge of appeal and was awarded an Officer of the Order of Australia.

It was not only constitutional cases that kept me busy in the High Court. There were applications for special leave in criminal cases, and occasionally civil cases were taken to the High Court after an unsuccessful appeal to the Full Court of Western Australia.

Applications for special leave to appeal in criminal cases, for many years, were heard before a bench of five justices, and the court heard argument on the merits of the actual appeal. Because of the workload that imposed on the justices, the *Judiciary Act* was amended to restrict special leave to questions of law of public importance, to resolve differences of opinion in different courts or in the interests of justice. Since the 1990s, advocates for special leave are restricted to twenty minutes each, with a five-minute reply for the applicant. On many occasions, appearing for the prosecution, I would see the Chief Justice's pen begin to write some minutes into the argument. When my time came to respond, I would often be told, 'The court does not need to trouble you, Mr McKechnie.' The response to such a direction is to rise in your seat, bow and sit down. Nothing need be said—sometimes to the disappointment of the junior prosecutor, who had spent hours preparing an argument.

The standard of advocacy in the High Court is very high, and over the years I had a front-row seat to watch the best barristers in Australia interact with the best judicial minds.

The High Court once had a reputation for rudeness and brusqueness. I began appearing in the High Court before Sir Garfield Barwick as Chief Justice, who was followed by Sir Harry Gibbs, Sir Anthony Mason, Sir Gerard Brennan and Murray Gleeson AC. They and other justices were polite and considerate. Their questions were to the point, and many appeared to enjoy an intellectual interchange with counsel. Justice Deane, later Governor-General of Australia, was softly spoken on the few occasions when he did enter the debate. By contrast, Justice McHugh seemed to enjoy the skirmishes with counsel, and it was wise not to take a backward step when discussing a submission with him. Justice Mason said almost nothing from the bench until he became the presiding judge, when he turned quite chatty. Justice Kirby would likely as not come at the problem in a different way, which always made an advocate cautious. Justice Gaudron seemed to smile on me, if not necessarily on my argument.

Kevin was always listened to with respect and could exchange a quip with the best. In 1974 Peter Wilsmore was acquitted of wilful murder on the grounds of unsoundness of mind and detained until Her Majesty's pleasure was known—that is, indefinitely. In 1979 he attempted to enrol as an elector, but his application was denied because of his status as detainee. He challenged the *Electoral Act* as unconstitutional and enlisted Robert (Bob) French, later Chief Justice of the High Court, and constitutional scholar Peter Johnson (PJ) to argue his case. Justice Brinsden ruled against Wilsmore, but the Full Court reversed that decision. A decision was made to seek leave to the Privy Council rather than the High Court.

I was quite looking forward to packing my bags for a trip to London, but it was not to be. The state required leave to appeal, which the Full Court refused. So off to Canberra we went, months out of time. Kevin was magnificent in explaining why we had not gone to the High Court in the first place. The court seemed disposed to grant special leave to appeal, but Justice Mason wanted to know who would pay Mr Wilsmore's costs, which were being disbursed by Legal Aid.

Kevin didn't hesitate. 'If your Honour is winking, I'll nod.'

Special leave was granted and in due course, for the first time, all seven justices travelled to Perth to hear the appeal. We spent an intense few weeks refining the argument. Late in the afternoon before the hearing, having had most of the Crown Solicitor's office engaged in photocopying, I arranged in order on the bar table the legal authorities we would rely on.

That night Kevin stayed up until dawn and completely reworked the argument. When he referred the court to the first case from which he wished to read—completely out of the order I had arranged them—I was flummoxed. We battled through, and in due course the High Court unanimously allowed the state's appeal. The *Electoral Act* was safe.

Next year, PJ thought up another constitutional argument and commenced a case that Chris Wheeler dubbed 'Son of Wilsmore'. Again, we were successful. PJ was a good friend and a legal gadfly who kept us on our toes until his sudden death in 2015. He was a constitutional law lecturer who greeted new students with the slogan 'Here we don't just teach constitutional law, we make it'.

As time passed, Kevin handed more matters to me and others. He was then busy with his responsibilities as a Group Captain in the Air Force and helping draft the *Australia Acts*, which in 1986 made Australia a fully independent nation.

In constitutional matters I could call upon the talents of Kevin's professional assistants, brilliant young lawyers who have gone on to great things, including one Chief Justice, three Appeal Judges, Supreme and District Court judges, senior counsel and a respected professor of political science.

I continued to appear regularly before the High Court until I went to the bench in March 1999.

The Wagyl

The Wagyl is a rainbow serpent. In the Dreamtime, the Wagyl was the giver of life and responsible for sources of fresh water. Among many other creations, the Wagyl is responsible for the Derbal Yerrigan (Swan River) and the Djarlgaroo Beeliar (Canning River). The Wagyl's spirit was said to be in many places, including the wetlands and watercourse known as Korndiny Karla Boodjar (Bennett Brook). The wetlands had long been a spiritual place as well as a rich source of food.

A camp was nearby to Bennett Brook. The leader was Robert Bropho. He regarded himself as a custodian of the lands on behalf of the Noongar people.

In the early 1980s the State Electricity Commission (SEC) wished to lay a pipeline to carry natural gas from the north to the metropolitan area. Extensive consultation took place with interested parties. The Noongar people accepted that the pipeline would have to be laid along the chosen route. The point of difference came when the pipeline reached Korndiny Karla Boodjar.

The SEC was adamant that the pipeline would have to be buried under the brook, it being too risky to allow a high-pressure gas mainline to be exposed. Mr Bropho and other Noongar people were opposed to this. It would disturb the Wagyl, whose spirit slept beneath the water. They had no objection to the pipe crossing the watercourse above the ground for a short distance before resuming its underground route. If the ground was disturbed by tunnelling, the Wagyl might be killed or become angry, with dire consequences for the Noongar people.

In February 1986, while the dispute was continuing, Mr Ernest Francis Bridge, known to all as Ernie Bridge, was appointed Honorary Minister assisting the Minister for Aboriginal Affairs. Following his success in *Bridge v Ridge*, it nevertheless took two elections before he became the member for Kimberley. He would be appointed Minister for Aboriginal Affairs (among other portfolios) in July 1986.

Ernie Bridge was an exceptional person. Born in Halls Creek, a country and western singer and former mayor, he was the first Aboriginal person to hold cabinet rank in Australia. He was effectively acting as the minister, as the incumbent—knowing a hot potato when he saw one—had passed the matter along to his honorary minister.

Bridge had to decide—or, technically, recommend to the minister—whether to grant consent to the excavation of an Aboriginal sacred site under the *Aboriginal Heritage Act*. He was torn between the two options. The SEC officials were steadfast in opposing the aerial option on engineering grounds. On the other hand, the arguments on behalf of the Noongar people were also powerful. Mr Bropho applied to the Supreme Court for an injunction to prevent the excavation.

The plaintiff was represented by R.L. Le Miere, an able barrister, and later a friend and colleague of mine on the Supreme Court. The SEC was represented by R.J. Anderson QC, a formidable advocate and later also a colleague on the court. I appeared for the minister, though in reality my client was Ernie Bridge. After argument, Justice Rowland granted the injunction to prevent work on the excavation under the brook until a full trial. And so the matter headed for a twelve-day contest.

The parties were obdurate. Engineers from both sides had different views about the safety and efficacy of an aerial crossing. An advisor from the SEC suggested that the minister should 'let loose the dogs'. I think he meant me.

I gently reminded the minister that I was here to look after his interests, not those of the SEC. The trial had barely begun when we told the judge we would trouble him no longer. The matter had been settled. The pipeline would be built over the brook, as Mr Bropho had first proposed.

As far as I know, the pipeline remains in place today. A lot of fuss, which, as events showed, could have been reasonably settled at an early stage.

Result: Wagyl 1, state 0.

*

Australians are known as a nation of beer drinkers. Beer means there must be a brewery. In 1857, Frederick Sherwood established the Swan Brewery in the Perth colony. After his death, other interests bought the brewery, and in 1879 it was moved from Sherwood Court in the city to a site by the Swan River beneath Mount Eliza. The brewery expanded the buildings on the site, which since 1838 had been used as a mill, a tannery and accommodation for convicts from England. The brewery continued making beer on the banks of the Swan River until 1966.

Swan Lager was the beer of choice for patriotic Sandgropers. It was not the only brew on offer. As a young boy, I went with Dad in his Rover 75 on several occasions to pick up a kilderkin of non-alcoholic ginger beer to be enjoyed at a Legacy Picnic.

After the beer-making operations were moved, first to the Emu Brewery site and then to Canning Vale, the riverside buildings became more and more dilapidated. Nobody wanted to buy them. They became a chokepoint for traffic on the busy Mounts Bay Road and an eyesore.

Then came the 1980s, the time of the 'four on the floor entrepreneurs' and a risk-taking government that would become known as WA Inc. In 1981, Alan Bond—of whom more later—bought the Swan Brewery, followed two years later by the purchase of Castlemaine Tooheys, putting the Bond Group for a while in control of half the nation's beer supply. All built on debt. Bond disposed of the Swan Brewery site as soon as he could, selling it to Yosse Goldberg, a property developer with links to the government. He in turn sold it to the WA Development Corporation (WADC).

The WADC was created in the early years of the Brian Burke government in 1983. It was to enjoy the freedom of a trading corporation without direction from a minister, while retaining the privileges and immunities of the Crown. The chief immunity was the right not to be bound by certain acts of parliament.

In a deal shrouded by commercial confidentiality, the WADC purchased the Swan Brewery site from Goldberg, and then set about planning to restore the buildings, with a view to making them into offices, apartments and restaurants.

Enter Robert Bropho—again.

In *Bropho v The WADC and Western Australia*, he argued that the site had strong spiritual and cultural significance to the Noongar people and was another place inhabited by the Wagyl. The proposed redevelopment would be in breach of the *Aboriginal Heritage Act*.

The WADC responded that the land on which the brewery was built had been reclaimed from the Swan River many years ago, and the site of spiritual significance was closer to Mount Eliza, in the vicinity of a freshwater spring known as Kennedy's Fountain.

The state argued that the WADC was protected by the doctrine of Crown immunity. The *Aboriginal Heritage Act* did not bind the Crown, and the WADC did not need to comply with the act as it was part of the Crown.

The brewery site was picketed every week for years. The WADC was obdurate. So was Mr Bropho. He and other Noongar people wanted the buildings removed and the land made into a natural reserve. At one point, a motion in parliament succeeded in calling for the buildings to be demolished, but the government ignored it. To complicate matters even further, another group was formed to argue that the buildings were of great heritage value, representing a bygone industrial age, and so should be preserved as is.

Mr Bropho sued the state and the WADC. Chris Wheeler appeared for the state before Master White, who held that the *Aboriginal Heritage Act* did not bind the Crown, and by extension the WADC. Mr Bropho appealed to the Full Court, which dismissed the appeal, accepting Ms Wheeler's persuasive analysis.

Mr Bropho sought leave to appeal to the High Court. It was early 1990. I had recently swapped jobs with Graeme Scott QC to become

Chief Crown Prosecutor. I had also just been appointed Queen's Counsel myself. For whatever reason, it was decided that I should lead Chris Wheeler in the High Court. We split the argument between us, as did the two counsel for Mr Bropho, Greg McIntyre (who had acted for Eddie Mabo) and Dr Stephen Churches.

The main issue was an ancient principle known as Crown immunity. Put simply, the Crown, monarch and government were generally immune from civil action in respect of decisions such as these. Unless the law expressly stated, as many do, that the act is intended to bind the Crown, it is not bound by that law. An issue was whether the immunity extended to governmental bodies that were independent to a degree, specifically the WADC.

We travelled to Canberra in March 1990 to respond to the appeal. The hearing took place in Court No. 1, a cavernous and intimidating space. On one wall hangs a Federation tapestry representing the states and territories. At that time, portraits of the first three judges also adorned the walls, staring down forbiddingly at counsel.

Unlike in many courts, counsel address the High Court from a central podium. The seven judges are ranged in a semicircle, slightly elevated. I have described that podium as the loneliest place in Australia.

The hearing had gone for a day and was well into the morning of the next day when Dr Churches finished his submissions. The court was conscious of time, as one of them was due to fly out that evening.

I approached the lectern and began my argument as to why the WADC was entitled to act as an instrument of the Crown.

I barely got a word in. From the start, each judge took issue with our central propositions, and I was responding to questions, sometimes three at a time, until, recognising what was happening, they smiled and invited me to answer at my own order. After what seemed an eternity but was likely only about thirty minutes, I finished my submissions, gathered my papers from the lectern and sat down.

Chris Wheeler took my place and, after a couple of opening comments, announced that her brief had gone missing. All the judges were instantly on her side, suggesting where she might look. I thought some of them were going to come down from the bench and help. After a time, I examined my papers. There were Chris's detailed notes. Sheepishly, I handed them to her.

'Never trust your leader,' said Justice Brennan with a grin.

Chris Wheeler and I went into the High Court with 400 years of unbroken authority in our favour, including a six–nil decision of the High Court ten years previously and a five–nil decision of the House of Lords four months before. We lost unanimously, seven–nil.

Result: Wagyl 2, state 0.

The lesson was that everything in the High Court might be in flux, as it is the supreme arbiter of the law and can adjust principles to suit modern circumstances if it considers it should do so. Throughout Australia during the 1980s, there had been a rise of semi-government trading bodies, often structured to avoid obligations that corporate law would have imposed, remaining free to trade like a normal company but, when necessary, under the protection of the state. After the stock market crash of 1987, some of these bodies were exposed to significant losses. The decision in *Bropho v The WADC* acted as a corrective to reckless governments or their entities.

I ascribe another possible reason for our loss: my slightly bedraggled appearance.

At that time, we owned a pet rabbit, which had the run of the house. When I was packing my suitcase before leaving home, my robes and wig sat on top. I left the room for a moment, and on my return there was the rabbit, grazing on my wig. There was no time to repair the damage before the hearing began.

Mr Bropho's success in the High Court was a pyrrhic victory. In due course, the premier, Dr Carmen Lawrence, allowed the work on the old brewery site to proceed. Mr Bropho again went to court. His action and, later, his appeal were each dismissed. Today the Old Swan Brewery site is home to corporations, private apartments and high-end restaurants, much as originally envisioned.

As an end note, Mr Bropho's actions in fighting for very strongly held beliefs about the nature of the Wagyl were commendable. Everything else about his life was not. He ran a Swan Valley camp as a fiefdom. Police and social workers were discouraged or prevented from entering. Only in 2001, when a former colleague of mine at the office of the Director of Public Prosecutions, Alistair Hope, as Coroner, handed down a scathing report on a suicide of a young girl in the camp, did the authorities act. Mr Bropho was convicted of multiple child sex offences and died in prison.

Justice Murphy

In August 1985 I represented Western Australia when it intervened in the High Court in an application by Justice Murphy to quash his conviction for attempting to pervert the course of justice. Under the *Judiciary Act*, any attorney-general can intervene in a case that relates to a matter under the Constitution or involving its interpretation.

Lionel Keith Murphy was a polarising figure. He took silk, becoming Queen's Counsel at the age of thirty-eight. As the Attorney-General of Australia in the Whitlam government, he reformed the matrimonial laws, establishing no-fault divorce and setting up the Family Court. He established the Law Reform Commission and the Australian Institute of Criminology.

Appointed to the High Court in 1975, following the death of Sir Douglas Menzies, his judgments were generally short and lacked the intellectual rigour necessary to persuade colleagues to his point of view. He publicly differed with the Chief Justice, Sir Garfield Barwick, over the latter's role in what has become known as 'the Dismissal'—the sacking of Prime Minister Whitlam's government by Governor-General Sir John Kerr.

In July 1985, Murphy was convicted of attempting to pervert the course of justice. He allegedly asked the Chief Magistrate in New South Wales, 'Now, what about my little mate?'—referring to a solicitor who was then charged and before the courts. After conviction, the trial judge reserved certain questions of law for consideration by the High Court. In summary, was a committal proceeding part of the judicial power of the Commonwealth? If not, justice could not have been perverted.

It was decided at the highest levels of government that Western Australia should intervene in the action in support of Justice Murphy. I was deputed to present the state's argument, with Chris Wheeler as my instructing solicitor. No one wanted us there. Our submissions, which Chris had largely prepared and which I thought were very good, were received in silence from the bench and thereafter ignored.

The hearing took place over three days. Court No. 1 in Canberra was packed, mainly with journalists. The arguments about the law were highly technical, and at the end of day one an enterprising journalist lawyer made a handy sum by explaining in lay terms what the arguments were about.

On the third day, after a short adjournment, a unanimous judgment was delivered forthwith, dismissing the contentions and returning the matter to the Court of Appeal in New South Wales.

One side-effect of my appearance was that I developed a friendship with Mary Gaudron QC, then Solicitor-General of New South Wales and later the first female High Court judge. I think she was touched that we had intervened to support her friend Lionel. Although she wouldn't remember, I appeared before her in Sydney when she was Deputy President of the Conciliation and Arbitration Commission in a dispute with the Printers' Union. The hearing was unremarkable but I will never forget the occasion.

I had flown to Sydney the day before, 8 December 1980. Leaving my bags in my hotel room, I went for a walk. Banner headlines from the afternoon newspapers proclaimed, 'John Lennon Killed'. It was true—the famous Beatle had been gunned down outside the Dakota building in New York.

Returning to the Murphy appeal, an oddity was that, apart from the associate who called the matter for hearing, no one, counsel or judge, ever mentioned Murphy's name. Even a judgment of his was referred to by Chief Justice Gibbs as 'a judgment to similar effect'. It reminded me of the trials I had prosecuted when the deceased was an Indigenous person. For cultural reasons, the name of the deceased would not be spoken. It was as if Justice Murphy—who was then a judge of the same High Court—was a phantom.

The New South Wales Court of Appeal allowed the appeal and ordered a retrial, at which Murphy was acquitted.

His troubles were not over. Parliament appointed three retired judges to enquire into whether his conduct amounted to prove misbehaviour under section 72 of the Constitution, justifying his removal from office. He brought an application in the High Court for an injunction to stop the inquiry. His six colleagues dismissed the application. The inquiry never reported.

Lionel Murphy contracted cancer, from which he died on 21 October 1986. Justice Murphy asked penetrating questions of counsel and always followed the debate. He frequently dissented, but unlike, for example, Justice Kirby, he did not bother to write judgments in a way that might gather support from colleagues or history.

Life as a Counsel

I joined the Crown Solicitor's office in 1976, when its clients included the State Government Insurance Office and many government departments including public hospitals. There was a fair amount of personal negligence work, always acting for the defendant, and usually losing.

One of the many attractions of law is learning about other people and their occupations. A lawyer becomes, temporarily, a mini expert on a contested topic. There are personal injuries lawyers who know as much about the structure and mechanics of the human back as any orthopaedic surgeon. I was engaged as junior counsel to Russell Bainton QC in an arbitration over the construction of part of the Derby–Darwin highway. For a time I knew all about the layered construction of a road and the importance of the correct placement of culverts. Our instructing solicitor, John Young, knew even more.

Most matters never get to trial. Advice is given by counsel that a case should be settled as there is no defence. So there was no trial against the country hospital that, scheduling a patient for the amputation of one leg, negligently amputated the other leg. Nor for the hospital when, near the end of an operation for a radical hysterectomy on a young woman, the anaesthetist, looking at the notes, discovered that she should have been undergoing a simple procedure for repair of an anal fissure.

Medical negligence cases were frightening in the 'it could happen to me' way, if one was unfortunate enough to be hospitalised. Scarily, there is even a name for it: iatrogenic injury.

In 1989, with an instructing solicitor, I travelled the world searching for experts to respond to a claim of negligence during a birth. The plaintiff child had been born with cerebral palsy and the question was whether this had been caused by negligence. Our client was the King Edward Memorial Hospital. Our defence was that, statistically, a small number of children were born with cerebral palsy regardless of the birthing procedure. Geoffrey Miller QC acted on behalf of the doctor. It might have been an interesting trial, but we settled it early with Bart Kakulas QC, one of Western Australia's leading personal injury lawyers.

The case left me with a sense of the unfairness of litigation. Two children might have cerebral palsy. One can point to a possible human intervention as a cause; the other cannot. The one might recover millions of dollars for lifetime care; the other gets nothing. There is a strong argument for a New Zealand–style universal insurance that takes the lottery out of negligence litigation.

In the late 1970s I did a stint as a solicitor to the Williams Royal Commission into the drug trade. By that decade the importation and consumption of illicit drugs were becoming major problems. The Commonwealth and the states combined in a Royal Commission headed by a Queensland judge, Sir Edward (Ned) Williams. For the West Australian portion of the Royal Commission, Geoffrey Miller was briefed as junior counsel. I was the instructing solicitor. The Royal Commission caused Australia to modernise its fight against the drug trade.

In 1986 I was seconded as counsel to the National Crime Authority for a period. That work, even now, must remain secret. It gave me early experience of lawyers working with investigators and the constant need to manage the relationship. That experience bore fruit when, as Director of Public Prosecutions, I established the WA Inc Royal Commission taskforce, and later in my work as Corruption and Crime Commissioner. Lawyers and investigators have different skill sets; while they generally work in harmony, they are apt to butt heads on occasion.

The work with the NCA was helpful. Kevin Parker was surprised that I returned when my secondment finished, as he expected I would be drawn to the bright lights of Canberra. However, I was an advocate and missed the cut and thrust of the courtroom.

Over time, I rose through the ranks of the Crown Solicitor's office and eventually I was appointed Crown Counsel in 1988. I had begun appearing regularly in the Full Court or the Court of Criminal Appeal (now merged into the Court of Appeal) since the late 1970s. As Crown Counsel, I was expected to handle the more complex civil appeals and occasional trials. Much of my work still involved prosecuting criminal trials before juries.

Within the first months of my joining the Crown, I had appeared as junior counsel to Geoffrey Miller in a murder trial in Port Hedland. The accused man—Angus—was convicted of wilful murder but successfully appealed. On a retrial, Angus was convicted of manslaughter and the jury made a strong recommendation for mercy.

Geoffrey was a close friend and a fearsome advocate, meticulous in preparation and deadly in cross-examination in the right case. In the Angus trial he was leading counsel. Later I briefed him for the prosecution and regularly appeared against him when he was acting for an accused.

I conducted my first murder trial as sole prosecuting counsel in 1981, and thereafter my life was a steady diet of cruel death, violence, rape, and fraud.

There is little quirkiness or amusement in criminal law. Every crime has a ripple effect, involving many victims. Fraud held special interest. The accused were often intelligent and, usually, superficially friendly and plausible. When interviewing victims prior to their giving evidence, I encountered a lot of anguish from them as to how they could be so stupid. However, it was not stupidity, by and large, but trustfulness that caused them loss.

Of particular note was the tendency to continue to pour money into a venture in the hope that things might change and the money be returned. Witnesses often could not understand how they could continue even though on one level they knew they were being conned. I coined a name for this phenomenon: 'the Kaa effect'. In Rudyard Kipling's *The Jungle Book*, Kaa is a snake that hypnotises the monkeys into walking towards their doom, even though they recognise what is happening.

Taking Silk

'Silk' is a colloquial term lawyers use to denote a barrister who has been appointed Senior Counsel. Senior Counsel wear gowns of silk, whereas all other counsel wear robes of stuff—cotton. Whereas a junior barrister's gown has a fee bag at the back (for a grateful client to reward the argument) and a tassel at the front (for a solicitor to attract the barrister's attention), a silk gown has a flat piece of material at the back, similar to a sailor's suit and for the same reason. The material protects the clothes below from long, greasy hair. The silk's gown has long sleeves that extend from the elbow to the floor.

Nomenclature gets confusing, because all other barristers are known as junior counsel. A barrister may be a senior junior counsel and have years more experience than a junior senior counsel.

A barrister appointed to the ranks of senior counsel without the general approval of the legal profession may be derisively referred to behind their back as a 'rayon'—that is, not a genuine silk.

The office of Senior Counsel is longstanding. At one time a Queen's Counsel would have to seek approval to appear against the Crown in, for example, a criminal defence. The role attaches directly to the monarch, notionally as an adviser. When Queen Elizabeth II passed away and was succeeded by King Charles III, all Queen's Counsels instantly became King's Counsels, courtesy of the *Demise of the Crown Act 1901*.

In 2003 some governments indicated that they would no longer recommend appointments of Queen's Counsel to their state governor.

The judges of the West Australian Supreme Court now appoint barristers to the office of Senior Counsel annually. Senior Counsel—SC—have all the privileges and responsibilities of King's Counsel—KC.

In 1989 it was the custom to wait for an invitation to apply to become 'one of Her Majesty's counsel learned in the law', to give the appointment its full title. Traditionally, and in my case, one was invited to tea with Chief Justice David Malcolm AC and asked, in effect, why hadn't one applied for silk already. The Chief Justice remarked that I had impressed the judges with my ability to concede a poor case.

'Great,' I thought, 'I'm becoming a silk because I am a good loser.'

I was appointed by the Governor of Western Australia on 12 December 1989, almost fifteen years to the day after my admission. To paraphrase a famous barrister, F.E. Smith KC, I had grown, if not wiser, better informed.

Applying for silk was not a given. Chris Steytler AO, later the first President of the Court of Appeal, was invited down for tea and duly put in his application, only to be told, sorry, not ready yet—perhaps next year! He was appointed in due course.

It is the custom for new Senior Counsel to announce their appearance in the High Court at a ceremonial sitting in February each year. In 1990, the five new West Australian silks—Alton Jackson, Len Roberts-Smith, Rob Pringle, Rob O'Connor and I—travelled to Canberra to make our appearance.

The leader of each state bar announces who has been appointed. Then the Chief Justice goes through the list, asking each new silk in turn, 'Do you move?' The silk bows, signalling no. This ancient ritual assigns the order of precedence. In court, a Senior Counsel has precedence over all junior counsel, with the privilege that their case will be called on first.

*

My mother used to say, 'Don't return a favour—pass it on.' During my journey to Senior Counsel, I had many mentors and teachers who unstintingly gave of their talents to assist young lawyers, instilling in us strong ethical boundaries. Following Mum's advice, I have tried to mentor lawyers in turn, and it gives great satisfaction to see where they are now and how far their hard work has carried them.

I taught criminal law at the University of Western Australia for two years, and in 1987 started the first undergraduate practical advocacy course. I moved the course to Murdoch University in 2006 and still teach the subject, which I have also taught at Curtin University and in the United States. Students routinely say it is the most terrifying but also one of the most rewarding subjects. I generally tell them at the commencement of the course that they will be very bad at it. At the end of the course, they will still be bad at it, but not quite so bad. That is because advocacy takes much practice and experience.

On one occasion, trying to be encouraging, I said to a group of neophytes at the end of the course, 'I look forward to seeing you one day at the other end of the bar table.'

A voice from the class responded, 'If I were you, so would I.'

Hundreds of students have completed the intensive practical course, and it gave me great pleasure as a judge when one of them appeared in a case before me. I was often tempted to offer a critique after the conclusion of their cross-examinations but generally resisted.

For many years, with other experienced judges, I presented 'the criminal trial from hell' at the National Judicial Orientation Program, mischievously known as the 'baby judges' school'. The course, run by the National Judicial College of Australia over a week, is designed to help newly appointed judges with aspects of the issues they will encounter for which there is often no clear answer.

In 2003 I was invited to co-author a textbook on criminal law in Queensland and Western Australia with a very talented criminal law academic, Professor Eric Colvin. We have now co-authored seven editions, together with other authors. During all that time, we met face-to-face only once, in Canberra, when we attended the same conference. The wonders of technology. It has been a happy collaboration. Associate Professor Liz Greene is our current third author.

Domestic Violence

My legal career in crime was bookended by domestic violence.

In my first trial as a prosecutor, the Angus trial, the accused fatally stabbed his de facto partner. My last trial as a judge was that of a Muslim man who murdered his wife by stabbing her in front of their children because she was becoming independent. He pleaded not guilty on the grounds of unsoundness of mind, but after a three-day trial without a jury, I found him guilty. He was sentenced to life imprisonment on the morning of my last day as a judge.

In the years between, as prosecutor and judge I had dealt with many stabbings, woundings and deaths in what is called domestic violence. That odd-sounding term is likely to disguise what is serious criminal conduct. After decades of silence about this blight, it is pleasing to see governments and media increasingly acknowledge that there is a major problem and seek solutions.

Some domestic violence is learned behaviour, often perpetrated by weak and cowardly men. Putting issues related to mental illness to one side for the moment, domestic violence originates from a desire to exercise control and a lack of respect for another human being.

Cases involving the deaths of children were the worst. Sometimes children are treated like possessions and are injured or killed for no better reason than if the perpetrator could not have them, no one could. The perpetrators were almost always men.

One man, separated from his wife, took his two children for a ride in his work van on the day of his wife's birthday. Driving along

Gnangara Road, in Perth's north, the van veered in front of a petrol tanker. The two boys strapped into booster seats were unharmed. Their father was terribly injured, and his arm amputated. The family gathered around him in sympathy. Eight weeks later, when the wreck of the van was returned to the business, a search revealed a suicide note, in which he had set out his plans to kill himself and his two boys. Sympathy turned to disgust. Why he strapped his sons into booster seats if he was set on killing them was never explained. He pleaded guilty to attempted murder of his sons and I passed sentence of twelve years' imprisonment.

A form of domestic violence occurred in 1991 when a lodger and his landlady began arguing over which was the national anthem of Scotland. The lodger reckoned on 'Flower of Scotland', written by the Corries and sung at national Scottish football and rugby games. His landlady asserted that the national anthem of Great Britain was 'God Save the Queen'. She might have overlooked a verse that at one time was sung:

> Lord grant that Marshal Wade,
> May by thy mighty aid,
> Victory bring.
> May he sedition hush,
> And like a torrent rush,
> Rebellious Scots to crush,
> God save the King.

At all events, the argument proceeded until, enraged, the lodger strangled the landlady with a scarf. I appeared for the prosecution in Bunbury, where Justice Neville Owen sentenced the lodger to life imprisonment. The case remains in memory as an example of how pointless and trivial a motive for murder may be.

There is no doubt that domestic violence is a scourge, and it is right that governments are waking to the need to implement programs that directly address the issue. Women and children suffer most, and there is a shortage of safe refuges and accommodation.

No matter how perpetrators might seek to control the narrative, domestic violence is never the victim's fault, even if sometimes they are gaslighted to believe that it is. Because of this, women sometimes seek to withdraw valid complaints of domestic violence, leaving police in an invidious position. Without the cooperation of the victim, there may be insufficient evidence to lay a charge. The offender might appeal to the victim's good nature with pleas like 'It will never happen again' or 'I only do it because I love you so much'. These self-serving statements are best ignored.

Domestic violence will not be solved by government. Passing more laws looks as if action is being taken but accomplishes little unless it is backed by effective policing, with appropriate increase in funding. A particular criminogenic characteristic is impulsivity. A person acts without thought of consequences. Counselling for violent offenders whose background has not included impulse control can be effective. It requires resources.

Courts cannot solve crime. Necessarily, the crime has occurred by the time it reaches the court. A court's role in sentencing is about more than providing general deterrence to others or deterrence to the offender. The High Court has held that a court, on behalf of society, has an obligation to vindicate the dignity of each victim of violence and to express the community's disapproval of that offending.

Domestic violence will only be reduced when society rises up against it, stops passively excusing it and provides safe spaces for victims. This is beginning—but as my experience has shown, little changed over nearly half a century.

Chief Crown Prosecutor and DPP

Shortly after I had taken silk, Kevin Parker proposed that I swap roles with Graeme Scott QC, then Chief Crown Prosecutor. Graeme needed a change from the pressures of the role. It was a straight swap: I would move from Crown Counsel to Chief Crown Prosecutor, and Graeme would move the other way. In fact, it was a short move for him because within two years he was appointed a Supreme Court judge.

I had served under three Chief Crown Prosecutors: Michael Murray QC, Ron Davies QC and Graeme Scott QC. Graeme and I were old friends. Graeme had purchased a Holman and Pye designed UFO 34 yacht, *Reverie*. In 1981 I was part of the crew when we sailed in an inaugural race from Fremantle to Bali. We had also sailed several ocean races during the 1980s, and raced on the Swan River most Saturdays.

Although I had done many civil trials as counsel, I had also done criminal trials and appeals. I thoroughly enjoyed civil work, as every brief seemed to contain something new to comprehend. I reflected on whether I wanted to give up arguably the best job in the Crown Law Department.

At that time, asbestosis and mesothelioma cases were beginning to come through the courts. Many defendants were government departments or clients of the state insurer. The cases were usually listed in the expedited list because the plaintiffs were dying. Everything would be under time pressure. Moreover, the nature of the cases meant that the defendants would probably lose most of them. That didn't particularly bother me, but I could see that when I won the odd case, it would be at the expense of someone who was dying. I would not feel very pleased with myself in those circumstances.

I decided to swap. My plan was to do five years and then leave the Crown to practise at the independent bar—but so much for those plans.

*

In the 1980s there was agitation for the creation of an office of the Director of Public Prosecutions (DPP), so that prosecutions could be independent of government pressure. The debate increased when the Attorney-General intervened to discontinue a prosecution against a union official.

As Chief Crown Prosecutor, I had prosecuted a young man who cowardly punched a taxi driver on the Mitchell Freeway. The taxi driver died from a contrecoup injury to the brain. This occurs when the brain bounces around inside the cranium and the injury is often opposite the site of the initial trauma. The accused was charged with murder and convicted of manslaughter by a jury after trial. Justice Franklyn sentenced him to a significant term of imprisonment.

The trial received a lot of publicity and led directly to better treatment for families and others who were victims of crime. During the public debate, I was described by a leading politician as 'a second-rate solicitor'. The case was seen by some as demonstrating the need for a professional dedicated prosecution service under a Director of Public Prosecutions.

Then came the Royal Commission into the Commercial Activities of Government, better known as the WA Inc. Royal Commission. This was long fought for, until eventually Premier Carmen Lawrence succumbed.

The commissioners were three eminent jurists. Justice Geoffrey Kennedy, then in the Supreme Court, was one of the finest, most measured and most polite judges I ever encountered. I had been in awe of him, and his sense of justice. In my youth at Scotch College, he judged the senior school public speaking competition and awarded me first prize. It was my great honour to be his colleague briefly when I joined the Supreme Court from 1999 until his retirement in 2001.

Sitting with him were Sir Ronald Wilson AC QC, then lately retired from the High Court, and the Hon. Peter Brinsden QC, who had recently retired from the Supreme Court, saying in his farewell speech that 'there are more things in life than law'. When I reminded him of this, he just smiled gently and shrugged his shoulders.

Leading counsel assisting the commission were A.J. (Tony) Templeman QC, later a Supreme Court judge and colleague of mine, and Brian Martin QC, later Commonwealth DPP and Chief Justice of the Northern Territory.

As the time drew near for the Royal Commission's report to be delivered, the pressure for a DPP intensified. Various names of eminent lawyers were publicly suggested, so I was surprised and honoured when Attorney-General Joe Berinson QC approached me to take on the role.

I accepted, and in December 1991 I was appointed the first state Director of Public Prosecutions. The separation from the Crown Solicitor's office was not harmonious. I had been given twelve as the maximum number of lawyers I could take across to the DPP. More than that number wanted to transfer.

For a time, relations between the Crown Solicitor, Peter Panegyres, Kevin Parker and I were strained. I contemplated resigning. Fortunately, Michael Murray, by then a Supreme Court judge, gave me sage advice and the DPP commenced with a small number of dedicated prosecutors. When the Liberal government took office a year later, Attorney-General Cheryl Edwardes recognised that the whole purpose of the DPP was to be independent of government and approved the transfer of the remaining lawyers to the DPP. I was lucky to obtain the services of highly capable committed lawyers and paralegals, each of whom had a strong commitment to justice and the rule of law.

In 1987 I had been given a secretary, Kate Black. Kate followed me as I progressed through the Crown and then became my executive secretary when I was DPP. When I joined the Supreme Court, Kate came as my associate, remaining at my side until she retired when I went to the Corruption and Crime Commission. Kate was enormously efficient, fiercely loyal and a good friend. As I discovered much later, Kate and others—including Helen Porter, later Chief Criminal Injuries Assessor, and Libby Woods, Deputy Chief Magistrate—formed an invisible protective barrier around the boss.

When I was at law school, I overheard a lecturer remark that women only went to law school to find a husband. I thought then that was the most sexist remark I had ever heard. It ignited in me a drive to champion the role of women in the law.

I have mentioned some women who were well ahead of their male contemporaries. They chose service in the Crown partly, I think, because there was less discrimination. Peter Panegyres was responsible for a hiring policy that looked solely at ability, not gender. I was a beneficiary of that policy when the DPP commenced and worked with brilliant lawyers such as Shauna Deane and Gail Archer. Both followed in the footsteps of Chris Wheeler, becoming successively Senior Counsel and judge. Shauna served sixteen years in the District Court and Gail is now a judge of the Western Australian Court of Appeal.

Without regard to gender, then, only ability, the office of the DPP forged ahead, applying a newly minted Statement of Prosecution Policy to exclude cases that, for a variety of reasons, should be discontinued. Other cases were taken to court for a jury to determine whether an accused was guilty or not guilty.

A busy nine years followed, including consideration of criminal charges following three Royal Commissions. For a time I was the only silk in the office, so I had to make myself available for the more complex matters, including prosecuting or directing prosecutions of three former premiers, a former deputy premier, other politicians and well-known business identities.

Rothwells Ltd

During my term as DPP, the longest criminal trial in Western Australia's history concluded. It was known as the Rothwells conspiracy trial and arose from the collapse of the merchant bank Rothwells Ltd.

Rothwells Outfitters Ltd was founded in 1897 by Thomas Rothwell OBE as a gentlemen's tailor and haberdasher. Although it later traded as a merchant bank, it never held a banking licence. In the crash of 1987, a rescue package had been put together by the Burke government, but this was not enough to prevent its descent into liquidation a year later.

The affairs of the firm were investigated by Malcolm McCusker QC. The Commissioner for Corporate Affairs had appointed him as an inspector into the Rothwells demise. He developed a competent taskforce of investigators, lawyers and accountants. I appeared for Mr McCusker when one of the Rothwells directors, Tom Hugall, made a late, unsuccessful attempt to prevent Mr McCusker from releasing his report.

As a result of Mr McCusker's work, several criminal prosecutions were initiated. The headquarters of the Rothwells taskforce was a floor of what was then known as Bond Tower, on the corner of St Georges Terrace and William Street, Perth. By this time, the Bond Corporation had collapsed and its links to Rothwells were being uncovered, so the irony did not escape any of us.

Louis Carter had been Rothwells' auditor. He brought successful injunction proceedings before Justice Ipp to remove all the lawyers from the private law firm that had been assisting to prepare the prosecution case as part of the taskforce. Overnight the taskforce went from many lawyers to one. That one was Michael Mischin, later Attorney-General, who was told of his transfer on a Friday and uncomplainingly started work on the taskforce on Monday. Little did he or I know it would be five years before his return.

Fresh from victory before Justice Ipp, a lawyer for Louis Carter approached me with an offer. If I withdrew the charges, Carter would not claim costs. This was audacious, as costs are not awarded against the Crown in criminal cases. With my fingers firmly crossed behind my back, I nonchalantly told the lawyer that we would continue, as I had already replaced the legal team. The three counsel, Ron Davies QC, David Parsons and Gerry Edwards, had not been affected. They laboured on to the end, with Michael as instructing solicitor.

The main accused, Laurence Robert Connell, died during the trial. He was a pugnacious bull of a man whom I had spent years pursuing. We occasionally met on the forecourt of a service station, of all places, when we were both refuelling our cars. On those occasions we would exchange pleasant and polite small talk about football or the weather without animosity.

The trial was originally set to commence while I was still Chief Crown Prosecutor. For several reasons, the trial date kept moving. The judge, my former mentor, Justice Seaman, eventually retired after making many rulings on evidence and applications to adjourn the trial. A new judge, Justice Kerry White, was appointed to take over.

Justice White had done limited criminal work as a judge. Appointed to the District Court, he was shortly moved to the position of Master of the Supreme Court before becoming a Supreme Court judge. He presided over what was to become Western Australia's longest criminal jury trial without blemish. He was courteous and softly spoken, and some advocates took these attributes as a sign of weakness. Big mistake. By observation, I learned an invaluable lesson from him. It is not necessary to argue with counsel as a judge always has the last word. Justice White would listen attentively to yet another adjournment application, reserve his decision and then dismiss the application.

One reason the trial took so long to start was because Connell overreached. He had been charged with rigging a horserace, and was more fearful of that trial because he thought it would be easier for a jury to understand. At the same time, he did not want to go to trial on the Rothwells conspiracy, so he instructed his lawyers to keep applying for adjournments. Some of his co-accused did likewise. Finally, Justice Seaman adjourned the start of the Rothwells trial for such a period that the horseracing trial could be heard in the District Court in the meantime. Connell had outsmarted himself. After a lengthy committal hearing and a trial lasting many months, he was convicted in the horseracing trial of one count of attempting to pervert the course of justice and acquitted of one count of conspiracy to defraud. The Chief Judge of the District Court, Judge Heenan, sentenced Connell to prison for five years.

And so, after many delays and setbacks, the Rothwells conspiracy trial finally commenced. Connell had exhausted his funds and was defending himself, despite the well-known aphorism that a person who defends themselves has a fool for a client.

On 26 February 1996, after the Rothwells trial had been going for some months, Justice White sent the jury home early while he dealt with a submission by Connell to exclude certain evidence.

Shortly after the first rescue of Rothwells following the market crash of 1987, Connell had engaged Jonathan Pope, a partner in accounting firm Price Waterhouse, to give him a report on Rothwells' viability. The records were in a deplorable condition, but Pope was able to conclude that Rothwells' position was terminal, and he so reported to Connell.

Pope was bound by a confidentiality agreement, which Connell now relied on, arguing that Pope could not give evidence. Justice White ruled that the confidentiality agreement did not override the criminal law and Pope could be called by the prosecution the following day.

That night, however, Connell suffered a massive heart attack at his home and could not be revived. At 5 am the next morning I was telephoned with the news by the duty police inspector. At 5.15 am

Commissioner Bob Falconer phoned me, and at 5.30 am the prosecutor, Ron Davies QC, was on the line. I attended court that morning, when Justice White adjourned the trial for some time in view of developments. Connell had died owing creditors nearly $400 million.

The Rothwells conspiracy trial resumed following Connell's death. In all, it lasted for fourteen months. Another co-conspirator, Tom Hugall, also passed away before the trial, but the remaining two accused were convicted by the jury and sentenced by Justice White to imprisonment. I left it to Ron Davies QC to argue against the appeal in the Court of Criminal Appeal. The appeal was dismissed.

Louis Carter, who had been Rothwells' auditor, sought special leave to appeal to the High Court. The High Court will only grant leave if there is a point of general importance or a verdict that is patently wrong. Few applications for leave are granted. I appeared for the prosecution to respond to the application for special leave. The counsel for the applicant was Wayne Martin QC.

Carter's instructing solicitors had copied the transcript and exhibits of the whole trial and appeal. It amounted to approximately forty-eight volumes, which, stacked on the bar table, were a looming presence. There were 12,500 pages of transcript from 176 witnesses, and 15,000 exhibits. The prosecutor's final address had lasted for six weeks.

As we were waiting for the court I remarked to Wayne, 'You are not going to get special leave.'

'Why not?' said Wayne. 'I have a good point.'

'You do,' I replied, 'but the court is going to take one look at the stack of volumes behind you and realise that if they grant special leave, the appeal would take months.'

Whether or not that was the reason, special leave was refused.

Justice Kirby asked how a fourteen-month trial was to be understood in its entirety, and to be absorbed by the court in the space of time the court would normally devote to it. I was not called upon. I was grateful that years of posturing and delay had failed to affect the course of justice.

The Nullarbor Plain

As I have recounted, I first crossed the Nullarbor Plain on the Eyre Highway when I was nine and the bitumen ended just outside Norseman, in the distant eastern goldfields of Western Australia. Many crossings followed. As my great-uncle Peter had been stationed at the telegraph station, we always stopped at Eucla. As I described earlier, the Nullarbor Plain finished off our venerable Rover 75, which gave up the ghost out of Southern Cross.

Sailing has always been my sport of choice. In the 1990s, I was part of a fleet of Windrush catamarans that raced against on the Swan River in summer and winter. Sometimes we would make the trek across the Nullarbor Plain to take part in a national regatta. This would involve leaving in the morning on Boxing Day, towing our boat and meeting with other sailors to form a convoy. Often we would travel by bus, and I would entertain the passengers by reciting Australian bush ballads or encouraging community singing. Well, it passed the time.

In 1998 the national regatta was to be held at Barmera, in South Australia, on Lake Bonney. I took one of my daughters as crew, and we towed our catamaran, which was perhaps aptly named *Stark Ravin Mad*. Other sailors shared the driving with us. We competed creditably but well back in the fleet. It was very hot. On one occasion a dust storm rolled across the lake, capsizing almost all the fleet, including us.

In early January 1999, on our return journey, we suffered a rollover. The accident occurred about 4 pm, fifteen kilometres from Norseman. We were travelling in convoy. I was in the back seat, snoozing after my driving shift. One of our number was driving. She had not, it later transpired, ever towed a trailer before. We had six boats on a trailer, stacked so high that it acted as a kind of sail. There was a fresh wind blowing. Rounding a bend, the wind caught the trailer and caused the trailer to wobble.

The correct technique when this happens is to speed up and bring the trailer back under control. It's advice that sounds good on paper— but in practice you are travelling at 100 kilometres per hour, out of control and you want to go faster?

The driver began to panic. I told her to let the vehicle slowly reduce speed. On no account should she brake. We were swaying all over the road. From the opposite direction, a car and truck appeared. Our driver braked. Over we went, rolling several times until—miraculously—we stopped upside down. No one was injured, although the seconds before my daughter in the front seat answered me were the longest in my life.

We emerged through the back window and surveyed the wreckage. Amazingly, the boats had received only minor damage. The trailer had broken loose at the first roll and finished upright on its wheels.

The approaching car had stopped, and we soon realised it had received significant damage to the front. I went over to see if they were all right. The driver asked if he could help. He offered a thermos of tea, which was accepted all around. I apologised for the state of his vehicle but he said it wasn't our fault. He and his wife had come up from Esperance a week ago while she had a pacemaker fitted at Kalgoorlie Hospital. They were on their way home and had got as far as Boulder when another car went through a stop sign and cleaned them up. After some running repairs to the now damaged front, they set off again—only to be met by the sight of us careening out of control.

I looked across at the wife, who was white-faced, clutching her chest. 'Glad to have road-tested the pacemaker?' I quipped.

As one of our number remarked, after we had walked away uninjured, all that was left was just metal and plastic. We arranged a truck to pick up the car and trailer and returned to Norseman for the night, where I sank two double whiskies in short order.

On the side of the road, I had realised that fate could always upset the best of plans. In its own peculiar way, the curse of the Nullarbor Plain ultimately led me to accepting appointment as a judge.

*

In 2003 there was a national Windrush regatta on Port Phillip Bay, at Sandringham Yacht Club. By then I had been a judge for some years and was looking forward to a break over Christmas. I thought I had plenty of time—the regatta was scheduled for two weeks—but I had misjudged things. I had to be back in Perth to preside over a trial of wilful murder. That meant we would only have a week for racing—long enough to compete in the two-person sloop championship, but not the single-handed super sloop races. We would only be in Melbourne for just a week.

Nevertheless, we decided to go. We drove 7000 kilometres in all, for a week of sailing. I took one daughter as crew and enlisted an older daughter as co-driver.

Coming out of Penong on the homeward journey, we spied a willy-willy heading to cross the road. 'Don't drive into that,' I shouted to my daughter.

She drove into it.

The car shook violently and the boat nearly took off. Fortunately, it passed on in seconds. All I could think of was Dorothy and *The Wizard of Oz*. That and my earlier experience.

Shakily, my daughter eased the car to a stop.

'Why did you drive through it?' I fumed. 'I urged you not to!'

'Not to!' she replied. 'You said, "Drive though that." I wanted to stop!'

It was my fault. Apologies all round, and off we drove, with me wondering whether the Eyre Highway was secretly cursed against me.

The Supreme Court

I was reappointed as DPP at the end of 1996 for a further five-year term. I decided that, on completion of that term, I would go to the independent bar as a barrister and see what would happen.

In August 1998, Geoffrey Miller QC accepted an appointment to the Supreme Court. When I rang with congratulations, I reminded him of a conversation we'd had on one of our 'picnic' cases, when he had said how content he was and that judicial life was not attractive to him. He replied that he had felt that at the time, but in the past month he had grown weary of life at the bar and the invitation was welcome. He went on to serve for eleven years, including as a Judge of Appeal, only retiring in 2009 due to ill health. He was a formidable opponent, a wise colleague and a good friend.

In late October 1998 I was approached by Bob Meadows QC, the Solicitor-General of Western Australia, to replace the recently retired Justice Terry Walsh on the Supreme Court. I declined. I still had things to do as DPP, although I remembered the words of Cheryl Edwardes, when she was Attorney-General and had broached the subject years earlier: 'Always leave something for the next person to do.'

Fittingly, perhaps, it was by the side of the road—not to Damascus but to Southern Cross—that I had an epiphany in January 1999. Plans for an ordered life are fragile.

Bob Meadows rang again in early February. He began by saying, 'I know what your answer will be, but—'

I interrupted him and said I would love to take the appointment.

It is a tremendous honour to be appointed a Supreme Court judge. You are entrusted with decisions that will change lives and prosperities. Any lawyer worth their salt should aspire to judicial office. In whatever capacity—magistrate, District or Supreme Court judge, Appeal or High Court judge—a judicial officer exercises the power of the state. Counsel make submissions. They do not decide things. Judicial officers deliver binding judgments. In the civil jurisdiction, a judge declares and vindicates rights. In the criminal jurisdiction, a judge presides over trials that will have a lasting impact on individuals and imposes sentences that must be appropriate and fair. Very few judgments reach the Court of Appeal for possible correction, so the judge is generally the first and final adjudicator. Being a judge is an awesome responsibility.

On 4 March 1999 I relinquished the office of Director of Public Prosecutions to become a judge of the Supreme Court. I would wander into court and stand in my accustomed place at the prosecutor's position no more. Instead, I would enter onto the bench while the court orderly commanded: 'All rise. Those who have business before this Honourable court shall draw nigh, give their attendance and they shall be heard.' All in court would solemnly bow in my direction, as I had once bowed in the direction of the presiding judge.

The custom of bowing to the court is, like many rituals, shrouded in mystery. After those in the court bow, the judge in turn bows to the court in acknowledgment. Some assert that bowing began in ancient Phoenician times as a mark of respect. Others trace its origins to 1399 in England. This belief is related to the coat of arms under which the judicial officer sits. The bow is not directed to the judge but to the institution the judge represents: the third arm of government known as 'the Judicature'.

In most modern courts in Australia, the judicial officer sits beneath an official Commonwealth or state crest. However, in Court Nos 1, 2 and 3 of the old Supreme Court building in St Georges Terrace, Perth, the judge sits beneath the coat of arms of the monarch of Great Britain. The historical anachronism, like the uncomfortable chairs and narrow bar table, is because all are heritage-listed. I tried to get the coat of arms changed, but in vain.

I would serve for sixteen years as a judge, trying a variety of civil cases and presiding over many criminal trials, often in Court No. 2, where I had first appeared as a nervous young defence lawyer so many years before. In all those years, I never once yearned to return to legal practice. I had enjoyed my years as an advocate and as DPP, but I had moved on.

Life as a Judge

My last few months as a judge were typical of the workload for a primary judge in the general division. While these days judges tend to specialise—perhaps in crime, perhaps in commercial cases—a judge is expected, if necessary, to turn their hand to any part of the court's jurisdiction.

However, a degree of specialisation is important. One judge may be well equipped to deal with a lengthy commercial dispute between large ASX-listed companies. Another may be expert at conducting a long jury trial with multiple accused. Court of Appeal judges are expected to deal with appeals from all parts of the jurisdiction.

It may surprise some readers to learn that very few cases, whether civil or criminal, ever come to trial. Most criminal cases are resolved by a plea of guilty. While the judge must still pass sentence, a trial is avoided. Accused are encouraged to enter an early plea of guilty by a provision in the *Sentencing Act* that provides for a discount on sentence for an early plea. There are similar provisions in other states. During the Covid pandemic and continuing, many criminal trials were heard by a judge sitting without a jury.

Civil writs, as the originating process is often known, are filed in their thousands; in most cases the defendant will not contest the claim. Those matters that proceed are required to undergo mediation, sometimes on multiple occasions. Many cases settle in some form after mediation. Professor Jim Klein, a US academic who visited Perth while

I was teaching at the University of Western Australia, would often say that only bad cases reach court; good cases settle.

If a civil matter has proceeded to a full trial, a judgment must be prepared and delivered. Sometimes a judge can do this at the conclusion of the hearing and will deliver an oral judgment then and there. This is known as an *ex tempore* judgment. More often a judge will adjourn the trial until they have written a judgment. This is known as reserving a decision. Sometimes, in law reports that set out that the dates on which a case was heard, the publisher will note 'cav'. This is short for '*curia advisari vult*', meaning 'the court wishes to advise itself'. It is a fancy way of a judge saying that a decision will be reserved.

Most judges carry a backlog of decisions. It is generally not possible to build in time for writing immediately following a trial. Sometimes a week out of court in which a judge plans to write a judgment is lost because an urgent application for an injunction has been made and must be listed before any judge who is available.

A jury trial, on the other hand, requires a judge to keep pace with the evidence and to sum up and direct the jury immediately after counsels' addresses are complete. The judge's work is all completed within the parameters of the trial and there is no need for a reserve decision.

Timeliness in delivering judgment is important. The parties, known as litigants, obviously want a decision as soon as possible. Well, at least one party does. But timeliness is not the only yardstick. Civil and criminal cases that reach the Supreme Court for trial are usually difficult and require contemplation to arrive at a correct and just result. Civil cases may cost the losing party millions of dollars.

The Supreme Court, in its criminal jurisdiction, deals with homicides, complex frauds, trafficking in narcotics, and armed robberies. Imposing a sentence on an offender requires a judge to weigh all manner of factors as to the appropriate disposition in each case. While a judge may prepare sentencing remarks, in keeping with the oral tradition of criminal law, a sentence is always delivered in open court. Although some sentences may be handed down through a video link with an offender in prison, in nearly all cases the sentence is delivered in court, face to face, with the offender standing to receive the sentence of the court.

Despite what the tabloids might say, this is never a mechanical exercise. A judge must consider whether deterrence is appropriate. The sentence must be consistent with the range of sentences imposed in similar cases. Imprisonment is the sentence of last resort. Has that stage been reached? What matters aggravate the crime, making it more serious than others of the same type? What matters are in the offender's favour?

The interests of the victim of the crime must also be considered. These are often made known to the judge through a victim impact statement, either in writing or delivered in court, so that the offender may understand the effect the crime has had on another citizen.

Professor Jim Raymond, an American teacher in a course for judges run by the National Judicial College of Australia, would tell his judicial students that, if asked their profession, they could honestly answer 'writer'. It is true for all judges who sit in the civil division.

A judge will analyse the case and write a judgment, which will be delivered to the parties and published on the court's website. It may be further published in an authorised law report. During my life as a judge, I authored or co-authored (in the Full Court) over 750 judgments. Other judges have delivered many more. When well written, a judgment can bring the parties to life and apply the law to the facts in a way that any member of the community can understand.

In preparing a judgment, a judge will start with the pleadings. These are formal documents that set out the plaintiff's claim in detail and specify what relief the plaintiff is seeking—damages, a declaration, an injunction? The pleadings also contain the detailed defence to the plaintiff's claim, and sometimes a counterclaim by the defendant against the plaintiff.

The judge will refresh their memory from detailed notes kept during the trial. All trials are now recorded, and the judge will read the transcripts of witnesses' evidence. There may be thousands of documents tendered as exhibits. Counsel for the parties will refer to legal principles and cases in support of their argument, and the judge will analyse them to reach a conclusion that fits the facts with the law to achieve a just result.

In the criminal division, where I sat frequently as a judge, there are fewer written judgments unless a trial before a judge alone has been ordered. The criminal jurisdiction remains an oral tradition. A judge presides over a trial, making rulings on points of law, and directing the jury before it retires to consider its verdict.

In my final months as a Supreme Court judge, I delivered judgment in a lengthy trial for a claim of negligence brought by an academic against Curtin University. He claimed that the university allowed him to be bullied over a period of years and took other actions that affected his mental health. The trial was completed in July 2014, but I told the parties I would not get to the judgment until 2015. The court was particularly busy and lacked its full complement of judges.

In between other cases, I wrote the judgment from late December 2014, delivering a 185-page judgment on 27 February 2015. I did not uphold the plaintiff's case and entered judgment for Curtin University. Writing the judgment involved late nights and the occasional ruined weekend (I did not allow weekend work to affect my sailing). An appeal against my judgment was dismissed.

I also delivered judgments on an appeal from a magistrate's decision, on a question of the intention of a testatrix in a will, on a dispute between a bank and a guarantor (an appeal was dismissed), on a review order challenging a magistrate's decision under the *Planning and Development Act*, on several contested applications for bail, on an appeal over the size of a fine for an assault by a police officer, and on applications under the *Dangerous Sexual Offenders Act* (now known as the *High Risk Offenders Act*).

As well, I presided over several criminal trials and sentencing days. The trials included that of a seventeen-year-old who had thrown a slab of paving at a stranger and killed him, and of a woman who fatally stabbed her partner while defending herself against a drunken attack. In sentencing her to imprisonment for three years, I noted that domestic violence is an intractable problem in the Aboriginal community. Sadly, I had dealt with many domestic violence cases from remote communities over the years.

My last trial was without a jury and involved a defence of insanity. A husband had stabbed his wife to death in front of their children, one of whom had been injured while defending his mother. A neighbour summoned by one of the children disarmed and restrained the husband until police arrived. The neighbour later received an award for bravery. I heard evidence from the children of the marriage who had intervened to try and save their mother. They were remarkable witnesses. The young women each wore a hijab.

There is debate and controversy within judicial circles as to whether the wearing of head or face covering should be permitted. As part of a National Judicial College course, I asked the judicial participants whether you could assess the credibility of a witness by their eyes. Could looking into another's eyes give an insight into truth? Each judge agreed, after discussion, that you could not tell if a witness was truthful or lying by looking at their eyes. It would be a false guide.

Well, I continued, you would not then have a problem with a witness who chose to wear sunglasses in court. Each judge indignantly rejected the proposal. 'You must be able to see a witness's eyes when they are giving evidence,' they said. Many judges insist that a Muslim woman giving evidence must do so with her head uncovered.

My practice, which I followed in the present case, was to allow a witness to dress as they wished. The presence or absence of a head covering was of no assistance in determining the reliability of the evidence. Besides, it is a trifle hypocritical to comment on another's head dress when you are part of a profession that for centuries adhered to the notion that justice could only be achieved if the main participants put a mop of horsehair over their heads.

The trial lasted three days and I spent the weekend preparing my judgment. The factual circumstances were not contested, and the issue was between the evidence of two psychiatrists. They were both eminent and persuasive. One was of the opinion that the accused was of unsound mind at the time. The other had a contrary opinion.

Some background on the law on insanity, which has its origins in nineteenth-century Britain.

Daniel M'Naghten was born in 1813, the son of a Glasgow woodturner. As a youth, he tried acting for a time before becoming a woodturner himself. By the age of thirty, he was beset by delusions involving the Tory Party, the Pope and a conspiracy between them to persecute him. In late 1842, he travelled to London and for a time haunted the streets around Parliament. He decided that, to prevent his persecution by the Tories, he would assassinate their leader, the prime minister, Sir Robert Peel.

On the afternoon of 20 January 1843, M'Naghten followed a man whom he believed was Peel. Near the Horse Guards Parade, he struck, shooting his victim in the back. The man he shot was not Peel but his private secretary, Edward Drummond, who died of his wounds five days later.

At M'Naghten's trial for wilful murder, evidence was given about his delusions and the jury returned a verdict of guilty but insane. Under the *Criminal Lunatics Act*, Chief Justice Tindal ordered that M'Naghten be held in a mental hospital until Her Majesty's pleasure was known. He died twenty-two years later at the age of fifty-two.

Her Majesty Queen Victoria was not amused. As a result, an unusual course was followed. The House of Lords summoned the judges before them and asked their opinion on five questions. The answers established what became known as the M'Naghten rules. They are enacted as part of the Queensland and Western Australian Criminal Code and are also applied throughout Australia.

Section 26 of the Criminal Code provides that a person is presumed to be sane unless the contrary is proved. This means that the prosecution does not have to prove that an accused is sane. It is one of the rare occasions where the accused has the burden of proving a fact, albeit on the balance of probabilities, not beyond reasonable doubt. An accused must establish that it is more probable than not that they were suffering some mental impairment and were deprived of one or more of three capacities:

- The capacity to understand what they were doing
- The capacity to control their actions
- The capacity to know that they ought not do the act.

If one of these is established on the balance of probabilities, then the accused is entitled to be acquitted on the grounds of unsoundness of mind.

After spending the weekend reviewing the evidence in this particular case, I decided that the accused had not discharged the burden of proof that he was of unsound mind, and therefore he was presumed to be sane. I found the offender guilty of murder and imposed sentence about three hours before the Supreme Court sat for my formal farewell.

The Corruption and Crime Commission

The Commonwealth, states and territories all have some form of anti-corruption commission. The first was established in New South Wales in 1988. The latest, the National Anti-Corruption Commission, in 2022. The West Australian Corruption and Crime Commission (CCC) was established in 2004, following a Royal Commission into the WA Police Force.

Anti-corruption commissions have similarities to royal commissions. They have powers of compulsion to seize documents and devices containing data. Witnesses may be compelled to answer questions even at the risk of self-incrimination, though evidence so provided generally cannot be used in any subsequent criminal trial. Both anti-corruption commissions and royal commissions can form opinions of misconduct and publish reports. The commissioners of each are likely to be judges, retired judges or senior members of the bar.

The principal difference between an anti-corruption commission and a royal commission is in the purpose of each. A government will set up a royal commission to examine a specific matter. A royal commission will usually be required to report by a set date. An anti-corruption commission, by contrast, is a standing commission. It chooses what it will investigate through the receipt of allegations of misconduct, or from its own knowledge and experience. It has no timeframe and can choose whether to publish a report.

Both commissions utilise investigative capabilities such as law enforcement. These include obtaining warrants for telephone intercepts and data retention.

Like commissions all over Australia, the West Australian CCC has a serious misconduct jurisdiction over public officers, including ministers and members of parliament. Misconduct is defined to include bribery, corruption and abuse of office. The CCC is also a police misconduct commission; its jurisdiction there is wider, extending to wrongful acts that could lead to dismissal. The CCC holds many secrets, and officers are required to take an oath of confidentiality.

In 2011 I was telephoned by Attorney-General of Western Australia, Christian Porter, to sound out my interest in becoming Corruption and Crime Commissioner. I was on holiday in Melk, Austria, at the time. I ended the call by inviting the Attorney-General to imagine a barge pole stretching from Perth to Melk. 'That still wouldn't be long enough for me to touch the job,' I said.

It is no secret that the CCC in Western Australia has been in the spotlight for the wrong reasons on occasions. No commissioner had ever completed a full five-year term. There were times when acting commissioners, who had other full-time jobs, were forced to run the CCC for more than twelve months.

In 2013, a scandal was uncovered that led to allegations of criminal conduct by some members of the CCC surveillance squad. Police were called in to investigate. The Commissioner retired, and Acting Commissioners Chris Shanahan SC (now Chief Justice of Tasmania) and Neil Douglas, both busy lawyers, were left to clean up the mess. They did a fine job. By 2014 there were still differences of opinion between the CCC and the Parliamentary Inspector, Michael Murray, once my boss and colleague, by now a close friend. The differences spilled into the media. I watched the goings-on at the CCC with detachment and mild interest but was too busy to pay much attention.

At the end of 2014, I turned sixty-four and reviewed my future. I decided I would remain a judge until the age of seventy, when judges are required to retire.

Despite the efforts of the two Acting Commissioners, there was still tension at the CCC with both the Parliamentary Inspector and the Commissioner of Police. One Saturday morning in November 2014, I read in the newspaper with dismay the continuing arguments and lack of morale. After reflecting for the rest of the weekend, I decided I might have something to contribute.

On Monday morning I telephoned the Chief Justice, the Hon. Wayne Martin AC to advise him of my intention to put my name forward. He was immediately enthusiastic. I knew why. He was chair of the nominating committee, which was obliged under the *Corruption, Crime and Misconduct Act* to nominate three names to the Premier. Both Wayne and I had spent the past year trying to persuade sitting and former members of the Supreme and District courts to apply. We were universally knocked back.

I'd found that, after concluding my sales pitch, I was usually met with a comment that if the job was so good, why didn't I take it.

After I discussed the role with Wayne for a time, there was a long pause in the conversation. Finally, he said, 'We'll miss you.'

'That pause was a bit too long, Wayne,' I laughed.

Wayne and I had known each other as habitués of the student common room at law school and had occasionally opposed each other in cases over the intervening years. He had also appeared in front of me from time to time until 2006, when he was the natural and obvious choice to replace the Hon. David Malcolm AC as Chief Justice.

I worked closely with Wayne when I succeeded Michael Murray as senior judge of the general division in 2012. This position is known as the senior puisne judge. The word 'puisne' is pronounced 'puny' and literally means 'later born'. All judges are puisne judges—that is, of lesser rank than the chief justice.

Judicial welcomes and farewells have one thing in common: everyone says nice things about the judge. It only happens at these two events. For the time in between, there are few bouquets and many brickbats.

At 4.15 pm on Wednesday, 23 April 2015, I was honoured to be joined on the bench for my farewell by the Chief Justice of the High

Court, Robert French AC, as well as Chief Justice Wayne Martin and my judicial colleagues. In the well of the court were many retired judges and friends, including Kevin Parker, Michael Murray, Graeme Scott and others from my days as DPP. It was a humbling and nostalgic moment.

With some amusement, Attorney-General Michael Mischin informed me that my appointment as Corruption and Crime Commissioner had been approved on April Fool's Day—1 April. He thought that was apt! On Tuesday, 28 April 2015 I took the oath of office before the Chief Justice and the next stage of my life began.

*

I have served as Corruption and Crime Commissioner since then, apart from a fourteen-month hiatus that coincided with the Covid pandemic. This was because the Parliamentary Joint Standing Committee on the CCC was unable to achieve the statutory requirement of majority and bipartisan majority for support for my reappointment to a second term.

Premier Mark McGowan made a campaign pledge to reinstate me if his Labor Party won the election in March 2021. Labor duly won and the Premier kept his word. And so, in May 2021, after vigorous debate in both houses, parliament passed an amendment to the *Corruption, Crime and Misconduct Act* stating that John Roderick McKechnie was reappointed Commissioner for a period of five years commencing the 28 June 2021.

Early on that Monday morning, accompanied by Acting Commissioner Scott Ellis, who had capably run the CCC for the fourteen months of my absence despite having a busy practice at the bar, I attended before the Chief Justice to take the oath of office once again. This time it was Chief Justice Peter Quinlan, and instead of the old Supreme Court we were ushered into his chambers in the new David Malcolm Justice Centre.

TAX INVOICE
INOKUNIYA BOOK STORES OF AUSTRALIA
THE GALLERIES
LEVEL 2, 500 GEORGE STREET
SYDNEY NSW 2000
TEL: (02) 9262-7996
ABN 78 072 525 949

Ship: 0000001302000387336
Staff: Mikayla   Trans: 396124
Terminal: POS 02
Date: 03/06/25 3:24

Description	Amount
Barcode: 2111763733154 My Life in Crime : a	32.98
Total A$	32.98
EFTPOS	-32.98
Number of Items:	1

GST%	Net Amt	GST	Amount
	29.98	3.00	32.98

F1302000396124

The Chief Justice, who had also been one of Kevin Parker's many proteges, is a devout Catholic. I was therefore surprised when he showed us his recent acquisition, a rare Martin Luther Bible, written in German. I had been baptised into the Lutheran faith at St John's Church in Newcastle Street by Pastor Graebner. The Chief Justice allowed me to swear the oath on that Bible. I took the oath of office with my right hand on the Luther Bible, open at the passage from Micah 6 that has guided me all my life: 'Do justice, love mercy, walk humbly with your God.'

A judge's life is a solitary one. As sole decision-maker, a judge must largely work alone and strive to arrive at a fair and just conclusion. Apart from some general suggestions from other judges on occasions when that may be appropriate, only the judge has responsibility for the decision.

Now I was back in a collegiate environment. As Commissioner, I returned to working alongside talented men and women who are investigators, analysts, lawyers and assessors, all of whom have a mission to call out corruption that affects the body politic.

Corruption in the World

During my time, the CCC has published many reports and exposed corruption and misconduct, sometimes on a large scale involving many people. These are some observations made after my time as Commissioner.

Corruption flourishes, sorry to say. According to Transparency International, $1 trillion is paid in bribes each year. An estimated and staggering $2.6 trillion—equivalent to 5 per cent of global GDP—is stolen every year by criminals and corrupt officials.

Australia is a party to the United Nations' Sustainable Development Goals. Goal 16 relates to 'Peace, Justice and Strong Institutions', and subgoal 16.5 is to 'substantially reduce corruption and bribery in all their forms'. The UN and the signatories to the treaty are making good progress on some goals, while lagging on others. The reduction of corruption and bribery, sadly, is one of those others.

The 1Malaysia Development Berhad (1MDB) scandal in Malaysia was about corruption and bribery. A shadowy figure known as Jho Low arranged with Prime Minister Najib Razak to raise funds for a development fund. These were raised from a Middle East country and were intended to form a sovereign fund to speed development in what had been one of the 'Asian tigers' in the 1990s but latterly had languished.

The Prime Minister never could convincingly explain how nearly US$700 million ended up in his account. When the Attorney-General launched an investigation, he was removed from his post. The investigation by the Public Action Committee was postponed when four of its members were given cabinet positions. In other words, there was a concerted effort to neuter any anti-corruption probe into the Prime Minister or his cronies.

In 2018, Razak lost power after an election. Shortly after, police raided his unit and took away US$220 million worth of items, including gold bars and jewellery. Razak was subsequently convicted of corruption and imprisoned. In October, Goldman Sachs, which had facilitated many transactions, in the process earning millions in fees, paid US$2.3 billion as a penalty and disgorged US$600 million, representing its fee income. Jho Low is in hiding and has not been charged but has given up US$1 billion in an effort to settle actions against him.

In Peru, the popular President Martín Vizcarra, who was taking action to clean up corruption, was stripped of office in 2020 under an obscure rule by a congress in which about half the members are under investigation for crimes including bribery and money laundering. Peru's turmoil saw three presidents within a week. Mass protests against corruption followed.

Corruption overwhelmingly is a burden on the poor and vulnerable, whether at local level, paying off officials, or at state level, where funds earmarked for aid go missing or drugs and medicines are swapped for counterfeits.

Corruption distorts the marketplace. When an official is bribed to make a certain decision, there is no guarantee that the state is getting the best or the most price-competitive service. Indeed, the cost of the bribes will generally be recouped in the price.

When a country becomes a kleptocracy, the battle is hopeless until there is regime change.

More insidious is when anti-corruption agencies are deployed against the government's political foes. The agency may appear effective but operates against a background of venality.

Transparency International publishes an annual Corruption Perceptions Index. Note that it is an index of *perceptions*. The real level of corruption may be more or less than the perception. Globally, Australia is one of a number of countries regarded as relatively corruption-free, ranking high on the index. It is vital for a trading nation such as ours to have a reputation for honest dealing by officials and an independent judicial system.

My view is that the forces of good may never win the battle against corruption. But if they stop fighting, evil will undoubtedly triumph. The battle requires commitment from every honest citizen. In the words of a British politician of several centuries ago, Edmund Burke: 'When bad men combine, the good must associate; else they will fall, one by one, an unpitied sacrifice in a contemptible struggle.'

Misconduct in Western Australia is more widespread than I had expected when I joined the CCC. Every allegation of serious misconduct must be reported to the commission. As there are over 5000 allegations a year, it can only investigate a tiny number. The vast majority are dealt with by agencies. This is appropriate, as the CEO of each agency is principally responsible for corruption risk and mitigation. The CCC tends to choose matters for investigation that raise wider issues of governance for the public sector. What surprised me was the nature and number of credible allegations of misconduct. Examination of CCC reports over twenty years shows instances of corruption and misconduct in almost every facet of government.

Corruption may be a serious threat to public safety. In my term and earlier, CCC reports into vehicle examiners uncovered bribery. More worryingly, vehicles were in some cases being passed fit for licensing without even being inspected. Any defects were never found or corrected.

A CCC report uncovered drivers who were not properly certified to possess a licence. In one case, bribes were given to an examiner to pass applicants for a motorcycle licence. In another investigation, persons were assessed as competent to drive heavy vehicles although they had not been properly tested. This licence enables them to drive an ordinary motor vehicle. Some of these applicants had previously failed a driving test in their own car, so they turned to a truck-driving school that would pass them. The prospect of an unqualified and unskilled driver of a heavy rigid truck driving beside you is terrifying.

A CCC report into procedures in handling dangerous drugs within hospitals identified some flawed security processes. When a medical professional illegally taps a patient's strong pain medication for their own use, the patient is left with a weaker, adulterated dose. And a health worker under the influence of a narcotic may be danger to patients and other workers.

A prison officer allowed sentenced prisoners unsupervised access to the public while on limited release.

Policies and procedures are of limited use against misconduct. A feature of nearly every report into a public-sector agency revealed that the agency had codes of conduct, policies and procedures designed to mitigate misconduct. They seem to be seldom used or reinforced. Knowledge of such documents by officers within an agency ranged from good to non-existent. Misconduct is a risk to be managed like any other risk facing an organisation but relatively few agencies had an active misconduct risk plan.

Accountability has a cost. Agencies develop an appetite for risk in other areas. It may be that low-level misconduct is not worth the expense of action. Only a CEO can make that determination. On the other hand, in many areas of misconduct, the costs of corruption are immense. Not only is there the direct cost of the malfeasance, but there are also flow-on costs, which are not always measured in financial terms. The reputational damage may last for years, as the CCC itself is painfully aware. It took five years for it to regain public trust after the matters I referred to earlier.

Abuse of power can mask other misconduct. The CCC reported on a number of individuals in positions of power who had improperly influenced others to bring mates on board or to gain something for themselves. These were almost all men. Conduct ranged from hiding a gambling problem, embezzlement, hiring a lover, and favouring certain contractors in breach of Finance Department requirements for tendering.

Government is a substantial purchaser of goods and services, so the misconduct risk in procurement is obvious. For this reason, there are tight procedures about purchasing, including tendering and probity audits.

Large-scale projects are not usually a risk. There is too much control over the process. Small-scale maintenance contracts, on the other hand, in schools, hospitals and local governments, among others, can be problematic. Often the person for whom an opinion of misconduct has been formed has a reputation for 'getting things done'. Only later do the reasons why emerge.

In every case reported upon by the CCC, there were red flags to be seen if anyone had looked.

Paul White was corrupt for years yet rose to a senior role in the Department of Communities. His false invoices were paid each month; his defalcation amounted to $22 million when the CCC finally uncovered his behaviour. He pleaded guilty and is serving a sentence of twelve years' imprisonment. Western Australia lagged somewhat but now all Australian jurisdictions have legislation and rules of practice governing procurement of government services. Nevertheless, the prospect of government funds for a business or activity remains enticing, and some parties are prepared to bribe or subvert government officials to gain contracts.

Use of force can be problematic. As part of its general misconduct function, the CCC conducted several investigations into the actions of uniformed personnel, police and prison officers, where the use of force was unjustified or problematic. In these days when methamphetamine is freely available, a frontline officer constantly is at risk. There are numerous use-of-force incidents each day—generally, when force is justified to protect the officer, innocent bystanders or the offender. The assessment as to what constitutes a reasonable response can be difficult, and it is always cautionary not to apply hindsight to the mind of an officer confronted with a dangerous situation.

Overall, police officers are professional. Complaints are generally dealt with satisfactorily within the agency. Only occasionally has it been necessary for the CCC to take over and investigate. Incidents reported on include the wrongful tasering of a driver, an assault against a drunken pedestrian who was slow to respond to a request, and a woman who was left in a lockup for hours with a broken hip.

The CCC has reported on several use-of-force incidents within West Australian prisons. Prisoners can be violent and unpredictable, and force is required on occasion to maintain order. However, prisoners are also vulnerable and can be at risk from overly zealous officers, who may lack the skill necessary to deal with a situation.

The work of the CCC is another layer of protection of the public purse and good governance. Its very presence undoubtedly has a deterrent effect on persons tempted to do the wrong thing. Some public servants who have not thought through the consequences of their actions are surprised when what they thought to be, at worst, unethical behaviour is in fact judged serious criminal activity, for which the punishment is not merely dismissal but imprisonment.

PART TWO
A SHORT EXPLANATION
OF LAW

There is an air of mystery about legal matters that many lawyers do little to dispel. Perhaps they still think of themselves as monks guarding the sacred spirit of the common law. In fact, law is nothing more than a tool that provides people with a set of rules to follow, enabling them to live in harmony. Law also allows disputes between citizens to be settled impartially and fairly.

Knowledge of all aspects of law is beyond any one human being. In the days when Latin was widely used in law, there was a maxim that *ignorantia juris non excusat*—ignorance of the law is no excuse. This rule applies today in criminal law. A driver caught doing seventy kilometres per hour in a school zone will get short shrift if they attempt to argue that they did not know such behaviour was an offence. And so an ordinary citizen is presumed to know every aspect of law, breach of which might lead to punishment. It works, mostly.

Law has always been complex. The application and interpretation rests on members of society who have devoted themselves to study and achieved recognition of their knowledge through exams. They join one of the three 'learned' professions: law, theology and medicine. They have been given various names at different times, depending on the area of law they have chosen: barrister, solicitor, proctor, attorney, notary, advocate, counsellor, sergeant at law, King's (or Queen's) Counsel, senior counsel, legal practitioner. The generic name is lawyer.

Every society has a set of laws, values or conventions that govern interaction between members. If you live alone on a deserted island, you have no need of laws. However, the moment another person arrives on your island, you must modify your behaviour to take account of their needs and desires, so that the two of you may live amicably.

Law is pervasive, like the air we breathe. It governs our everyday life, our relationships and our activities, and grants us permission to undertake certain tasks without penalty. In Australia, the parliaments of the Commonwealth and the states are empowered to make laws for 'peace, order (welfare) and good government'.

The sources of law in Australia, in brief, are limited to two: the common law, sometimes called case law, and statutory law. In what follows, I will also touch on the differences between criminal and civil law.

Common law

Common law is judge-made law. When Australia was colonised by the British, common law was imported, and it remains an important source of law in Australia and other former British colonies such as the United States and Canada.

Two parties are in dispute. A judge applies the law to the particular facts and announces a result. The law the judge applies might stretch from past centuries (precedent). The development of common law is like playing with Lego. Piece by piece, a structure emerges. After perhaps ten similar cases all decided the same way, a principle may emerge.

A famous example is *Donoghue v Stevenson*, where the highest court of the time, the House of Lords, laid down a principle of duty of care in negligence that is still followed today in Australia.

On a warm afternoon in August 1928, a friend bought Ms Donoghue, a lady of straitened circumstances, a bottle of ginger beer at the Wellmeadow café in Paisley, Scotland. After Ms Donoghue had consumed about half the bottle, she poured the remainder into a glass—and out floated the decomposed remains of a snail. Ms Donoghue was treated for gastroenteritis and shock. When she recovered, she sued Mr Stevenson, the soft drink manufacturer.

The law of negligence, which today we take for granted, was then in development, with the principles of duty of care and standards of care not completely settled. This was illustrated by the judgments. Although three law lords found in favour of the plaintiff, Ms Donoghue, two eminent law lords dissented and would have dismissed her claim. Were they wrong, or was it simply that they applied a different principle? The case-by-case approach of the common law allows development in many directions. By contrast, statutory law, if it is clear, permits no divergence.

Statutory law

The second source of law in Australia is that made by one of the parliaments, via their statutes or acts—the terms are interchangeable. When a document known as a bill is agreed to by a majority of members of both houses of parliament, and subsequently assented to by the King's representative, the Governor or Governor-General, the bill becomes law and is known as an Act of Parliament.

This is now the main source of law. Whereas a judge's task in a common law case is to find facts and apply a principle developed over the ages by other judges, in a statutory law case the judge will find facts, if necessary, interpret the statute to see what it means, and then apply the words of the statute to the facts to resolve the dispute.

Parliaments may pass laws on any subject. They may intend to regulate a developing issue, to amend the criminal law to deal with a specific threat or to enact promises made at elections.

There is sometimes a tendency to think of legislation as the solution to any problem. Of course, it is not. Parliaments that attempt to legislate for every situation tend to get into strife. It is courts that must resolve disputes, in particular factual situations. As a judge said many years ago, parliament enacts the outlines of the picture, leaving courts to colour in the detail.

Civil law and criminal law

Finally, a word about the difference between civil law and criminal law.

Civil law is the vindication of rights and may be based on the common law, statute law or both. In civil law, a person comes to court to seek vindication of a right. It might be a right under contract, a claim of a breach of duty of care, or a complaint that a government department has acted unlawfully. Most civil cases are settled either by the parties directly or through mediation. With disputes that proceed to trial, the judge will decide, on the balance of probabilities, which side's facts resolve the legal issue.

A side note: many parties will choose to resolve their dispute privately, without a judge. Instead, they will submit their dispute to an arbitrator appointed by them. This may be useful if the dispute involves complex technical evidence, such as a breach of patent or an engineering dispute. An arbitrator does not have to be a lawyer, though many are.

Criminal law is different to civil law. The primary purpose of criminal law is not to resolve disputes but to determine if it is proved beyond reasonable doubt that the conduct of a person has breached a statutory law, such as a section of the criminal code. If so, the person is to be punished in a manner the statute permits. The state takes over what might otherwise be a private dispute between an offender and a victim to keep the peace, to prevent retribution and revenge, and to inform and deter others by means of the penalties it imposes.

Criminal law in Western Australia, Queensland, Tasmania, the Northern Territory and the Australian Capital Territory is entirely statutory, in the form of a criminal code. In New South Wales, Victoria and South Australia, while most criminal law is now the subject of statutes, there remains some operation of the common law. Criminal or regulatory acts, such as the *Work Health and Safety Act*, prescribe maximum penalties—length of imprisonment or amount of fine—leaving a judge to fix a just penalty within the range the statute allows. The most severe punishment legislated in Australia is loss of liberty or imprisonment.

In an imaginary perfect community, citizens would know all the law, rather than the state imposing an artificial and unrealistic presumption of knowledge. Until we reach that enlightened Shangri-La, we will continue to need pilots who can navigate us through the complexities of law in the modern age.

For the time being, then, lawyers will remain with us. Though I suspect developers of machine learning and large language models may have other ideas. Artificial intelligence is already widely used in many professions, including law. It can be a great aid in complex cases involving terabytes of data. There are many critics of the use of juries to determine guilt and critics of judgments by one person, albeit with the possibility of an appeal. However, I suspect that most people would prefer to have their dispute resolved by a human being rather than by an impersonal algorithm.

PART THREE
CRIMINAL CASES THAT
CHANGED THE LAW

Three Murderers

In 1980, three men awaited death by hanging following convictions for wilful murder. This is how their imminent executions changed the law in Western Australia.

The law of homicide set out in the state's Criminal Code had been virtually unchanged for a century. There were three types of homicide, with penalties for each reflecting the seriousness.

Wilful murder was defined as an unlawful killing accompanied by an intention to kill. The penalty for wilful murder was death.

Murder was an unlawful killing accompanied by an intention short of killing—to do grievous bodily harm. Another form of murder, popularly called *felony murder*, was the killing of a person during a crime. The penalty for murder was a mandatory sentence of life imprisonment.

The third form of unlawful killing was *manslaughter*. This might encompass an unlawful killing without an intention to either kill or do grievous bodily harm. It might also include an unlawful killing caused by gross negligence. The penalty for manslaughter was imprisonment up to, and including, life imprisonment.

A person accused of a crime might claim they were of unsound mind at the time. This is generally known as the defence of insanity. If a verdict was not guilty on account of unsoundness of mind, the accused was usually confined to a prison 'until Her Majesty's pleasure was known'—that is, for an indefinite period. It was hard for a defence counsel to persuade a jury that a person who had deliberately killed a victim was insane. Even when the defence was successful, there appeared little difference in result, as the person found to be insane was confined in prison just as was a person convicted of murder, and was subject to similar conditions.

If a person was found guilty of wilful murder, the judge passed sentence: 'You are to suffer death in a manner prescribed by law.'

The last two executions in Western Australia were carried out in Fremantle Prison. Death was by hanging, and each time on a Monday morning. One story is well known; the other less so.

On 9 February 1963, Constable Noel Iles was called to a minor domestic disturbance in Epsom Avenue, in outer-suburban Belmont. An argument had broken out between a father and his son, possibly over a rumour that the son's sister was also his mother. As there was a double-barrelled shotgun in the house, and with the possibility of violence, police were summoned. When Constable Iles arrived, he was shot in the face by Brian Robinson, aged twenty-four, who had been arguing with his father. With Constable Iles rendered helpless by his wound, Robinson approached and, at point-blank range, shot him in the head, killing him instantly.

Trying to make his escape, Robinson flagged down a micro sports car, a Goggomobil Dart driven by a young woman with a passenger, Andrew McDougall. McDougall resisted and was shot dead by Robinson. Robinson then hailed a taxi, forcing the driver to take him to the Gnangara pine plantation, north of Perth.

The taxi driver managed to send an emergency message, and when they arrived at the pine plantation the driver deliberately bogged the taxi. Robinson took off into the trees. A huge manhunt—which, extraordinarily, included armed citizens as well as police and the Air Force—failed to find him. He was captured the next day after being wounded by a police officer.

Robinson was convicted of wilful murder and on 29 May 1963 was sentenced to death by Justice Hale. An appeal was dismissed, as was a further appeal to the High Court.

Perhaps to try to delay the execution, Robinson's lawyer, Dr J.S. Marian, charged the police officer who had arrested Robinson with unlawful grievous bodily harm, and asked for a stay of execution so that Robinson could give evidence at the trial. This was refused and Robinson was hanged on 20 January 1964, a Monday, at 8 am.

Eric Edgar Cooke, the last man executed in Western Australia, was hanged later that year. He was a serial killer. His story is well known to locals, and nowhere better told than in *The Shark Net* by Robert Drewe. For an excellent, though fictionalised, version, *Cloudstreet* by Tim Winton is hard to beat.

On 26 January 1963, Cooke shot five people chosen randomly by him, killing three.

The city was in fear. Doors habitually left unlocked began to be locked. Although Perth was known internationally as the City of Lights, because astronaut John Glenn had so described it in 1962 as he orbited the Earth, many streetlights were still extinguished at 1 am, leaving suburbs in darkness. The entire city entered an unofficial curfew.

Then there was the plight of the milkos. Bottles of milk would be delivered in the early hours. Panicky residents began to take potshots at milkmen running up the path to leave milk at the front door. Eventually milk vans carried lights to reassure anxious householders that all that was happening was a routine delivery.

As I related earlier, when our Dalkeith house was built in 1952 there were still shortages of building materials, so my room was a sleepout with louvred windows. Anyone going around the back of the house could easily peek in, or indeed break in if they were so minded.

In 1963 I was twelve years old. After the night of death in January, there were for a time no further killings. My brother died in a car crash in Geelong that June. On 10 August my parents, deeming me old enough to look after myself, went out to seek comfort with some old friends. At about 9 pm I went to bed.

Early the next morning, we were awakened by police officers at the door, seeking to fingerprint my father and me. A hundred metres up our street, Wavell Road, an eighteen-year-old student, Shirley McLeod, had been shot dead through the window of the house where she was babysitting for the evening. It transpired that she was yet another victim of Eric Edgar Cooke.

Cooke was captured when he attempted to retrieve a rifle hidden in a tree on the Mount Pleasant foreshore, south of the city. A cartridge found in his car matched the bullet that had killed Shirley McLeod.

Cooke claimed insanity as a defence, but after a three-day trial the jury rejected the claim. He was convicted of wilful murder and sentenced to death by Justice Virtue. Although he did not appeal against the verdict, in an effort to avoid death he confessed to a number of crimes. He was hanged on Monday, 26 October 1964.

After the execution of those two men, Robinson and Cooke, sentences of death following verdicts of wilful murder were routinely commuted to life imprisonment by the West Australian Governor, following a recommendation from cabinet.

And so we come to 1979.

Donald Irwin Parre

Shortly after joining the Crown Solicitor's office, I received a file about a local court action in Mount Barker brought against the State Electricity Commission (SEC). The plaintiff, Donald Irwin Parre, was a former US Marine who had settled in Western Australia with his family and owned a small farm.

The SEC was improving its network, and for that purpose took an easement over Parre's land to build a transmission tower. This was perfectly legal, but Mr Parre had views of property ownership more suited to parts of the United States. In his view, he was an allodial owner and entitled to charge the SEC rent for the land on which the tower stood.

I drafted a summons and affidavit to strike out the plaintiff's action on the grounds that it was ill-conceived. In due course, the summons came before a magistrate, who agreed that the legal action by Mr Parre was doomed to fail and dismissed his claim. He ordered the plaintiff to pay $153.10 to the defendant in costs. And so the scene was set for tragedy.

After obtaining judgment for the defendant, I passed the file to the recovery unit. They issued several demands for payment of $153.10, which Mr Parre ignored. Finally, the recovery unit engaged the local bailiff to serve what is called a writ of *fieri facias*, or 'fi fa', to seize property to the value of the debt.

The local bailiff was also the officer in charge of the Mount Barker Police Station, Sergeant James Keelan. Together with First Class Constable William (Bill) Pense, he set off for Parre's farm in a police van on 12 October 1979. His purpose was to try to negotiate a settlement, failing which he would serve the writ.

Nothing seemed out of the ordinary as they turned into the drive leading to the house. Little did they know that Parre had prepared himself for their arrival. He armed himself with a .22 rifle and concealed a loaded Beretta pistol in his shirt pocket. As Keelan walked to the front door, Parre burst from a shed. Pense shouted a warning: 'He's got a gun!'

The rifle had a telescopic sight and Parre aimed directly at Keelan. Keelan attempted to retreat to the police vehicle, but Parre opened fire before he could reach safety. Keelan was hit and severely wounded. Showing great bravery, Pense ran towards Parre, firing his police pistol as he went. Parre returned fire, hitting Pense four times. Despite his wounds, Pense continued running towards Parre until he reached him and wrestled the rifle from his hands. Pense managed to subdue Parre, and it appeared for a moment that the struggle was over. However, Parre pulled out the Beretta pistol and shot Pense in the heart, killing him instantly.

Meanwhile, Keelan reached the safety of the police vehicle. Parre called out, saying he'd had enough. Leaving his weapons, Parre went into his house.

Keelan tried to radio for help but had difficulty in getting through. Looking up, he was alarmed to see Parre, armed with another rifle, approaching him again. Later examination showed nine bullet holes in the police van. Keelan was able to drive away in the police van, eventually reaching a safe place where he was able to telephone for help and get medical assistance for his wounds.

That telephone call started a massive police response. Eventually, reinforcements arrived in Mount Barker, led by Detective Sergeant

Bruce Scott. They stormed the house, subduing Parre, who had been seriously wounded himself in the earlier exchange.

Parre had made the mistake of believing the law allowed him to take the actions he did. However, although a mistaken belief in a matter of fact might excuse criminal responsibility, a mistaken belief in law does not. Parre pleaded not guilty to wilful murder, relying on a defence of insanity, but on 12 March 1980 he was convicted after trial by jury, and a mandatory sentence of death was pronounced by Justice Smith. Parre appealed against his conviction but was unsuccessful.

Less than a month after he was murdered, First Class Constable Bill Pense was posthumously awarded the George Cross for his bravery in saving Keelan's life. His bravery is acknowledged at the National Police Memorial Day every September.

Parre was lodged in Fremantle Prison to await execution by hanging.

Brian William Edwards

Brian Edwards was only ten when he stole a toy gun from a shop in the wheatbelt town of Dowerin, where he grew up. This was an early indication of lawlessness and a fascination with firearms. He grew into a violent adult. When he was twenty, he shattered a man's thigh with a shotgun blast because he 'just felt like shooting someone'.

Although he began his sentence for that crime in Fremantle Prison, due to overcrowding he and others were sent to a medium-security prison in Bunbury.

On 27 October 1979, Edwards was one of a party of prisoners attending a sporting event outside the prison when he escaped—his second attempt. While on the run, he stole a .303 rifle, ammunition and a Toyota Land Cruiser. Three weeks after his escape, he encountered a seventeen-year-old woman, whom he threatened with the rifle and then viciously raped. He left her alive. Edwards then made his way to a small track near the Mandurah estuary, where he slept the night.

The next morning, a newly engaged young couple, childhood sweethearts, had the ill- fortune to drive down that same track on their way to a picnic. Edwards shot the man in the chest as he got out of the car, then shot the young woman, who was still seated in the car, before shooting each of them again, fatally.

Edwards headed north but was apprehended by an armed police contingent outside Port Hedland. He pleaded guilty before Justice Smith in Supreme Court No. 2. He was twenty-three years old.

Edwards blamed his violent actions on racist discrimination and humiliation he had suffered as a child in Dowerin. 'I have grown up with an unreasoning hatred towards white people which at times I find uncontrollable,' he said. He expressed sorrow for his actions and said that the only way he could atone for his actions was to save their parents, relatives and friends the ordeal of a trial.

In view of the consequence of a conviction for wilful murder, counsel for Edwards, experienced barrister and author Lloyd Davies arranged for two lawyers to separately advise Edwards and for two psychiatrists to examine him. Both psychiatrists pronounced him sane.

I was present in court when he was sentenced. Like many murderers, there was nothing in his outward appearance that gave any hint of the evil within. He looked like an ordinary young man, though slightly dishevelled. When the indictment was read to him, he responded, 'Guilty,' both times without visible expression. A letter he had written to the judge was read aloud.

The judge then pronounced sentence: 'For the crimes of wilful murder, you are sentenced to death in a manner prescribed by law.'

Peter John Maloney

At about 5 am on Friday, 15 December 1978, an early-morning walker discovered the battered naked body of a young woman hidden in the bush near The Esplanade, a beachside drive in the small southern town of Esperance. Her identity was soon discovered—I will call her Ann. She was sixteen and lived in the town. Her body bore distinctive markings caused by whatever had been used in her assault.

How she had got there and who had killed her were to be a mystery for eleven months, despite an intensive police investigation. To answer those questions, it is necessary to go back to the night before.

It was a warm Thursday evening shortly before Christmas when Peter Maloney, a young man of twenty-one, decided to go out to a local tavern. As often happened, he fell in with a group of friends and joined them for a few drinks. Ann was part of the group.

The evening finished quietly, and when the tavern closed each went their separate way. Maloney took a friend home and then drove down to the waterfront for a few stubbies. On his way home, he saw Ann walking on the other side of the road. Maloney stopped and offered her a lift, which she accepted. Initial plans to find a party were abandoned when Maloney parked up and they began kissing. When he wanted to go further, she said, 'Stop.'

Enraged and intent on rape, Maloney pushed Ann from the car. Ann hit her nose, causing it to bleed. The sight set Maloney off and he started hitting Ann in earnest.

On one of his fingers, Maloney wore a distinctive signet ring. A rectangular mark above Ann's eyebrow was later matched to the ring.

At some point, Maloney took the car jack from the boot of the car and began to hit Ann ferociously with it, to such an extent that the shape of the jack's base was stamped on her skin. It was later proved to have been the weapon of death.

All of that was sometime in the future. For the moment, Maloney was free.

Eleven months later, he was working as a barman in an Esperance motel. A group of elderly citizens from Gosnells, touring the south-west by coach, arrived for the night and checked in before going out for dinner.

The day's travelling had been long and tiring. Mrs Catherine Burden, a member of the group, was given a first-floor room. Instead of accompanying the others for dinner, she decided to relax in her room with a nice hot cup of tea. Unfortunately, there was no milk or sugar in the room. Mrs Burden rang the front desk and spoke with Maloney, who promised to bring some up shortly. He then forgot all about it.

Finishing his shift at 11 pm, he went out drinking with mates. Staggering home at 3 am, Maloney suddenly remembered the milk and sugar. Despite the hour, he decided to wake Mrs Burden and apologise. He banged on her door until she answered it. Mrs Burden was not pleased at being woken and let Maloney know. Angered, Maloney grabbed whatever was at hand and hit her, causing her to fall back onto the bed. He continued to hit her with a chair. After leaving the room for a time, he returned with a length of cord, a rag and a plastic tube. He tied Mrs Burden's hands together and gagged her, before helping himself to a large glass of water, carelessly leaving his fingerprints on the glass and other objects.

Mrs Burden's body was discovered next morning. It did not take the police long to identify Maloney as the main suspect, and he was interviewed. During the interview about the killing of Mrs Burden, which he freely admitted, Maloney volunteered that he had also caused Ann's death. He was charged with two counts of wilful murder.

The first trial—for the murder of Ann—was before Justice Smith and a jury. Ron Davies led for the Crown. I was junior prosecuting counsel. Maloney was defended by Henry Wallwork, a big-hearted criminal lawyer who was constantly in demand for homicide cases. Years later we became colleagues on the Supreme Court. The single issue was Maloney's intention at the time he unlawfully killed Ann. The jury returned a verdict of not guilty of wilful murder, but guilty of murder. They were satisfied that Maloney intended to cause Ann at least some grievous bodily harm. He was sentenced to a mandatory term of life imprisonment.

The second trial followed within two months. Again, Ron Davies was the lead prosecutor. His junior counsel for this trial was a new addition to the Crown Prosecutor's office, Michael Muller, polite, softly spoken and effective. Michael later served with distinction as a District Court judge for many years. Henry Wallwork again appeared for Maloney.

This time a defence of insanity was raised. This defence requires the accused person to prove, on the balance of probabilities, that he was insane at the time of the offence. The defence is found in section 27 of the Criminal Code, and mirrors the famous M'Naghten rules, formulated by English judges a century before.

Maloney argued that long-term drinking had caused brain damage, and that this, coupled with his intoxication on the night, meant he fell within the definition of insanity in section 27, as he lacked the capacity to understand what he was doing or to control his actions.

The jury did not accept that Maloney was insane. He was convicted of wilful murder. Justice Wallace, who had presided over the trial, passed the mandatory sentence of death.

How did the law change?
In 1980 the penalty for wilful murder, an intentional killing, was death. The penalty for murder, a killing intending not to kill but to cause grievous bodily harm, was imprisonment for life. A prisoner whose sentence of death was commuted to life imprisonment was eligible for parole in less than twenty years.

The three individuals—Parre, Edwards and Maloney—presented a conundrum. Each had committed evil crimes. One had killed a police officer in the execution of their duty. The other two, though still young men, had each killed two people. Many in the community thought death was the appropriate punishment—an eye for an eye. But there was a strong body of the community who argued passionately against the death penalty.

The judicial process had concluded. Orders had been made by a court that each man suffer the penalty of death. There remained one option to avoid execution. The royal prerogative of mercy vests in the Governor, who must act on advice from the executive council—the cabinet of the government of the day. By exercising the prerogative, the Governor can alter a sentence or, in some cases, remit the sentence entirely or pardon the offender. Cabinet advises the Governor whether to exercise the prerogative. There is no judicial intervention.

The death penalty had not been carried out in Western Australia since Eric Edgar Cooke was hanged in Fremantle Prison sixteen years earlier. The death sentence for wilful murderers since then had been commuted to life imprisonment. This, in turn, meant eligibility for parole in due course.

Community feelings ran high. In July 1980, a Liberal Party conference passed overwhelmingly a motion calling for the death penalty to be enforced. A later conference of Young Liberals also called for enforcement. The Police Union issued a strong statement that the death penalty should be enforced.

The Australian Labor Party, then in opposition, together with many church leaders, called for the abolition of the death penalty. The Women's Guild had been seeking its abolition for years. Petitions were tabled in parliament. By 1980, Western Australia was an outlier. Other states had abolished the death penalty.

This was the quandary faced by the cabinet as it grappled with the issue: whether to allow three wilful murderers to hang, or to be merciful and commute the sentences to life imprisonment. Parre, Edwards and Maloney were all on death row. Something had to be done.

Shortly before Christmas 1980, the government acted. Parliament introduced a new sentence: strict security life imprisonment. A person under this regime would be required to serve at least twenty years before parole could be considered. Strict security life imprisonment was expressed to be an option if the royal prerogative of mercy was extended to an offender. The prerogative of mercy was exercised. The sentences of death were commuted to strict security life imprisonment.

Parre died in prison in 2005. No one mourned his passing. In 2005 Edwards escaped from a minimum-security prison and spent eleven days on the run before being recaptured. Maloney's request for parole was denied in 2017. At the time of writing, he remains in prison.

In 1984, a new West Australian government, formed by the Australian Labor Party under Premier Brian Burke, passed legislation abolishing the death penalty. Forty years on, the discussion about the death penalty is likely still to provoke heated discussion on both sides, with very few people changing their minds.

There are practical reasons to support the lack of a death penalty. Australia has treaties with many countries and organisations. For some, the presence of the death penalty in the law of the land is an impediment to a treaty for extradition.

The death penalty might also affect extraditions. In the late 1980s, attempts to extradite an accused person from the United Kingdom ran into difficulty because Western Australia retained in its Criminal Code whipping as a punishment for some offences. The last person to be whipped was a youth of nineteen for the offence of unlawful carnal knowledge of a girl under the age of sixteen. He had received twelve strokes of the birch. As Chief Crown Prosecutor, I made urgent representations to Attorney-General Joe Berinson QC. The punishment was abolished by a Criminal Code amendment that came into effect from 6 January 1993. If a state were ever to reintroduce the death penalty, it is certain that extraditions would be severely affected.

The Case that Shocked the Public Conscience

In June 2006 the whole of Australia was shocked by the horrific murder of an eight-year-old girl who, while in a suburban shopping centre with her family, had left them for a moment to go to the toilet. Her terribly injured body was found a few minutes later by a member of the family who were searching frantically for her.

Suspicion soon fell on a young man named Dante William Arthurs. He had come under police notice before. Three years earlier, police had interviewed him over the assault of another young girl at a playground near his home. On that occasion, a forensic analysis of his shorts was not undertaken, and so traces of the girl's blood on them, which might have led to his conviction, were not found until years later. Furthermore, the police interview was so poorly conducted that the DPP refused to prosecute.

To return to the present: Arthurs lived with his parents and was planning to go to the United Kingdom on holiday the next day, having saved up for the trip. His bedroom was searched and a disturbing discovery was made. In a bag, police discovered photographs of young women, directions to their houses, gloves, tape, handcuffs and a knife. Arthurs was interviewed in relation to the killing and charged with wilful murder, sexual assault and deprivation of liberty.

The community outcry was enormous, and wild rumours circulated that he was a notorious English child killer sent to Australia to live anonymously. Adverse publicity was so great that the Chief

Justice ordered the trial should take place in front of a judge alone, not a jury. I was assigned the trial.

Before the trial began, defence counsel Bob Richardson asked for a pre-trial hearing to challenge the admissibility of Arthurs' videotaped interview with police. To ensure that, as the trial judge, I did not hear any inadmissible evidence, Justice Blaxell presided over the pre-trial hearing and ruled that the interview was involuntary. It would not be permitted in the trial.

Twice in three years, police had failed to conduct an interview with Arthurs according to the proper procedures, which were designed to ensure that any confession was made voluntarily and would be admissible in court.

The DPP concluded that the prosecution could not prove beyond reasonable doubt that Arthurs had intended to kill the child. In other words, the prosecution could not prove the crime of wilful murder. It could prove, however, that Arthurs was guilty of murder, either because he intended to do the child grievous bodily harm or by way of felony murder—that is, that in the course of an unlawful act, sexual assault, he did an act likely to endanger the girl's life by stopping her breathing.

The penalty of life imprisonment was the same, but the effective difference between wilful murder and murder was the length of time before the offender could be considered for parole. A person convicted of wilful murder must serve a minimum of fifteen years before parole, though a non-parole period could be much longer and include strict security life imprisonment. By contrast, a judge was required to set a lower minimum period—between seven and fourteen years—for a person convicted of murder.

There were also technical difficulties with the crimes of sexual assault alleged against Arthurs, as it could not be determined whether the child was dead before or after the assaults had taken place.

The DPP and the defence, through Bob Richardson, reached agreement that Arthurs would plead guilty to murder and deprivation of liberty. My forthcoming trial therefore became a sentencing day.

Sam Vandongen, a very able counsel, now a judge of the Federal Court of Australia, took me through the facts asserted by the prosecution. These were so disturbing that some people left the courtroom in anguish. Arthurs' clothing from the earlier incident had now been analysed, and I was invited to take that crime into account. The items in his bag were given prominence.

I was shown the record of interview from 2003. The police conduct was appalling. Had that incident been fully investigated and the rules followed, there might not have been a death three years later.

Victim impact statements were tendered.

Bob Richardson acted in the best traditions of the bar. A barrister practising in criminal law must accept a brief for defence without regard to the nature of the crime alleged. A barrister is not permitted to refuse to act simply because the crime is horrific, or because the accused person is evil. Richardson did not attempt to justify or excuse his client's conduct, but pointed to some matters, such as a psychological examination, which I should consider. Arthurs showed no remorse for his crime. However, he had a condition, then referred to as Asperger's syndrome, which prevented him from feeling such emotions, and I did not take his lack of remorse into account.

When Bob Richardson concluded his address, I adjourned the court until late in the afternoon. The decision on sentence was not difficult. Obviously, it must be life imprisonment. The only question was how long before Arthurs would be eligible for parole.

Court resumed after 4 pm. The media desk was crowded. The family of the young girl could not bear to be present. Their priest represented them and spoke on their behalf. Arthurs stood alone in the dock, trembling as I began to address him.

'Your brutal crime is so evil it has shocked the public conscience,' I said. 'Your actions have made every parent feel less safe, less trusting, more worried.'

Then came the sentence. Arthurs remained looking down. For the crime of deprivation of liberty, he was sentenced to a term of imprisonment for two years. This was to be served concurrently with the sentence for murder. For the crime of murder, he was sentenced to imprisonment for life. I set a minimum term of thirteen years before he could be considered for parole.

'You should clearly understand that the sentence is one of life imprisonment,' I cautioned. 'You may never be released. Stand down.'

The parole was one year less than the maximum of fourteen years to take account of his plea of guilty, which had saved the family from the further trauma of a trial, and such other matters in mitigation as I could find. There were not many.

Was the non-parole period too lenient? Of course it was. It was effectively the maximum that could be imposed but still fell way short of the punishment such an evil and heinous crime deserved. As a result of this and some other cases, the government moved swiftly to amend the law in accordance with a Law Reform Commission recommendation.

In 2008, the criminal law on homicide was changed. The distinction between wilful murder and murder was abolished. Judges were required to impose a minimum of ten years before parole but were given discretion to impose a sentence of life imprisonment with a minimum before parole suited to the particular facts.

Since that time, judges have regularly imposed minimum terms above twenty years, and some terms above thirty. One sentence with a minimum of forty-two years has been handed down, and one sentence with no parole eligibility—in other words, life, never to be released.

Arthurs became eligible for parole after thirteen years but was refused parole. The attorney-general at the time of Arthurs' crime, Jim McGinty, has said he doubts that any future Attorney-General of Western Australia will ever recommend Arthurs' release on parole.

That was not the only change. After persistent efforts by the family in 2012, the Community Protection (Offenders Reporting) Act was amended to allow for a sex offenders' register, which meant some details of known sex offenders could be accessed by the public.

This was not my first case of child killing or sexual assault. Over the years, I had seen the depths of depravity and the cruelty one person could inflict on another. However, I had not seen this extent of violence inflicted on a child before.

Indeed, it would be another seven years before I saw it again, in the trial by judge alone of Mervyn Kenneth Bell, who inflicted gross injuries on a nine-month-old infant as revenge against the child's mother.

A Pretend Robber

It was March 1983 and Carl, twenty-one, had a problem. He had no money. Banks have money. Solution: rob a bank. And that's just what he did.

Carl grabbed the key to his mate's motorbike, rode into Perth and parked across from the Supreme Court. Then he walked up to the Hay Street branch of the Westpac Bank and, in the time-honoured phrase, said, 'This is a hold-up.'

Carl did not say anything else to threaten the bank teller, but he did not have to. For he was holding a bag, and protruding out through the zipper was a rifle barrel. In fear of being shot, the teller handed over some fifties and twenties. Then Carl fled from the bank. Remorse soon set in, and when he was arrested most of the money was returned.

I prosecuted Carl in the Supreme Court. The charge was stealing $1100 with actual violence, and at the time being armed with an offensive weapon—namely, a portion of a rifle barrel. Immediately after Carl had pleaded not guilty, veteran defence counsel Malcolm Hall explained to the jury that Carl admitted almost everything. The only issue was whether he was armed with an offensive weapon.

This issue was important, because being armed with a dangerous or offensive weapon was a circumstance of aggravation to the crime of robbery, increasing the penalty to life imprisonment.

So was a three-inch length of a rifle barrel an offensive weapon? The jury thought so, and Carl was convicted as charged.

Subsequently, two of three appeal judges thought otherwise. Carl did not intend to use the rifle barrel to inflict bodily harm, they said, and it was therefore not an offensive weapon. The circumstance of aggravation was quashed.

It was somewhat of a pyrrhic victory, however, because his sentence remained the same. The effect of the pretence on the victim was the real mischief. The bank teller was not to know that the bit of rifle barrel was harmless. She was terrified.

Parliament acted swiftly to cover similar situations in the future, amending the definition by adding six words to the circumstance of aggravation:

> If immediately, before, during, or immediately after the commission of the offence, the offender is armed with any dangerous or offensive weapon *or pretends to be so armed*, to imprisonment for life.

Over the years, people have been convicted of pretending to be armed with a variety of 'weapons':

- A Smurf
- A tin of Nugget shoe polish ('give me money or I will drop this')
- A pencil
- A water pistol
- A pair of secateurs
- A finger

The Baby in the Fridge

Abortion is a subject on which there are strong opinions, for and against. I am bemused by those I've met who are against abortion, which they regard as taking a life, but in favour of capital punishment, which is taking a life. Like capital punishment, abortion is a subject where views are entrenched. This is the story of how Western Australia led the nation in abortion law reform—accidentally.

In 1972, a Labor member of parliament introduced a private member's bill to reform the law relating to abortion, but, as with many highly contentious social issues, it was impossible to span the political divide and reach a consensus. The bill went nowhere.

The West Australian Family Planning Association was active in counselling and advising women on medical and social matters including termination. It tried to keep within the bounds of the law at the same time as offering a comprehensive service.

There was a general belief that terminations, if not strictly legal, were tolerated. This belief in what the law allowed was bolstered by directions to the jury by judges in particular cases, but there was no definitive decision, and no court of appeal or High Court ruling to settle the issue.

It was widely believed that a termination was legal if performed to save the mother's life, or if necessary for her continued physical or mental wellbeing. The lack of clarity was about the issue of mental wellbeing. At what point did an abortion for the woman's wellbeing become 'abortion on demand'? Abortion clinics were staffed by highly skilled and properly qualified doctors and nurses, a far cry from back-yard abortionists, whose awful ministrations sometimes led to the death of young women. Yet the doctors were working in a grey area of the law. And at some risk of prosecution to themselves.

In 1974 the Commonwealth government allowed Medicare bene-fits for women who had undergone a termination. This was a major change. On the other side, there was a push to shut down abortion clinics. Many churches, including the influential Catholic Church, preached and fought to maintain the right to life. In the mid-1970s, in response to pressure to 'do something', police executed several search warrants against clinics and other services. Ultimately, nothing came of them.

Some respectable people were prepared to go to gaol if neces-sary for supporting these services. Others held religious beliefs that regarded termination as akin to murder. As still happens today in some parts of the world, emotions ran high and the debate got out of hand. Out of curiosity, I attended a community meeting near my local suburb where one speaker spoke of aborted foetuses climbing out of the bucket they had been dropped in. Even my limited medical knowl-edge rebelled at such a notion.

After this flurry of activity, officials fell into a sort of 'don't ask, don't tell' position. Periodically, people would write to the attor-ney-general and other ministers and provide photographic proof that abortions were being performed, or at least advertised. The response of the government and police was to ignore the problem and hope it would go away.

By 1998 it was reported in the *West Australian* that about 160 termination procedures were performed in the state each week, or nearly 9000 a year.

Parliament had many opportunities to reform the law, but to do so risked alienating at least one influential section of the voting pop-ulation. So politicians did what they do best: nothing. Until a primary school kid lit a fuse.

A tradition in primary schools is for a teacher to ask for news. Children will stand and share their piece of information. 'We went camping on the weekend. It was fun.' 'I have a new guinea pig.' One morning in 1997 a boy stood up and announced the following to his startled teacher: 'We have a dead baby in the fridge.'

The teacher informed police. Upon investigation, it was discovered that the boy's mother had attended a clinic staffed by doctors and nurses, where a termination was performed. At her request, she was given the foetus and was storing it in the freezer until she could take it back to her homelands for a proper burial. She was forthcoming about the name of the clinic and the doctors who had performed the procedure.

The police went to the clinic and interviewed the doctors, who freely admitted what they had done, perhaps seeing nothing wrong in their actions. Recognising that they had the thorniest of all dilemmas on their hands, police sought the advice of the Director of Public Prosecutions. So it was that I received the brief to advise whether an offence had been committed.

Early in my time as DPP, I had sought to shape the approach towards prosecutions, publishing a statement of prosecution policy and guidelines. Successive directors have improved and refined it. With another prosecutor, we assessed the brief according to basic principles, as to the sufficiency of evidence and the application of the prosecution policy. In general terms, under the law at that time, performing an abortion was illegal unless the purpose was to preserve life. The grey area was what was regarded as preservation of life for the mother's benefit.

The leading case was an unusual one. In 1938 a respected English gynaecologist, Aleck Bourne, was charged with procuring an abortion. He had not charged a fee for the operation, which was performed on a fifteen-year-old girl who had been raped by five British Army officers and become pregnant as a result. The judge had given a direction to the jury that if the probable consequence of the continuance of the pregnancy would be to make the woman a physical or mental wreck, the jury was entitled to take the view that the doctor was operating for the purpose of preserving the life of the mother. And so Dr Bourne was acquitted.

In 1969, Justice Menhennit of the Supreme Court of Victoria gave evidential rulings to the effect that an abortion might be lawful to preserve the physical or mental health of the woman. Again, the accused was acquitted. In each case, the acquittal meant that there was no opportunity to test the ruling of the primary judge by way of an appeal.

The decision of a single judge, especially when it is not a written judgment but a charge to a jury, has limited precedential value in the law. There is a hierarchy of judgments. A judge or court of appeal must follow and apply any principle laid down by the High Court. Next in the hierarchy is a Court of Appeal, federal and state. A single judge, as a matter of comity, should follow judgments from such courts. A judgment by a single judge might be followed if it is not in conflict with decisions of a higher court.

Directions on law to a jury in a case with unique facts do not have the same status as a judgment. Nevertheless, for more than a half-century, the law on terminations was based on directions to the jury in a handful of cases.

The brief against the West Australian doctors disclosed credible evidence that an offence of procuring or performing an abortion may have been committed. That was simply the first step.

It has never been the case that every suspected crime must be prosecuted. A prosecution must also be in the public interest. Many factors listed in the prosecution policy inform the answer to that question. We began to run through them.

Was there a prima facie case—that is, enough evidence that a jury could convict? Yes, especially with the admissions from the woman who'd had the procedure, and from the medical team who'd conducted it.

Was the law obsolete or in desuetude? No. There had been prosecutions within the last thirty years.

Were there objectively reasonable prospects of conviction? Yes.

Were there other factors weighing against the prosecution? There were. First, a large proportion of the population was in favour of abortion if the woman wanted it. It is her body, after all. Second, a termination is a routine medical procedure. But there was also a large proportion of the population who regarded abortion as equivalent to murder and never to be countenanced. They supported a right to life for the unborn.

In these circumstances, I decided it was a matter for a jury to decide and advised the police that there was no impediment to a charge of illegally procuring an abortion against each doctor. On signing the advice, I remarked to the other counsel in the words of warning on most fireworks: 'Light blue touch paper and retire to a safe distance.'

The two doctors were charged with procuring an abortion. The resultant firestorm consumed the media for the next few weeks as the community was suddenly confronted by an issue that had been avoided for many years. Doctors at the main maternity hospital threatened to refuse to undertake termination procedures unless the law was clarified. A senior doctor said that 99 per cent of terminations carried out in Western Australia were illegal. Abortion clinics were picketed. Newspapers were full of angry words for and against. Radio airwaves were replete with voices arguing both sides. Replica foetuses were sent to cabinet ministers.

As I had fully expected, I received letters praising my decision and letters condemning it. I was accused of being a Catholic, a zealot, arrogant and ignorant of the law. Early on in my career, I had learned to ignore personal criticism. In this instance I was a convenient lightning rod for people who held strong views. It is easy to have strong views when you are not charged with the responsibility of decision.

Reasoned critique of an action by the office or by me was a different matter. We routinely examined such critiques carefully and corrected our decisions if necessary.

I was advised that abortion was not a crime, which came as something of a surprise, in view of the explicit words of the Criminal Code. One Calvinistic lawyer, who visited to implore me to hold fast, quoted the Old Testament as authority for my actions.

Some politicians wrote, imploring me to change my mind. Anything to pass the buck. One was the former Premier and Federal Minister for Health Dr Carmen Lawrence, who started a petition, also signed by other prominent women, calling for me to discontinue. As she could have influenced a change in the law but did nothing, my response to her was, in retrospect, somewhat less than gracious.

How did the law change? Both houses of the West Australian parliament passed bills addressing the issue, but confusion as to which was the better bill remained. Finally, the Attorney-General, Peter Foss QC, and an Opposition member, Cheryl Davenport, in a bipartisan effort, drafted a compromise law that decriminalised abortion in language that appeased at least some of the anti-abortion group. Effectively, it moved the issue from the sanctions of the criminal law and into the regime of health.

The Criminal Code offence was rewritten. It was unlawful to perform an abortion unless performed by a medical practitioner in good faith, and with reasonable care and skill, and justified under the terms of the *Health Act*, which required informed consent from the woman and an independent medical practitioner to have provided her with counselling about the medical risk both of termination and of carrying to term. After twenty weeks, there was a requirement that two doctors from a panel agree that a severe medical condition in the mother or the unborn child justified the termination.

Penalties were different. A medical practitioner breaking the law was liable to a fine of up to $50,000. A non-doctor who committed a crime was liable to imprisonment for five years. This was clearly to discourage backyard abortionists, who had been a scourge for years.

The bill ultimately passed the Legislative Assembly and the Legislative Council on a conscience vote. By default, Western Australia led the country in abortion reform. The maternity hospital resumed terminations and other doctors were free to do the best for their patients.

After the new law was proclaimed, I waited a decent interval for the dust to settle and announced that, in view of the change in the law, it was no longer in the public interest to proceed with the prosecution of the doctors.

I told Ron Cannon, who acted as counsel for one of them, what I would do as soon as prominent people stopped going to the media to tell me what to do. Ever the pragmatist, Ron understood and made no public comment himself. Nor did the other lawyer, Ron Birmingham. Of course, I duly received letters both praising my decision and condemning it.

As I look back on this episode, I would not change any action of mine. I did not give advice to police to change the law or in the hope that debate should be encouraged. I followed Ron Cannon's advice from long ago: 'I fight cases, not causes.'

Years ago, in Queensland, the title of my counterpart was 'Director of Prosecutions'. The incumbent, Royce Miller QC, successfully lobbied the government to amend the title to 'Director of Public Prosecutions', so importantly did he regard the role as acting in the public interest, not allied with any particular cause, or indeed with any complainant or victim.

If a DPP takes account of their personal views as to social justice, or the righteousness of some cause, however well-meaning, they are no longer acting on behalf of the public but according to their own beliefs. They are not paid for that.

The change of law was a consequence not of my decision, but of the refusal of successive governments and parliaments to grapple with the issue. Having searched my conscience, I am content that my decision was made within the legal framework that governs all prosecutions. To have injected my personal views into the decision would have been an abrogation of responsibility.

Twenty-five years later, parliament revisited the issue and simplified and streamlined the process. Unlike in 1998, the passage of the *Abortion Legislation Reform Act 2023* proceeded without significant community interest or debate.

PART FOUR
A TAPESTRY OF CASES

My life in the law has been enthralling. Let me share some of my cases with you, before we journey back in time to delight in the rich canvas of human endeavour and emotion illustrated in a collection of quirky cases from Australia, New Zealand and Papua New Guinea.

The following cases have been chosen almost at random to illustrate the diversity of the law in the life of a counsel or judge. Some of the cases in which I appeared attracted great public attention at the time. Now they have faded from memory. Other cases passed without the media spotlight. Every case was important to the participants.

Nowhere in this book have I sought to glamourise my role or to pretend that my advocacy won the day. Lord Birkett, a famous English barrister, used to say that of every hundred cases, ninety are won on the facts. Only three are won on advocacy. As I tell my students, Lord Birkett added that seven are lost on advocacy.

It was not my initial purpose to write about my cases at all, but the cases that follow are ones in which I had some involvement. I have selected them because I found them interesting at the time. I hope you do too.

A Tale of Money and Trickery

Alan Bond was one of Australia's greatest fraudsters, though it must be acknowledged he had some stiff competition. He cost his victims and creditors billions of dollars. The financial excesses and collapses of the late twentieth century, Bond's time, are nowhere better captured than in three books by Trevor Sykes: *The Money Miners*, *Two Centuries of Panic* and *The Bold Riders*.

Bond rose from a signwriter who claimed to have repainted a prominent Fremantle landmark—the red dingo on the flour mills facing the Indian Ocean—to an international business identity. In 1978 he was named joint Australian of the Year with the activist Galarrwuy Yunupingu. After Bond backed the yacht *Australia II*, which won the America's Cup in 1983, his company, Bond Corporation, embarked on a series of increasingly audacious and ultimately ruinous investments. For a time, he was feted as a financial wizard. Bond was awarded Officer of the Order of Australia in 1984, though this was rescinded in 1997.

By 1992, he declared bankruptcy with debts totalling $1.8 billion. Notwithstanding, he maintained a lavish lifestyle through the assistance of a Swiss friend, Jurgen Bollag. The law eventually caught up with Bond and he spent time in gaol for federal offences. He died in 2015, largely disgraced but still admired in some quarters as the man who won the America's Cup for Australia. Bond Corp did in fact contribute millions to the competition but then claimed it as a deduction for research and development, so in reality it was the taxpayer who helped win the America's Cup.

Here I will tell the story of how Bond was prosecuted for dishonestly concealing facts from prominent Perth businessman Brian Coppin. He was convicted and sentenced to imprisonment. Then, in a twist reminiscent of a James Patterson thriller, he won an appeal and, after a retrial, was acquitted.

The story starts with Rothwells Ltd and another financial rogue, Lawrence Robert Connell, also known as 'Earn' for his prodigious success fees and 'Last Resort Laurie' for his ability to finance dubious ventures.

As I explained earlier, Rothwells was never a licensed merchant bank, but by 1980 it had achieved authorised trustee status by returning dividends for at least fifteen years. This meant it was a safe investment for trusts and estates. Laurie Connell purchased it in 1980 and the business was transferred to Perth, Western Australia, though the registered office and auditors remained in Brisbane, Queensland. Rothwells began to trade as a merchant bank in tandem with L.R. Connell and Partners, Connell's partnership with his wife, and his own company Oakhill Pty Ltd. The funds of these enterprises soon became intermingled.

Malcolm McCusker QC—later Governor of Western Australia and Companion of the Order of Australia—was appointed an inspector to understand what happened when Rothwells collapsed. He reported that over three years, 1985 to 1987, Connell and his entities borrowed huge sums from Rothwells. No hint of the borrowings appeared in either the published accounts or the annual reports. At year's end, Connell's indebtedness to Rothwells was removed from the books of Rothwells by journal entries that were either totally or substantially fictitious.

Rothwells eventually collapsed after three rescue efforts. It was likely insolvent shortly after Connell took control. The collapse of Rothwells was a major driver in the creation of the Royal Commission into the public-private partnerships known as 'WA Inc.'.

Tuesday, 20 October 1987 was the day the Australian share market lost 25 per cent of its value. Australia was not alone but followed other countries, including the United States, off a fiscal cliff. The month earlier, Western Australia had been rocked by the collapse of the Swan Building Society, followed by the Teachers' Credit Society, which for a very brief time, as it turned out, was Australia's largest corporate collapse.

Rothwells was in a vulnerable position. It had taken money from mum and dad investors and institutions such as the Catholic Education Commission. Its collapse would have a serious effect on the West Australian economy and beyond, not to mention political pain for the government. A rescue was imperative but had to be achieved in less than a week, as Rothwells' bank would not honour cheques written from the following Monday.

Something had to be done. Put simply, it was decided that Rothwells would make a $150 million share issue, to be underwritten by prominent businesspeople and companies. This would be backed by a guarantee to the bank from the state government in like amount.

Alan Bond was a great salesman, being relatively unburdened by the need to tell the truth. Bond promised to help raise the funds. Bond Corporation contributed $17.5 million. Bond approached several people, who pledged various amounts to the rescue by way of underwriting the share issue. He worked tirelessly throughout the weekend, persuading and negotiating. Bond was holding himself and his company out as being motivated essentially by a public concern to see that Rothwells should not collapse, lest that cause a domino effect on other financial institutions.

Bond had an old friend, Brian Coppin, a prominent businessperson with multiple interests. Bond went to see him at his home to ask him to take part. After some hesitation, because he did not have that kind of money, Mr Coppin agreed to underwrite a maximum subscription amounting to $20 million, but added the words 'or such amount as can be underwritten'.

These words were a serious barrier to the whole arrangement. Early the next morning, Bond returned to Mr Coppin's house and told him the whole deal could fall over unless Mr Coppin removed those words. There was no time to lose. Mr Coppin did so after his commitment was reduced to $15 million.

What Mr Coppin did not know was that the night before, Bond and Connell had met.

Rothwells was close to being saved, due in fair part to the efforts by Bond to find underwriters for the share subscription, and Bond wanted to be paid. He said to Connell, 'You're used to charging big fees, Laurie. How about $20 million.'

Connell, feeling he had no choice, eventually agreed to Rothwells paying a fee of $16 million to Bond Corporation. Peter Beckwith, one of Connell's lieutenants, drafted a letter, which was put on Rothwells' letterhead and signed by Connell and another director, David Hurley. Of course, the success fee in effect reduced the Bond Corporation contribution from $17.5 million to $1.5 million.

Other contributors to the underwriting were also left in the dark about the success fee.

Mr Coppin gave evidence to Mr McCusker that if he had known about the fee, he would 'not have gone into it'—that is, he would not have participated in the rescue. Mr Coppin learned about the fee the following month and believed at that point there was nothing he could do about it.

Bond was charged with dishonestly concealing the success fee from Mr Coppin, thereby inducing him to delete the sub-underwriting condition.

The trial was listed before Judge Blaxell for 25 May 1992. I led Michael Corboy for the prosecution. Michael Mischin was the instructing solicitor. The formidable Ian Callinan QC, with Chris Steytler, appeared for the defence.[5]

It was game on from the get-go.

At the heart of the trial was what had happened at the meeting between Bond and Connell. David Hurley, a director who was expected to give vital evidence about the circumstances of the letter, did not do so. The prosecution case then depended on the jury being satisfied

---

5 Later in life, Judge Blaxell and Michael Corboy both became Supreme Court Judges. Michael Mischin became Attorney-General. Ian Callinan became a High Court judge. Chris Steytler became the first President of the Court of Appeal.

that Connell's evidence—that an agreement had been sealed that night—was true. Bond did not deny that a success fee was discussed, but said agreement was not reached with Peter Beckwith, a Bond lieutenant, until a few days later. As there was no agreement about a success fee when he met with Mr Coppin the following morning, he contended, there was no concealment.

The trial took place over four days and ended with Bond's conviction. The public gallery was crowded. One person seated in the centre was Bond's ex-wife, Eileen, from whom he had recently divorced. I looked at Bond as the verdict of guilty was pronounced. At that moment he only had eyes for one person: Eileen. The next day, he was sentenced to two and a half years in prison.

Now the story gets strange: enter Max Healy.

I expected Bond's lawyers to lodge an immediate appeal and so they did. The first four grounds raised technical legal points. The fifth was a doozy.

A feature of some trials of the time was that a witness in one trial might well be an accused in another trial. So was the case with Connell. He was facing two trials. One was a conspiracy to defraud Rothwells over many years. His other criminal trial arose out of a horserace in Bunbury, in Western Australia's south. Connell had allegedly paid an apprentice jockey, Danny Hobby, $5000 to fall off a horse named Strike Softly so that Connell's horse, Saratoga Express, might win.

Hobby's fall was so laughably contrived that the race stewards opened an enquiry. Connell paid Hobby to flee the country, and for the next few years the jockey lived the high life, travelling the world at Connell's expense. Eventually Hobby returned to Australia, and he and a trainer, Bob Meyers, were key witnesses against Connell as he fought the charge of conspiracy to pervert the course of justice arising from the horse race. (I will explore this in more detail in 'The Strike Softly Affair'.)

The fifth ground of appeal claimed that fresh evidence had been discovered, rendering the verdict unsafe. It was said that Connell had confessed to lying about the success fee agreement in order to involve others in the downfall of Rothwells and to make himself look better when he fronted a jury.

How had this fresh evidence come about? Maxwell Raymond Healy was an undischarged bankrupt who had written, unbidden, to Bond shortly before the appeal. This is what he said in evidence to the Court of Appeal.

Healy had met Connell briefly some eighteen months ago at the races. He had no discussion with Connell, simply being introduced to him in a group of people. Connell was charged with the horseracing conspiracy on 18 January 1992. A couple of days later, Connell telephoned him out of the blue. He called himself Ivan and arranged to meet Healy in a room at the Hyatt Hotel in Perth. They met. Healy said Connell wanted him to give perjured evidence at his horseracing trial, to place the blame for the action taken to rig the race upon Meyers. Healy rejected the proposition but told Connell not to worry as he could trust Healy.

A week or so later, Connell telephoned again with a different proposition. The scheme was that Healy would write anonymously to Connell to arrange a meeting which was to take place at a motel. The conversation would be scripted and taped. The plan was to silence Hobby and Meyers by presenting an offer from an anonymous person, unknown to Connell. Healy apparently didn't understand the plan but went along with it anyway. He was to be paid a substantial sum of money. The offer was increased because Healy was hesitant. It was initially $25,000, then $50,000, then $100,000.

At his own expense, Healy hired a mobile phone—a rarity back then—and booked a motel room for two nights. He wrote a letter giving the number of the mobile phone and asking Connell to contact him urgently. He signed the letter 'D. Hancock'—who was a senior police officer. Shortly afterwards, he wrote a further letter dated 15 April 1992. This letter was signed 'Don', a reference to the same senior police officer. It spoke of efforts being made by a person called Max to contact Connell so that certain files could be removed without interference over the Easter weekend. The name 'Max' referred to a person whose surname was Rogers, who was supposedly a drug squad detective.

Healy's evidence was that, in accordance with Connell's scheme, a meeting was held at the Great Eastern Motel in Belmont. Healy played the part of the detective Max Rogers, and a tape was made of a conversation. A second tape was made with a conversation held in a motor vehicle. This recording was done by a private investigator hiding in the boot of the car. The possibility of getting rid of key witnesses was discussed, and of seizing or disposing of files that had been delivered to the Royal Commission in relation to Connell. All the material on the tapes was made with Connell's knowledge and consent, as Connell instructed it should be.

Healy said Connell's motivation was to secure his acquittal of the race-fixing charges so that he would appear as a good guy before the Rothwells charges went to trial. He also told Healy that it would be helpful to Connell if other people were convicted of Rothwells offences. Connell said that the more people who were convicted of Rothwells offences, the better it would be for him, as the jury would associate Rothwells with other people rather than him.

Then came Connell's confession to Healy:

> I said, 'Isn't Alan Bond on a Rothwells charge?' He said, 'Yes.' I said, 'What did he do?' Connell said he didn't do anything. I asked what the offence was about. Connell told me it was over a commission and that Bond didn't do anything as he had arranged the commission with Beckwith. Connell said I must give false evidence in the Bond trial.
>
> 'Why can't you do it to someone you don't know?' I said, then I continued—'Yeah, but you're doing it for self-preservation.'

By the time Healy gave this full account, Connell had reported his approaches to police and Healy had been charged with attempting to pervert the course of justice.

If this all seems extremely far-fetched, two members of the court thought there was enough in it to allow the appeal and send the matter back for retrial.

The third judge would have dismissed the appeal, leaving Michael Mischin to quip that they must have a competition to see who wears the brain for the day.

In February 1995 Healy was convicted of attempting to pervert the course of justice and imprisoned. The jury acquitted him of fraudulently attempting to obtain money from Connell, suggesting that they preferred Healy's version of events over Connell's.

On to Bond's retrial. This took place before Chief Judge Hammond and a jury. I thought the prosecution may be in trouble when I saw Mr Coppin sitting in the courtroom with his arm around Eileen Bond before the case began.

Mr Coppin's evidence on the retrial was substantially watered down from both his evidence to Mr McCusker—that if he had known about the fee he would 'not have gone into it'—and in the first trial, when he would not have underwritten the shares if he had known of the agreement for a success fee which took from Rothwells the equivalent of Mr Coppin's contribution and then some.

In evidence, I asked Coppin how his knowledge of the success fee might have affected his decision to commit funds to the Rothwells rescue. Instead of the unequivocal answer he had given previously, his response was: 'I don't think it's a fair question because the events had occurred so long ago.'

The judge held that the defence had no case to answer on the charge alleged, but allowed the prosecution to proceed on the basis there was some evidence of an attempted concealment. The trial limped to its conclusion and Bond was acquitted.

Some weeks later I had to fly east to a conference. Arriving early at the airport, I struck up a conversation with Ansett Airlines' state manager, Geoff Court, whom I had known since primary school. With a twinkle in his eye, Geoff told me how, a few weeks before the retrial, Brian Coppin had booked a first-class ticket to Sydney. Alan Bond was on the same flight. Bond asked to change seats to be next to Mr Coppin. They spent the flight together in close conversation.

Alan always was a master salesman!

The Strike Softly Affair

Laurie Connell was only forty-nine when he died, leaving behind a trail of debt, broken promises and betrayed friendships. He corrupted everything he touched. He was responsible in part for the fall of the Labor government after the scandal of its commercial activities was exposed. He contaminated sporting endeavours. He tried to buy his way into society with other people's money. Only death relieved him of accountability for the massive fraud which was Rothwells Ltd.

This chapter is about how Laurie Connell paid a jockey to travel the world to keep out of reach of the authorities. Along the way, the scandal ensnared Brian Singleton QC, who was charged with a criminal offence, tried by Judge Gunning without a jury and acquitted.

After he was charged, Connell tried every legal option to avoid trial. He was brought down by a small team of prosecutors, amply backed up by Inspector Graeme Lienert and his trusted crew of experienced detectives.

Connell had a genuine interest in horses, so far as may be judged. He owned a stable of thoroughbreds, at one time nearly the largest in Australia. He was a competent and keen polo player. He had, however, more interest in money. It was said that the most dangerous place on Earth was standing between Laurie Connell and a bag of cash.

In 1975 Connell was responsible for the 'Kalgoorlie Sting', so named because it resembled the Paul Newman and Robert Redford movie *The Sting*, released a couple of years earlier. Connell was in the betting ring at the Kalgoorlie racetrack. Across the country in Melbourne, his horse His Worship was to run.

'And they're off and racing ...' Those words were broadcast live on radio. Well, it was live in Melbourne. In Perth, a radio station delayed the broadcast, and it was further delayed in Kalgoorlie. So by the time Connell placed his bets in Kalgoorlie, the race had been run. Connell had known the winner. The bookies were unhappy. An inquiry was held and Connell was 'warned off' racetracks for two years for dishonourable action.

By the early 1980s, Connell was back on the racecourse. His fortunes were looking up. His merchant bank, Rothwells, and his firm, L.R. Connell and Partners, were apparently thriving. The Liberal government, under Premier Ray O'Connor, was in terminal decline, soon to be replaced by Labor's team led by Brian Burke. This would unleash the 'four on the floor entrepreneurs', whom Labour courted, some of whom would cause misery and loss in the years to come. Connell and Bond were determined to be part of the new order.

It was a sunny January day in 1983 for the running of the AHA Cup in Bunbury, Western Australia. Connell had a horse running in the race: Saratoga Express. It was almost certain to be a winner. Note the word 'almost'. Connell had backed it for $29,000 and didn't like to lose money—or horseraces.

But there was a problem. Strike Softly, another horse in the race, to be ridden by an up-and-coming nineteen-year-old rider called Danny Hobby, was even faster than Saratoga Express. The night before the race, Hobby was visited by a trainer, Bob Meyers, on behalf of Connell. Meyers offered Hobby $3000 to pull up the horse. Hobby agreed to do so for $5000. However, Hobby decided that Strike Softly was too good to be pulled up, so he would 'fall' off shortly after the start and tell everyone that his foot had not been properly in the stirrups.

The race started and shortly after, as planned, Hobby came off his mount. This was not enough to enrich Connell, however, because in a thrilling final furlong Saratoga Express was pipped at the post by another horse whose jockey was trying to win.

Hobby's fall was so risible that the stewards mounted an inquiry. Obviously, Hobby would be the key witness. An investigation was opened immediately and then adjourned to Perth. Hobby gave his explanation but was not believed; he received a two-year suspension. He lodged an appeal that was dismissed.

Meanwhile, the stewards had launched a betting inquiry. Connell was in danger if Hobby spoke the truth. At this point, Sam Franchina, a prominent Perth identity and a relative of Meyer's wife, entered the story. Hobby was made an offer too good to refuse. If he and his girlfriend left Australia for two years, he would be paid a monthly allowance and expenses. Hobby and his girlfriend accepted and in mid-April 1983 flew to England and spent some time at Newmarket, the home of British horseracing.

Back in Perth, allegations were made in a newspaper about corruption in racing. The Turf Club requested a police investigation. Control of it was given to Superintendent Graeme Lienert, who put together a team he could trust and commenced making inquiries. Lienert was known to the conspirators Connell, Meyers, Franchina and others as a man who could not be bought off.

In October 1983, Hobby was visited by police in Newmarket, England, and made a statement, falsely repeating his evidence to the stewards' inquiry. Panicking, he closed his bank accounts in England, destroyed documents and flew to Paris. He and his girlfriend spent several months travelling Europe, all the while receiving payments.

From Europe they travelled to the United States, arriving in January 1984. They then visited Canada, and in July 1984 returned to Australia. Although Lienert had arranged for a 'stop order' to be activated if Hobby returned, Franchina managed to have it lifted by a corrupt police officer, so Hobby's arrival back into Australia through Sydney was not known to the police.

Hobby was visited by Franchina and left the town of Esperance, in Western Australia's far-flung south-west, where he had been visiting his sick grandmother, returning to Canada before going to New Zealand. In January 1985 Hobby left New Zealand for England. There he was visited by Brian Singleton QC, then shortly after he flew to

Singapore. From Singapore, declining an offer from Franchina to go to Sicily, Hobby instead flew to Rome.

During this time, he met and married Ivy. They moved to Singapore and flew back to Perth on 26 October 1986. In Perth Hobby negotiated a further arrangement whereby he would be paid $300,000 to stay away for a further three years. The Hobbys then returned to Singapore.

In May 1987 Hobby returned from Singapore and went to Esperance, where on 28 May 1987 he was visited by Lienert, who had not given up the investigation. Spooked by this, Hobby contacted the barrister Singleton, who rang him back and recorded the conversation. A third voice, probably Connell's, could be heard saying, in respect of Lienert's investigation, 'Does that mean that without the kid, he's got nothing?' Money was regularly transferred to fund Hobby's itinerant lifestyle. It came from several sources, including Laverock Pty Ltd, a Connell company domiciled in Jersey, and accounts in Rome, Hong Kong and Singapore.

Meyers dropped out of the conspiracy early on and liaison with Hobby was conducted by others. They included Sam Franchina and Jack Walsh, who worked for Connell from time to time and was a Labor strategist. Only death in each case prevented them being fellow conspirators in the dock with Connell.

Lienert's team did not give up, but without Hobby there were few avenues of inquiry. Try as they might, for years the team made little progress. Lienert was pressured to drop the investigation more than once as Connell's star rose. Until ...

In 1989 Meyers was convicted of breaking and entering a building and seriously assaulting the householder. He had arranged for a couple of thugs to go to a former girlfriend's house and give her a hiding to teach her a lesson. He was sentenced to a cumulative term of ten years' imprisonment. In June 1990 he appealed against his conviction but was unsuccessful. I appeared for the prosecution to respond to the appeal. By December 1991, Meyers was depressed and despondent at the idea of years in prison. He reached out to Lienert. He was prepared to tell all in exchange for some leniency.

By this time, Danny and Ivy Hobby were in Singapore with a baby.

I had taken some leave shortly before Christmas to paint the house when I received a call from Lienert to see him and the team. We sat in my partly painted living room as they recounted Meyer's confession and discussed what to do. Eventually we agreed that detectives should travel to Singapore to interview Hobby.

This had to remain a closely guarded secret. Apart from the team, it was known only to the Police Commissioner, the Deputy Police Commissioner and the Head of the Detectives, Don Hancock.

On 1 January 1992, the wife of a prominent criminal lawyer telephoned Ivy Hobby to warn her police were on their way.[6] Someone had leaked.

By now Hobby had grown weary of the nomadic life and agreed to return to Western Australia, plead guilty and give evidence against Connell for the prosecution. Connell was arrested and charged with conspiracy to defraud by fixing the horserace, and with conspiracy to pervert the course of justice by paying to keep Hobby away.

This prosecution would need a crack team to complement the hand-picked band of detectives. After some consideration, I selected as lead prosecuting counsel Shauna Deane, whom I knew as a quietly spoken lawyer with meticulous attention to detail. Her gentle demeanour hid a strong and determined personality that would not be intimidated by the task before her, or the personalities involved. To support her as counsel, there was no one better than Bruno Fiannaca, then a young, committed prosecutor, now a respected Supreme Court judge. Instructing them as solicitor I appointed Virginia Campbell, calm and steady. For the next two years they worked long hours and weekends to ensure that the brief was as strong as could be. I was criticised from time to time in putting a couple of young prosecutors—one a woman at that—to confront two 'wise men from the east' alpha males for the

---

6 She later gave evidence at the committal hearing denying she had made the call. She was convicted of perjury for that statement, despite the best efforts of Geoffrey Miller QC on her behalf. Christine Wheeler prosecuted with her usual attention to every detail.

defence, Alec Shand QC and Stephen Archer. I never once regretted my choice.

The preparation for the committal and trial was arduous. At one point I flew to London, Jersey, Eire, Canandaigua in New York State, Rome and Singapore to obtain evidence of financial transactions and examine witnesses. I was given leave to appear in the Four Courts in Dublin, where my silk gown was much remarked upon.

In Rome I briefed an Italian *avvocato*, Signore Della Vedova, who introduced me to the Director Générale of the Department of Justice and Grace. He invited me to coffee. His hand trembled with each sip from his cup. Poor man. Two prominent prosecutors, Giovanni Falcone and Paolo Borsellino, had just been murdered by the Mafia with bombs. He was heavily guarded.

Connell elected to have a committal hearing. A committal hearing is held in front of a magistrate. The purpose is to determine if there is enough evidence to justify committing the matter for trial in the District Court. The magistrate has a limited function. The strength of the evidence is unimportant. The question is sufficiency of evidence. The magistrate does not decide whether there is proof beyond reasonable doubt.

By 1992, committal hearings were a rarity. Because of the low threshold, magistrates almost always committed an accused for trial. And even if an accused was discharged after committal, the prosecution could in any event present an 'ex officio' indictment.

Connell showed remarkable tenacity to prevent a trial by a sustained series of legal actions.

His committal was before Magistrate Dennis Reynolds, later the President of the Children's Court. It lasted sixty sitting days and produced 5593 pages of transcript from thirty-five witnesses. Those called by the prosecution were subjected to a searching, sometimes searing cross-examination.

In the middle of the committal, Connell's lawyers sought the intervention of the Supreme Court to dismiss the charges or correct the magistrate's alleged errors. I appeared for the prosecution. The matter was argued before Justice Pidgeon on 27 November 1992 and the application for an injunction was dismissed. Connell immediately appealed to the Full Court, which heard the matter on 9 December 1992. The legendary Tom Hughes QC led Stephen Archer for Connell. Shauna and I appeared for the prosecution. Again, Connell's application for an injunction to restrain further proceedings was dismissed.

The magistrate committed Connell for trial on 2 February 1993. On 5 March 1993, Connell sought leave to appeal against the committal. Justice White refused leave. I appeared against Stephen Archer to respond to the application.

Finally, the matter was listed for a jury trial before Judge Gunning. This produced a flurry of applications to the Supreme Court just before the trial, as Justice Rowland, then Justice White, refused the ever more desperate demands that the proceedings be stayed. To allow the team to concentrate on the trial, I appeared for the prosecution on these attempts, with Michael Mischin as my junior counsel. By this time, with his long preparation in the Rothwells trial, Michael knew more about Connell's affairs than anyone.

Judge Gunning was a competent trial judge with many years' experience, but he was apt to get irritable. He and Shand had already clashed, and I was fearful that the trial would degenerate into a shouting match.

In the event, I need not have worried. Shortly after the trial began, the judge suffered a heart attack. The trial had to begin again before a different judge. On the directions hearing before Chief Judge Heenan, he announced that he would take over the trial. I breathed a sigh of relief. Des Heenan, as his close friend Brian Singleton always called him, was in my opinion one of the best judges I appeared before. Learned, scrupulously fair, his only blemish was a tendency to pedantry. On one occasion years ago, after I had reframed a question in cross-examination several times, Judge Heenan looked at me, smiled and said, 'Mr McKechnie, that last question was very, very, very nearly proper.'

Connell's trial, which began on 16 November 1994 and lasted almost six months, was hard-fought. Almost every point was taken and argued. One hundred and ten witnesses were called. Finally, the jury was sent away to deliberate their verdict. They took thirty-five hours, punctuated by returns to court for the judge to read them selected parts of the transcript.

I was in Darwin attending a Heads of Prosecution Agencies meeting on 9 May 1994 when the verdicts were announced. The result: not guilty on the charge of conspiracy to defraud; guilty of conspiring to pervert the course of justice. The verdict was huge news. I gave a short media interview.

The verdicts seemed inconsistent, but Shauna assured me there was logic to them. The first charge hinged on the evidence of Meyers as to the date of a meeting between him and Connell. The judge clearly directed the jury that they had to be satisfied beyond reasonable doubt as to the date. There was confusion about the date and evidence that Connell was elsewhere at the time of the alleged meeting. The verdict of guilty to perverting justice did not require proof of a motive. The evidence of money transfers to Hobby on his travels, and direct evidence of meetings were more than enough to satisfy the standard of proof beyond reasonable doubt.

After the verdict, Connell was stripped of his belt, tie and shoelaces, bundled into a police van and driven to prison. Two days later, Judge Heenan sentenced him to five years' imprisonment.

I congratulated Shauna, Bruno and Virginia, Graeme Lienert and his faithful team and generously told them they could have the weekend off. 'Then back on Monday to prepare for the inevitable appeal,' I said.

The notice of appeal was not long in coming. There were more than fifty grounds of appeal, alleging errors on the part of the trial judge, inadmissible evidence, refusals to permanently stay the proceedings because of adverse publicity, jury prejudice and more. It took a while to get to ground fifty-three (inconsistency of the verdicts) and ground fifty-four (unsafe verdict).

Back the team went into the bunker, as the trial preparation room was nicknamed. After discussion, it was decided that I would argue the appeal from the prosecution, with Shauna and Bruno ready to put me right when I tripped up.

Connell had changed senior counsel, so I faced Roger Gyles QC, an experienced and daunting opponent but quieter and more measured than Alec Shand. Because Connell was in prison, the appeal was listed quickly for five days, beginning Monday, 11 August 1994.

We were well prepared when the appeal commenced but were immediately thrown a googly. Mr Gyles cunningly opened with ground fifty-three and suggested that the appeal might readily be disposed of on that ground alone. The issue, striking in its simplicity, was that the inconsistency between the not guilty and guilty verdicts meant the court could have no confidence in the result, which might have been due to compromise.

To my horror, the court, Chief Justice Malcolm and Justices Pidgeon and Nicholson, seemed well disposed to that idea, with the consequence that within an hour I was on my feet defending the verdict. I had not expected to do so until Wednesday.

As I rose to respond, I made myself a promise. I would not sit down until I had persuaded them to hear the whole appeal. I was fending off penetrating questions from the Chief Justice until nearly 4 pm, following which the court announced a short adjournment. On their return, the Chief Justice spoke the words I had been waiting for: 'The court will hear argument on all grounds tomorrow morning.'

Just before Christmas on 22 December 1994, judgment was handed down. It was not an early present for Laurie Connell. The court unanimously dismissed the appeal against conviction and sentence. For good measure, they agreed with our argument on several issues which I had thought were losers, but which Bruno Fiannaca had strongly pressed that we should make.

Connell's next step was an application for special leave to appeal to the High Court.

The High Court will only grant leave if there is a point of public importance. Such was the significance of the application that I decided we should travel to Canberra to respond to the application rather than appear by video-link from Perth. So we packed our bags and off we went. On 16 March 1995 we appeared before Justices Dawson, Toohey and McHugh. Roger Gyles QC again appeared for Connell.

I enjoyed appearing in the High Court, where, as an advocate, you are challenged by intelligence and experience greater than your own. Some judges stay sphinx-like and silent, while others engage in a direct, almost combative way.

Special leave applications are governed by strict rules. Each party has twenty minutes to make their argument, and the applicant has a further five minutes to respond. Times are strictly enforced with orange warning and red final lights. I have heard counsel cut off in mid-sentence as the clock ticks past twenty minutes. Usually, in applications for special leave, we did a lot of preparation and ended up not being called on, with the words from the presiding justice: 'We do not need to trouble you, Mr McKechnie.' Not this time.

Mr Gyles had refashioned his argument somewhat, but the essence was still a complaint about inconsistent verdicts. The court was engaged from the start, debating with him. When my turn came, Justice McHugh focused on the verdicts, and it was a relief to resume my seat. After Mr Gyles had concluded his five-minute response, to my surprise Justice McHugh had more questions for me, expressing some scepticism at my responses. Eventually I said, 'All I can do, your Honour, for a special leave application, is to point in very, very short form to their Honour's reasoning. To develop the point about inconsistency necessarily of course would take a long time and go through the evidence ...' This was an argument *in terrorem* (Latin for 'in terror'). If they really thought there was something in the point, I was prepared to stand there until they understood. Shades of the first day of the appeal in Western Australia.

After a short adjournment, Justice Dawson announced there was no sufficient reason to doubt the conclusion of the Court of Criminal Appeal that the verdicts were open to the jury. Special leave was refused. Shauna and I were left shaking our heads and wondering what the previous hour had all been about.

Connell served just over a year in prison, then was released to stand trial for conspiracy to defraud relating to Rothwells, another trial he had spent a fortune on in vain to delay or permanently stay. By then he had used up all his money—other people's money—and could not afford a lawyer, so he defended himself. The trial commenced in November 1996 with a three-day opening by Ron Davies QC.

To further complicate Connell's life, Alec Shand QC sued his solicitors for unpaid fees. The matter went to trial and Justice Wheeler reserved her decision. She was about to hand down judgment when the parties advised they had reached a settlement.

On 26 February 1996, I had lunch with Michael Mischin, who was the instructing solicitor. He remarked that the air conditioning wasn't working in the courtroom and if the trial continued in the heat, it was likely to turn into a homicide trial.

That afternoon, Connell argued that Justice White should not allow evidence from an accountant, Jonathan Pope, who had told Connell at the beginning of 1989 that Rothwells was insolvent. Connell had Pope sign a confidentiality clause to prevent him telling anyone. Connell then let Rothwells continue to trade and amass further debt. This evidence went to the heart of Connell's involvement in the conspiracy to defraud, but Connell argued that Pope was bound by the confidentiality clause and could not give evidence as a consequence.

Justice White was having none of it and rejected Connell's argument. The court adjourned until the next morning, when Ron Davies would call Pope into the witness box.

In the early hours of 27 February 1996, Connell suffered a massive heart attack at his home and died. He was forty-nine.

Contacted for comment, Danny Hobby said he had lost the best travel agent a man ever had.

Murder

There is nothing humorous about murder. A life is cut short, often in a brutal way. It has been my lot to prosecute many murders, and as a judge to preside over the trial of many more accused of this most serious of all crimes.

Lawyers and judges can become hardened to some of the more graphic details. A jury of ordinary men and women, by contrast, might never have been confronted with making a decision that could send a person to prison for life, or that might disappoint the deceased's family and friends, who are looking for what they regard as justice.

In a sense, there can never be justice. The one thing the victims most desire is the return of the deceased, which of course is impossible. The best the law can do is deprive the killer of liberty for a time. It can never replace the deceased.

We do not subscribe to the dictum 'a life for a life', as no state or territory in Australia has the death penalty. Opinions will always differ as to what length of incarceration relates to taking from the deceased that person's most precious right—the right to life.

Domestic violence appears to have recently been discovered by politicians. It is a scourge but not a new one. As already recounted, my first trial as a prosecutor was as junior counsel to Geoffrey Miller in Port Hedland. The accused, Angus, was charged with wilful murder. He had killed his wife in circumstances typical of domestic violence. He was convicted, successfully appealed and on retrial was convicted of manslaughter. It was my introduction to domestic violence. Over the years I would see many examples. Heartbreakingly, they included men who had killed not only their wives but their children as well.

My next murder as the prosecutor was a tawdry affair. Newly arrived at the Crown Law Department, I was led by Ron Davies, a prosecutor's prosecutor who could expose the heartless and remorseless mind of an accused like no other. He had a prodigious memory and could sum up a complex case for the jury with few, if any, notes.

Two men, Hakala and Saunders, were chronically hard up for cash. Living together in a flat in Mount Lawley, they decided to rob a defenceless old man who was the proprietor of a small post office in East Parade. The shop and its surrounds have long since been demolished. One morning they entered the shop, one of them carrying a large knife. A scuffle ensued and the old man, bleeding from fatal wounds, staggered outside and died. Even though they were wearing gloves of the sort used for washing dishes, the two were soon arrested.

At trial, the defence counsel adopted what lawyers call, macabrely, a 'cut-throat defence'—each blaming the other. The jury were not persuaded and convicted both of having a common intention to rob the post office, during which one of them—it mattered not who—stabbed the old man, intending to do him what is quaintly called grievous bodily harm. That fulfils the definition of murder. The men were sentenced to life imprisonment. On appeal, Saunders was convicted instead of manslaughter.

Murder in the Warehouse

Frank La Rosa, a man of many parts. He was a distinguished Vietnam War veteran. He was a family man. He was a major drug dealer.

In 1996, La Rosa was convicted of importing a large quantity of heroin and amphetamines from Thailand in hollowed-out books. He pleaded guilty before District Court Judge Viol and, despite the best efforts of Geoffrey Miller QC on his behalf, received a sentence of twelve years and four and a half months. He appealed against both his conviction and the sentence. He abandoned his appeal against conviction and his appeal against sentence was dismissed.

Three years later he attempted to overturn his conviction. This was legally difficult for two reasons. First, he had pleaded guilty, which was a strong obstacle. He alleged incorrect advice from his lawyer and an inducement from the National Crime Authority (NCA). Second, he had abandoned his appeal. Unless he could persuade the judges that his abandonment was a nullity, he was bound by his earlier decision. There was also a Commonwealth indictment and sentence to set aside.

In one of my last appearances before the Court of Criminal Appeal, I appeared for the State Crown to oppose his application.

The essence of Mr La Rosa's argument was that he was acting on behalf of the NCA and the WA Drug Squad, who had encouraged and enabled him in his drug business. Things became personal when he accused me of being part of the conspiracy, which earned him a rebuke from the bench. In the event, Mr LaRosa's application was denied. He returned to prison to serve out the rest of his sentence.

Mr La Rosa had more success in the Federal Court. During a botched drug deal, Mr La Rosa claimed that some $220,000 had been stolen from him by unscrupulous thieves. Clearly there was no honour among them. The Australian Taxation Office assessed the money as income. Mr La Rosa said it was a business loss. Appearing for himself, he argued that it was earned in the course of business—drug dealing— and lost while he was trying to obtain stock. The Full Court agreed.

Shall I repeat? The Full Court agreed that the theft of $220,000 of drug money was a tax write-off for the drug dealer. Little wonder the Commonwealth Government immediately changed the rules to prevent others from succeeding with a similar argument.

La Rosa continued his chosen trade of drug dealing. He also married Kim in 2007. They were inseparable. Indeed, they were together when La Rosa conducted business with another drug dealer at a coffee shop in Victoria Park, Western Australia, on 8 June 2008. Which was the last time they were seen alive.

After that meeting, they disappeared. The usual signs of sudden departure were there—food left out, lights not on and, later, bank accounts not accessed and appointments missed. Police became involved and the major crimes unit took over the investigation. La Rosa had made a lot of enemies during his life and there was no shortage of suspects.

Among his acquaintances was a young man of twenty-one, Adam Mikhail. Adam was a bit of a whiz with computers and would help the La Rosas with computer glitches. He attended their wedding and photographed the proceedings. La Rosa had loaned Adam $20,000 to pay for his own wedding in Vietnam, though the loan had come with conditions. Payments of $3000 a month were required, and interest kept accumulating. Frank Mikhail, Adam's father, did not like drugs or La Rosa. He said, 'To owe Frank La Rosa a dollar was to owe too much.'

Adam had an interest in a business that imported bathroom and floor tiles from Vietnam. On 8 June 2008 the business received a shipment of tiles in containers that were loaded into the warehouse. That evening, Frank and Kim La Rosa were summoned to the warehouse by

Adam. He had fixed a computer for them and wanted to give it back. The La Rosas drove in their distinctive red Jeep Cherokee.

During the weeks after the La Rosas went missing, the Jeep was the subject of several sightings. There was a nurse stationed in Lancelin who was moving to another location. A friend owned a helicopter and offered to give her a sightseeing tour before she left Lancelin. While taking photos, something odd caught her eye. Bogged into the side of a sand dune was a red Jeep Cherokee. She took photos of it and reported the sighting to police. Thus, from a few days after the disappearance, police knew where the La Rosas' Jeep was. The honest people who gave evidence later at trial as to recognition of the La Rosas in the red Jeep after the date it was located were mistaken.

Suspicion fell on Adam in view of his accumulating debt to La Rosa. In the week prior to the disappearance, Adam and Frank had made several trips to a rural property in the outer-city suburb of Chittering. Adam had used a TomTom GPS device to navigate. TomTom is a company based in the Netherlands. Police sent the device to Amsterdam, where its contents were downloaded. It disclosed four separate journeys to the Chittering property in the week before the La Rosas went missing.

Armed with the information about the destination, police made two unsuccessful searches. After the first, Adam rang his father to report a television broadcast of the search.

'They are at a certain location at the moment with an extensive team surveying the area, capish?' he said.

'Si si, capish,' the father replied.

Police grilled the Mikhails, who gave nothing away. After one such interview, Frank Mikhail commented to his son: 'That's the only problem, it's the fucking TomTom.'

Police did a final search of the Chittering property in January 2009. They had searched for hours and were on the point of giving up when Detective Senior Sergeant Rowson ordered a final dig. As the scoop emerged from deep within a pit, it was carrying two bodies—Frank and Kim La Rosa.

Remember the coffee shop meeting in June? Undercover police officers had photographed the meeting. Frank and Kim were dressed in the same clothes six months later when their bodies were discovered. Police arrested the Mikhails the same day.

The next day the warehouse was emptied. Hidden under the containers of tiles and waiting for discovery were fragments of shotgun cartridges. Frank and Kim had been shot in the back at close range.

I presided over the jury trial. It took place over many weeks in May and June 2011. The prosecution was represented by Linda Petrusa, now a District Court judge, and Michelle Radley, now a magistrate. The accused were represented by Jonathan Davies for Adam Mikhail, and Peter Ash for Frank Mikhail.

The trial was hard-fought. The prosecution had a jigsaw puzzle to put together to prove not only that the Mikhails were the killers, but also that, beyond reasonable doubt, no other person was. Intercepted telephone calls and mobile phone locations played their part. The TomTom evidence was critical. I convened court one evening to take evidence from the TomTom software engineer in the Netherlands. The proceedings were conducted in Dutch under Dutch law. The judge, the witness and the witness's lawyer all spoke perfect English; on occasion the witness would interrupt his evidence to correct the Perth-based interpreter in English before resuming his evidence in Dutch.

A possible alibi from Adam was disproved by the prosecution. A friend had claimed they were watching a particular movie on a subscription channel on the fatal Friday night. A witness from the channel proved that the movie was unavailable at that date. It had been broadcast earlier.[7]

Neither accused gave evidence. Mr Davies concentrated on the number of Frank's enemies who had reason to see him dead. He had been stabbed a few months earlier and was on bail for drug offences.

---

7 This was not the first time I had encountered this issue. While prosecuting an alleged rape many years earlier, the accused claimed that the victim consented. She reputedly made a reference to Sylvester Stallone using the words 'Italian stallion'. This was topical, he said, because they had been to see *Rambo: First Blood Part II*. In fact, the film had not been released until months after the alleged conversation. He was convicted.

There was no doubt that Frank La Rosa had serious competition in the drug trade and, possibly, people who wished him harm. To no avail.

I thought that the evidence was overwhelming, but it was not my job to decide. That duty rested entirely on the jury. After a retirement of some days, the jury returned unanimous verdicts of guilty. Yet again I was in awe of twelve men and women taken from their usual routine and occupations, who listened to some harrowing evidence for more than two months and then carefully considered their verdict.

Before sentencing, I heard a remarkable victim impact statement from Frank La Rosa's daughter from an earlier marriage. She looked at both the Mikhails, motionless in the dock, and said that she chose to forgive them. She chose not to carry the burden. She finished by quoting Frank La Rosa: 'If you do the crime, be prepared to do the time.' The crime was nothing less than a cold-blooded execution.

The entire story may never be known. I remain sceptical of the wedding debt story and suspect the real reason for La Rosa's death was something to do with drugs. He was summoned to the warehouse on the evening a shipment of tiles arrived from Vietnam. Regardless, Kim La Rosa was an innocent victim. She accompanied her husband everywhere, and for that reason she was murdered with him.

I sentenced each of the Mikhails to a mandatory sentence of life imprisonment for each murder. I set a minimum term of thirty-seven years before either would become eligible for parole.

Each appealed against their sentence. The appeals were dismissed. President McLure of the Court of Appeal, in giving judgment, said there were no mitigating factors of any significance and no remorse: 'The circumstances as a whole provide a particularly barren environment with little promise for any realistic prospect of rehabilitation or reform.'

In sentencing Frank Mikhail, who was fifty-six at the time, I noted that whatever sentence I imposed would likely be one that confined him until his death. On 23 February 2023, Frank was found unresponsive in his cell and could not be revived. There were no suspicious circumstances. He was sixty-eight. Adam Mikhail will be sixty-one when he becomes eligible for parole.

The Body Under the Slab

In January 2003 I had to cut short my participation in a sailing regatta to return to Perth for a trial. It was on this journey that we drove through the willy-willy, as I have recounted earlier.

Bruce Jones and his wife Barbara (not their real names) lived in a suburb to the south of Perth with their two children. The marriage appeared happy, but all was not well. Bruce's wife was a constant marijuana smoker, which left her without energy or drive. It was the source of frequent arguments between them.

They were a social couple and entertained a group of friends regularly with barbecues in the backyard. When people needed the convenience of the bathroom, the ladies would go inside, while the men, sorry to say, would line up behind the back shed.

One Friday night, as their friends gathered for the usual barbecue, Bruce had some bad news for them: Barbara had gone away. They'd had an argument and she had walked out on the kids and him. His friends consoled Bruce, telling him she would soon be back and all would be forgiven. She just needed a few hours. She adored her children and would never do anything to hurt them. Unusually, on this night, when the men in the party needed to use the toilet, Bruce suggested they go inside rather than use the back of the shed.

Barbara did not come back that night. Or Saturday. Or Sunday. By now Bruce was getting worried. So were their friends. 'Have you called the police, Bruce?' they asked. No, he had not. 'Don't you think you should?' 'I don't want to embarrass her if she comes home,' he told them.

By Monday, people were really worried. Bruce reluctantly called the police and reported Barbara as a missing person. A television station heard about Barbara's disappearance and sent out a reporter and crew. On the six o'clock news, the station showed a heartfelt plea from Bruce, standing there with his downcast children. 'Wherever you are, Barbara, please come back. I need you. The kids need you. We miss you.'

Bruce had not been idle that day, however. He had a motorcycle of which he was very proud, and he'd arranged to have a company pour a concrete slab at the back of the shed so he could park the bike there. This was done, and when the concrete was dry Bruce moved the bike onto it.

By Tuesday, Barbara was still missing and the police were involved. Detectives had taken the case over from the missing persons squad and had begun to make enquiries. By Wednesday, the family's property had been declared a crime scene. Bruce and the children had to move in temporarily with friends.

The detectives were particularly interested in the new concrete slab. In a voluntary record of interview with Bruce, video-recorded, detectives asked Bruce if he had killed his wife. Bruce was indignant. Of course not. The slab was a coincidence. If they dug it up, the detectives asked, what would they find? Nothing, said Bruce. In fact, they could go and dig it up right now. But who would pay for the replacement?

Bruce was very convincing, as plausible as he had been on television. No one watching the recording could think him capable of killing his wife and burying her body. It would be an impossible bluff to offer to dig up the slab if there was anything to hide.

Early the next morning, Bruce left the house where he was staying and rode his bicycle to his house, just in time to see a government contractor unloading a mechanical concrete cutter from a trailer. Bruce looked thoughtful for a while, then quietly rode his bike to the nearest train station, caught a train to Perth's Central Station and then a bus to the airport, where he purchased a one-way ticket to Melbourne. When the plane took off shortly after, Bruce was strapped in his seat.

Back at the house, it had taken a while to manoeuvre the concrete cutter into position and remove the motorbike. Finally, all was ready and the cutter did its work. Immediately the detectives could see the outline of a body. It was Barbara buried under the slab, as had been suspected all along.

Because of daylight saving time, Bruce arrived into Melbourne late in the evening. Having checked into a hotel, he telephoned his children at the friend's house where they were staying. Don't believe everything people are saying, was the gist of his message. As he put the phone down, detectives also carefully replaced the receiver at their end.

Ten minutes later, Bruce was rudely awoken by armed members of the Victorian Police entering the room in full tactical gear. Bruce went quietly and was extradited back to Western Australia to stand trial for murder.

Mr Phillip Urquhart, now a coroner, was the prosecutor—fair but deadly. The redoubtable Gail Archer SC appeared for Bruce.

Bruce gave evidence that around lunchtime on the Friday, while he and Barbara were in the backyard preparing the evening barbecue, they began arguing yet again about Barbara's marijuana use. In frustration, Bruce grabbed her round the throat, intending only to shut her up. But, to his horror, she collapsed and died. Her death, according to Bruce, was an accident, not murder.

'Why did you not own up immediately? Why did you bury the body?'

'Because,' said Bruce, 'I didn't think anyone would believe me.'

And in that he was completely right. Bruce was convicted of murder and sentenced to life imprisonment.

The Death of Mr Shortbread

Joe Hollomby was a Geraldton stalwart. For many years he would get up at 5 am and bake shortbread and pies using dough he had prepared the day before. By 9 am he was out the door, making his deliveries. Long retired, he baked as a labour of love for his community. All the profits he made were given away—to the Royal Flying Doctor Service, Silver Chain and other charities. Age did not deter him. At ninety-four he was still going strong—an institution in a country town that had bestowed on him the nickname 'Mr Shortbread'.

Since the death of his wife some years before, Joe had lived in a quiet suburb with his son. The son kept firearms at the home, locked securely in a gun safe. This fact, though not well known, was not a secret either.

Eric Pedersen was a violent, self-absorbed criminal. Addicted to amphetamines, he lived a life of petty lawlessness while generally managing to hold down a job. When his life crossed with that of Joe Hollomby with fatal results, he was nearly fifty.

Bill (a pseudonym) had crossed Eric in a deal, or so Eric thought. He brooded on this for a time before deciding that Bill should die. On 15 November 2008, his rage exploded. He knew where there were guns to be had—Joe Hollomby's home. Arming himself with a knife, he made his way to the house and broke in.

It was the early evening and Joe was at home. He had no chance. In vain he put up his hand to ward off repeated stabs but to no avail. He died at his home from a wound that pierced his aorta.

Eric tried to hide the body. After that, he broke open the gun safe, armed himself with a .270-calibre rifle and ammunition, and set off for Bill's house.

Bill and his family were at home when suddenly shots whistled past their heads, embedding in the wall. Fortunately, no one was hit.

Eric continued. His sister had a property just outside Geraldton. Pride of place in the animals stocking the farm was Banjo, a South American llama. Eric shot the llama dead.

Still, he was not finished. His brother was holding a small barbecue with friends to celebrate a successful outcome from recent hospitalisation with his care group. In came Eric. Again, making it all about him, he threatened to commit suicide in front of everyone. Police who were called had to administer several tasers before Eric could be apprehended.

Was Eric remorseful once he sobered up? Who knows. Remorse is a difficult emotion to assess, being close to regret, which is something else entirely. What is clear is that Eric took five months to come clean. Initially he blamed another man for the killing, going so far as to make a statement through his lawyers detailing how the other man went inside the Hollomby home while Eric stayed outside, keeping watch.

Naturally, the police investigated the other man as a suspect. He was confronted and interrogated. Fortunately for him, at the time in question he was 400 kilometres away in Perth at a party. Photographs of him taken at the party and the testimony of other guests proved conclusively that he was not involved.

Finally, Eric pleaded guilty to murder, on the basis that he did not intend to kill Joe Hollomby but only to do him some grievous bodily harm.

Many years before, when I was still new to the bench, Justice Bill Pidgeon had gently chided me for conducting sentencing proceedings for a murder in Perth, rather than in Esperance, where the crime had occurred. Bill was a country boy and had practised law for years in Bunbury, so he knew better than I about local communities. The jurisdiction of the Supreme Court is statewide, and they were entitled to see justice done in their own town. I followed his advice thereafter.

And so I so flew to Geraldton for the sentencing hearing. I was glad I did as the courtroom was packed. Joe Hollomby had been much loved.

As I listened to the prosecutor, Linda Petrusa, outline the facts, and then George Giudice on behalf of Eric Pedersen draw my attention to matters that might provide some mitigation of punishment, I reflected on how fate had brought these two opposites together one November evening, and the ensuing destruction of both lives. I sentenced Pedersen to life imprisonment with a minimum before parole consideration of nineteen years. Pedersen's appeal was dismissed and his application to the High Court was unsuccessful.

In 2010 the Geraldton community launched the Hollomby Foundation to support local students. In this way, the work of an unselfish local hero lives on.

Pedersen remains in prison.

The Fate of a Good Samaritan

North Bannister, on the Albany Highway, is hardly a town, just a roadhouse. One Friday night, the chance meeting of two strangers, coincidentally both named Edwards, led to the death of one and a sentence of death for the other.

Gary Edwards, his brother Warren and their friend Ron Nightingale decided one Friday evening, 27 March 1981, to drive to Albany, intending to visit friends. They set off at dusk down the Albany Highway.

They were travelling in Nightingale's station wagon. It was not in good condition. Before they had left Armadale behind, the differential began to overheat, eventually glowing red as a cherry. They limped into the North Bannister Roadhouse after dark. Now they were miles from home and without transport.

But help was at hand. Jeffrey Edwards was there too, refuelling his panel van. He had worked all week and was trying to cash a wages cheque of $200. He was on his way home to Pingelly. After hearing their story, and being kind-hearted, he offered to go out of his way in the other direction and tow them back to Perth.

Gary had been drinking. Taking a sawn-off shotgun from Ron's vehicle, he decided to ride with Jeffrey in the panel van. Warren and Ron sat in the station wagon, which was now hitched to Jeffrey's panel van with a rope.

From North Bannister, the Albany Highway threads its way through a jarrah forest to Armadale. For many years, small forestry townships had dotted the forest. Glen Eagles was once a thriving township in the forest just off the Albany Highway. Abandoned in the 1960s, by 1981 it had become what it is today, a picnic area. The little convoy stopped at the turn-off to Glen Eagles.

Jeffrey began to check the tow rope in the headlights of the station wagon. It was pitch-dark and there was no one else about. Ron, who had stayed in his vehicle, looked out of the window and was horrified to see Gary lining up the shotgun on the unsuspecting Jeffrey. He called out but it was too late. Gary fired, hitting Jeffrey in the back and knocking him to the ground.

Warren got out of the station wagon and helped Gary drag the body off the highway. 'You'd better make sure that he's dead,' he said.

Gary fired again, this time into Jeffrey's head.

Ron now joined them, and the three men dragged the body to a hollowed-out tree, dug a shallow grave and covered it with branches. Two days later they would return and throw a kangaroo carcass on top of the grave to further disguise it.

After the burial, they resumed the journey to Perth. Jeffrey's panel van was dismantled and stripped of parts that were subsequently sold, the proceeds being shared among the men. The shotgun was thrown into the Swan River from the Garratt Road Bridge.

To all intents and purposes, Jeffrey had just disappeared. His parents contacted the police, who posted him as a missing person. It was the perfect crime. Perhaps.

Ron Nightingale had been deeply affected by the senseless murder and confided in a few friends the events of that awful night. Word reached the ears of a police informant, who whispered the story to Detective Sergeant Ken Wells. He started investigating and found the missing persons report. It aroused his suspicions, especially as no attempt had been made to cash the pay cheque or to collect $400 that police were holding on Jeffrey's behalf at Narrogin.

By November 1982, Ron was working in Karratha. With no more than a cop's instinct, Wells flew to Karratha and confronted Ron, urging him to tell the truth. It was a relief for Ron, and he quickly told Wells what had happened. Returning together to Perth, Ron led detectives to the hollow tree and grave. So it was that, twenty months after his disappearance, Jeffrey's remains were uncovered. His parents finally knew what had happened to their son.

Gary, Warren and Ron were arrested. Gary was charged with wilful murder. Warren and Ron were charged as accessories after the fact. They had no knowledge that a crime was going to be committed, but had assisted afterwards in order to enable Gary to escape punishment.

I was briefed to lead George Tannin for the prosecution. Ian Temby QC, soon to be the first Commonwealth Director of Public Prosecutions, appeared for Gary with Kate O'Brien, later a District Court judge.

The police had been thorough and put together a very strong brief. For example, after three days diving in the muddy and turbid waters of the Swan River, they located the remains of the shotgun. They were helped by the evidence of a young woman, who was later a witness for the prosecution. When I interviewed her before trial, she said that she was a passenger in the car when Gary threw the shotgun into the water between the eighth and ninth light poles. When I asked her how she knew that, she gave the surprising answer that she always counted the light poles when she went over a bridge.

The trial was held before Justice Brinsden and a jury in March 1983. Gary's defence was that the shooting was accidental, but he had difficulty in accounting for two shots, not one. During cross-examination, I asked him to show the jury how he was holding the shotgun. He declined on the basis that it would be too painful to recollect. The judge ordered him to take up the weapon and answer the question. His squeamishness was too late.

Gary never explained to anyone why he had killed his Good Samaritan that dark night. When asked by his brother Warren, he said that he did not know. No crime is ever motiveless, although it may seem to be to others. The offender always has a reason, even if that reason is difficult to discern. This case is one of the few where I have been unable to see any motive for a murder.

The court was quiet when the jury filed in to deliver the verdict: Gary was guilty of wilful murder; Warren and Ron were guilty of being accessories.

When called on to say whether there was any reason why sentence of death should not be pronounced, Kate was too overcome to speak.

Justice Brinsden pronounced that Gary was sentenced to death in a manner prescribed by law. The sentence was later commuted to imprisonment for life. The two accomplices were sentenced to an effective term of three years' imprisonment, with parole eligibility.

Manslaughter

Manslaughter, despite its evocative name, is the least serious form of homicide. It is a crime to unlawfully kill another person, even if there is no intention either to do so or to cause grievous bodily harm. The maximum sentence for manslaughter has varied over the years and is presently imprisonment for life. Unlike for murder, life imprisonment for manslaughter is not mandatory.

Shortly before Christmas 2008 I was rostered for three sentencing days. I sentenced twenty-four offenders that week. Three were sentenced for manslaughter, but only two were the subject of publicity and comment.

The sentence that received no publicity involved an Aboriginal woman who, on New Year's Day, had fatally stabbed her partner in front of their young children. Her sentence of five years' imprisonment received no comment. No angry letters complaining of inadequacy, no callers to radio programs in a rage.

The second case, like the first, was tragic. All homicides are dreadful crimes, robbing the victim of that most fundamental human right—the right to live.

Christmas Day and the beginning of 2007 in Geraldton had started well, with parties at the beach and goodwill in plentiful supply. Mr Bill Rowe and his family were celebrating Christmas when a few youths stole beer from an esky nearby. Some retaliation followed. The boys ran away and returned with reinforcements. One of the returning group was a young man named Matthew McDonald, aged twenty-one.

For a while there was a running brawl between the group and members of the public who had been enjoying a day at the beach. Meanwhile, Bill Rowe had gone for a walk and was not involved in the disturbance.

McDonald played little part in the fighting. At one point he was grabbed and his head was held underwater for nearly a minute, which was terrifying because he could not swim. However, that is no real excuse. Mr Rowe returned from his walk. McDonald was heavily intoxicated with cannabis and alcohol when he picked up a cricket bat and hit Mr Rowe over the head, causing his death.

On Tuesday, 2 December 2008 McDonald pleaded guilty to manslaughter. Noting that no punishment could ever fit the crime, I sentenced McDonald to five years' imprisonment and activated a nine-month suspended sentence to be served consecutively.

The community outrage was sudden and vocal. Calls were made for my removal. Citizens expressed strong support for mandatory sentences in cases of manslaughter. There seemed to be near universal opinion that the sentence was grossly inadequate.

Were they right? The answer lies in the convoluted sentencing regime enacted by parliament.

At the time, the maximum penalty for manslaughter was imprisonment for twenty years. But under so called 'truth in sentencing' laws—an oxymoron if ever there was one—the maximum sentence had to be reduced by a third. This brought the maximum down to thirteen years and four months. McDonald had pleaded guilty in the early stages, and so was entitled to a further reduction of 25 per cent, or three years and four months, reducing the maximum available penalty to ten years and four months. So before I had taken account of any matters of mitigation, such as McDonald's age, prior record or other factors, the maximum sentence had already almost halved.

Also to be considered were other sentences and Court of Appeal decisions. Consistency is important and guidance is gained by reference to similar cases where they can be found. Youth remains an important mitigating factor.

The DPP, Robert Cock QC, evidently thought that the sentence, even if light, was within the range of a sentencing discretion, and with courage he resisted the many voices imploring him to appeal.

'Oh well, another day at the office,' I thought, as the airwaves continued to shout about the ridiculousness of the sentence and the need for mandatory sentencing to correct ignorant and out-of-touch judges living in an ivory tower.

Then came Friday, 5 December 2008 and another plea of guilty to manslaughter.

Alice Tarbuck (not her real name) and her husband spent years trying for a child using IVF treatment until eventually a little boy was born. For the first eighteen months Alice was a model mum, nurturing and breastfeeding the baby. But her world was collapsing. Deep depression meant she was psychologically separating from the baby. Her marriage crumbled. Her suicidal thoughts were generally kept at bay by tablets prescribed by her psychiatrist.

On 5 November 2007, overwhelmed and alone, Alice decided to end her life and that of her son. She drove into the hills and fed a hose from her car's exhaust into the cabin. Although she became affected by carbon monoxide, it failed to kill them. Now quite beside herself, she drove back to Perth and climbed to the top of the tall apartment block where she and her husband had once lived in happiness. With the baby cradled in her arms, she climbed over the safety rail and jumped. Alice survived but was terribly injured, with multiple fractures. The baby was killed.

Immediately arrested and charged with wilful murder, Alice was remanded in custody, first in hospital and then at Bandyup Women's Prison.

The prosecutor was a very experienced and humane lawyer, Dave Dempster. Defence counsel was the equally experienced and sensible Paul O'Brien. Together, they agreed that the charge would be reduced to manslaughter and she would plead guilty.

So it was that, on that Friday morning, Alice and I came face to face. She had her head down and was in tears as the facts were read, letters tendered and victim impact statements made.

It was difficult to decide on an appropriate sentence. Alice had robbed her son of a future life and caused great grief to his grandparents and father. On the other hand, here was a woman of unblemished character who was deeply affected by mental illness and, even at sentencing, in significant physical pain.

There is an aphorism in the law that when justice ends, mercy begins. I decided to apply that aphorism. No sentence I gave her could match the remorse she felt. Having regard to the eleven months she had already spent in custody, and all the other matters which a judge must consider, I asked her to stand.

'You are sentenced to imprisonment until the rising of the court,' I said. 'Court is adjourned.'

Alice was free, at least physically. Her family rushed to support her.

And how did the media and all those calling for mandatory sentences and my removal take it? What a wise, compassionate judge, they said. What a good thing it is that there is no mandatory sentencing.

Every crime is different.

A Pair of Wills

Phil and Gertrude Moss, brother and sister, ran a small shop on Scarborough Beach Road in inner-city Mount Hawthorn. Their relatives would infrequently look in on them, but otherwise they kept to themselves. They had some friends, in particular a widow, Mrs Winifred Dixon, and Mrs Angela Benetti, who would help in the shop from time to time.

Both were in their late seventies when they died within six weeks of each other, Phil on 14 October 1978 and Gertrude on 29 November 1978. Relatives were unaware of their passing for some months until one of them visited the shop and met the new owner—Mrs Benetti.

On Gertrude's death, all her property had been left in her will to Mrs Benetti and her husband. The wills contained a clause stipulating that the relatives were to get nothing if they 'detested the will'. Clearly, the writer meant 'contested the will'.

The relatives were suspicious and further inquiries were made. The wills had been admitted to probate by a well-respected solicitor. He had not drawn the wills, but advised on the requirements to meet the Probate Office queries, particularly about the number of signatures on each will. The wills were unusual in that they had purportedly been signed by the testator up to six times. They were witnessed by Mrs Benetti's sister and brother-in-law, who swore affidavits that they had been present when each will was executed.

Further inquiries were made, and the matter was reported to police. When Detective Sergeant Ayton knocked on Mrs Benetti's door, her response was, 'Oh, those bitches— forgive me—they are detesting the will.'

A great quantity of written material was seized, including a pension cheque signed 'Gertrude E. Moss'. The signature appeared to have been traced over and was similar to the signatures on the will.

Sergeant Jack Billing, a handwriting expert, compared the signatures with the proven handwriting and other signatures known to be of the two elderly shopkeepers, and declared that the signatures on both wills were forgeries. Mrs Benetti, her sister and her brother-in-law were arrested and committed for trial in the District Court before Judge O'Dea and a jury.

I appeared for the prosecution. The accused were represented by Ron Cannon. By then, Ron was one of the leading defence lawyers in Western Australia. He was a favourite before juries and a formidable opponent. He was clever, though he tried to keep it hidden by saying things like 'when I start reading law books, I start losing money'. Ron had graduated from law school with first-class honours. When I was at Jackson, McDonald, I had briefed Ron and appeared as his junior counsel for the trial of a lady accused of stealing from her employers. Ron had obtained an acquittal.

The chief prosecution witness was Sergeant Jack Billing, who explained to the jury how he had formed his opinion by reference to the acknowledged handwriting of Phil and Gertrude Moss. In his opinion, the multiple signatures of Phil and Gertrude Moss on their wills were forged. The signature of Gertrude Moss on the will bore a strong resemblance to the real signature on the cheque, as if it had been traced.

Mr Cannon then commenced his cross-examination. After a time, he produced a set of twelve Christmas cards said to have been sent by the Mosses to Mrs Dixon. Mr Cannon said she would be called as a defence witness in due course. The cards were addressed 'To Wyn' and signed 'Phil e Gert'. Sergeant Billing conceded that the handwriting on the cards was like that on the wills, which meant, logically, that the signatures on each will were not forged. There were other fragments of writing produced which Billing agreed were consistent with the writing on the wills. One such item was a card of the type handed out at funerals. It bore the signature of Phil Moss, evidencing his attendance at the funeral of Mrs Dixon's late husband.

The prosecution case was taking on water and beginning to sink. At the end of the day, I asked the judge if the cards could be released into my custody. Mr Cannon strongly opposed my motion, but the judge allowed the request.

I said to Detective Sergeant Ayton, 'Just find me one card that was printed after 29 November 1978'—Gertrude's date of death.

I was working late on the brief at about 10.30 pm that night when I received a phone call from Ayton. 'I haven't found you one,' he said. After a pause, he added, 'I've found you two.' The detectives had been busy. They contacted the Australian distributor of Hallmark greeting cards, who confirmed the date each card had been printed. At least two had been printed after Gertrude Moss had died. A representative from Hallmark Cards was flown to Perth and gave evidence for the prosecution.

There was more to follow. Mrs Dixon was interviewed and gave a different story to that suggested by Mr Cannon. She was called to give evidence by the prosecution, not the defence. This was her evidence as to the cards.

She was friendly with Phil and Gertrude, she said. She was sad when they passed away. Sometime after their deaths, she received a visit out of the blue from Mrs Benetti, who professed an interest in some photograph albums and scrapbooks. Mrs Dixon went into the kitchen to make coffee; when she returned, Mrs Benetti was holding a bundle of cards, which she said she had found in a photograph album. She also found the funeral card. Mrs Benetti asked to keep all the Christmas cards and Mrs Dixon agreed.

As to her husband's funeral, Mrs Dixon said Phil Moss was ill and did not attend. Mrs Dixon had never seen the funeral card before. On being shown the Christmas cards in court, Mrs Dixon said she had never seen them until Mrs Benetti produced them from the album. The Mosses never called her 'Wyn'. They always called her 'Winifred'.

After the evidence was presented by Mrs Dixon and the Hallmark Cards representative, the prosecution case began to recover. However, the case was far from over. More documents appeared from the defence with similarities to the signatures on the will.

An accused person is under no obligation to give evidence in a criminal trial. No one can force them to do so. It is the right of every citizen to require the state to prove its allegation beyond reasonable doubt.

Although an accused cannot be compelled to give evidence, they may do so voluntarily. Mrs Benetti decided to do so. In her evidence, Mrs Benetti had an answer of sorts to everything. When it was suggested that 'e' was Italian for 'and', she said that she did not speak Italian or write it. Mr Moss was helping her to learn how to speak it. She did not know what 'e' meant. Mrs Benetti was of Italian heritage. The prosecution produced a journal she kept, written entirely in Italian. As might be expected, 'e'—meaning 'and' in English—appeared a lot.

All three were convicted of forging and uttering. In addition, the brother-in-law was convicted of perjury for swearing in an affidavit that he had witnessed the wills being signed by each of the testators. The sister was spared gaol to care for the children. Mrs Benetti and her brother-in-law each received a heavy sentence. An appeal against conviction was dismissed. Probate was in due course set aside and letters of administration granted to the relatives.

Appearances Are Deceptive

I was prosecuting a dry-as-dust fraud trial. One Friday I was to lead the evidence of two important witnesses, a mother and her equally respectable son. That morning I took them through the testimony they would give, a process known as 'proofing the witness'.

In due course I called each of them in turn to the witness box. They gave truthful evidence and withstood cross-examination. After that they passed out of the court and out of my memory.

Until about eight months later, when I received a brief to prosecute a kidnapping and sexual assault case. The facts were particularly bad. A young woman was renting a cottage on a property in the hills of Perth. The landlord was a married man with children who lived in a big house nearby. On a Thursday night he broke into the woman's cottage and abducted her, locking her in the basement. He sexually assaulted her repeatedly.

As you may have guessed, it was the same apparently respectable man who had been my witness. On the Friday when I was leading his evidence, he had left the poor woman imprisoned in chains. Worse was to follow. He built a box to fit over her head. It was then bolted shut, leaving her in darkness. Her screams caused him to remove the box, but he continued to keep her chained up. He raped her.

She would commute to work on a motorbike. To put any inquirers off the scent, he took the bike a few kilometres down the valley and left it in such a position as to pretend that she had run off the road and crashed. By the Sunday, police were actively searching for her. He made the woman promise not to tell anyone what had happened and to stick to the motorcycle accident story. Of course, she agreed. He then let her go.

At the first opportunity she told of her ordeal. He was arrested, the house was searched, and the box and other materials such as the chains were discovered.

Videotaping interviews was still a novelty but he fully participated in an interview and confessed. It made for chilling viewing. He pleaded guilty before Justice Walsh and received a heavy sentence.

It demonstrated to me yet again that it is impossible to judge a person, either from their appearance or from brief association. Few murderers look the part: their ordinariness is their distinguishing characteristic. A witness may look shifty and refuse to make eye contact. They may mumble as if to conceal a lie. Yet they might be perfectly truthful, and their evidence is often confirmed by other evidence.

There was nothing about this middle-aged man that gave any hint of the depravity within.

The Thirsty Finn

People from Finland have a reputation as hard drinkers. The manifestation of that reputation in the hottest town in Western Australia meant that fireworks were likely.

Ari Heike Vaitenen, a Finnish prospector, had been banned from drinking at Marble Bar's only pub, the Iron Clad Hotel. This was in the same town where bottles of methylated spirits were kept on ice. On 7 October 1976 he tried to get a drink from the pub but was refused.

He decided to get his revenge. Taking two sticks of dynamite, he attached a fuse and detonators, and, in a somewhat foolhardy act, tucked them into the front of his trousers before making his way to the laundry at the back of the pub.

No doubt thankful that there had not been a premature eruption, he dropped the sticks behind the washing machine, lit the fuse and hurried away. The resultant explosion was spectacular. It was heard all over the town. When the dust had settled, there was no more laundry. The iron and asbestos structure had disintegrated, and the washing machines were destroyed.

In due course, Vaitenen pleaded guilty to setting an explosion and was sentenced to two years' imprisonment with a five-month minimum.

Third Time's the Charm

Bunning v Cross is a leading High Court case on the admissibility of unlawfully obtained evidence. Like many famous cases, it started in an almost humdrum way—low interest was just the beginning, one might say. In 1886, two brothers, Arthur and Robert Bunning, arrived in Western Australia and acquired a sawmill.

By the 1970s, Bunnings had expanded from wood products to DIY with a chain of hardware stores. This was due to the efforts of Robert's son Charles Bunning and his brothers.

Charles lived in leafy Peppermint Grove, and it was his habit after work to drop into the exclusive Weld Club for a whisky (or three). Driving home one night in his Rover, he was stopped on Stirling Highway in Claremont because he had crossed the lanes and was speeding. Constable Leslie smelt liquor on his breath. He asked Mr Bunning to get out of his car.

As Mr Bunning did so, the Rover, still in drive, began to move forward. Constable Leslie hopped in, applied the brake and turned off the engine. When stepping onto the footpath Mr Bunning staggered back onto the roadway.

At this point, Constable Leslie made an error. He should have administered a preliminary breath test. Instead, he took Mr Bunning directly to the police station, where he blew 0.190, which is an offence of driving under the influence—the charge he eventually faced. A DUI charge is appropriate when the blood alcohol reading is or exceeds

0.150, so even on the most favourable view Mr Bunning was well over the limit.

Mr Bunning pleaded not guilty and went to trial in the Magistrates Court. The magistrate was Robert Huck Burton, appointed three years earlier and not perhaps the finest intellect to have graced the bench. Mr Bunning was represented by Mr Terence Walsh, later the Supreme Court judge I replaced, and Mr Robert French, later Chief Justice of the High Court of Australia and an extraordinarily accomplished lawyer. After hearing argument from Mr French, the magistrate acquitted Mr Bunning on the basis that since no preliminary test had been performed, the subsequent test was illegal and evidence from it was inadmissible.

The prosecution commenced what was to be the first of three appeals. The appeal came before Justice Jones, who allowed the appeal, commenting that 'it is not very easy to draw from the decision any connected pattern of reasoning'. The judge sent the matter back to Mr Burton to decide whether, even though the evidence was unlawfully obtained, it could nevertheless be admitted into the trial as a matter of discretion.

The matter came before the magistrate a week later. Here I entered the case, appearing for the prosecution. Despite my citation of some fifteen cases in support of the proposition that the evidence should be admitted, the magistrate was more than equal to the task and managed to distinguish all fifteen. He dismissed the charge again.

The prosecution launched the second appeal, this time to the Full Court. I was led by Kevin Parker. Kevin gave his usual masterclass in advocacy and the prosecution succeeded on appeal, though the Chief Justice dissented. The court ordered that the matter be returned to the magistrate with a direction to convict.

This time it was Mr Bunning's turn to appeal, which he duly did to the High Court.

I was led by Kevin Parker again. While the majority of the court dismissed Mr Bunning's appeal, Justice Murphy would have allowed it. He was particularly offended by the repeated appeals. 'This "third time proves it" approach is not appropriate to the administration of criminal justice,' he said.

A short time later I attended before the magistrate again, who calmly followed the direction and entered a conviction. Robert Burton—'Beefy' to his friends—continued in office for another twenty-seven years, fending off the occasional appeal.

Charles Bunning had built up a successful and formidable business supplying building materials and dispensing a large number of barbecued sausages, before Bunnings was taken over by Wesfarmers in 1994. He lived until he was eighty-nine.

One Flew Over the Kookaburra's Nest

Following the success of the book (and later film) *One Flew Over the Cuckoo's Nest*, it is hard to believe that electro-convulsive therapy, or ECT, was still practised in the 1980s. In fact, it is still in use today, hopefully without Nurse Ratched.

A man, whom I shall call John Doe, had several jobs over his lifetime and was working as a fisherman in Fremantle at the time of these events. Mr Doe claimed that a lady was making unwanted sexual advances towards him. She would, he said, constantly ask him to sit with her and talk. They went 'parking' late into the night on several occasions and he became embarrassed, as everyone in Fremantle, he said, would know what was going on, although they never had sexual intercourse.

Eventually there was a falling-out. She and a friend of hers would roundly abuse him whenever they saw him, call him names and make faces at him in the street.

This was driving Mr Doe mad, and he decided that the only way to stop this was to slap the lady's face, thereby committing an assault. He could then be able to tell a magistrate the whole story. That would end the affair and get the lady off his back. Mr Doe went to her premises intending indeed to slap her, but the lady would not open the door. So he broke the flywire screen on a window as the next best thing, then sat quietly and waited for the police, who arrived in due course and arrested him.

Now his troubles began. When he appeared before the magistrate in the Fremantle Court of Petty Sessions, things did not go as planned. His behaviour was such that a magistrate ordered he be psychiatrically assessed before he could enter a plea, and remanded Doe in custody for that purpose. He was transferred to Heathcote Hospital.

An experienced psychiatrist diagnosed paranoid schizophrenia and admitted Mr Doe as an involuntary patient. He was in the hospital for some time and, despite his strenuous and violent objections, was administered drugs and underwent a regime of ECT.

This therapy was controversial, though there had been some claimed success in treating certain forms of schizophrenia. Unlike depictions on screen, a patient was sedated before treatment. Nevertheless, Mr Doe didn't want to be administered ECT. But he was an involuntary patient, so he had no choice. The doctors were empowered to prescribe whatever they considered was in the patient's best interests, regardless of the patient's own views.

On the psychiatrist's recommendation, the charge against Mr Doe was discontinued. He recovered and in due course consulted a solicitor, Mr Jack Courtis. Mr Doe sued the state for negligent medical treatment. In opening his case, Mr Courtis said that his client was not really seeking pecuniary compensation at all, but rather trying to prove a point. I appeared for the state and the doctors, leading Shauna Deane.

The plaintiff, Mr Doe, gave evidence in a manner Justice Jones, the trial judge, described as 'unique in my experience'. Mr Doe told his story, virtually uninterrupted, in a continuous flow for a little more than an hour and a half. I remember being unable to keep up taking notes.

Mr Courtis called two psychiatrists in support of Mr Doe's case. Neither diagnosed Mr Doe as suffering from paranoia. However, the difficulty was that each had seen him after the treatment of both the drug Modecate and the ECT. They could not deny that the treatment might have worked, and that while he was not now ill, he may have been suffering paranoid schizophrenia at the time he was admitted to hospital.

On the state of the evidence and the law, Justice Jones had little choice and dismissed the action. In doing so, he added that the judgment did not reflect in any way on the sincerity or truthfulness of the plaintiff, Mr Doe. 'The brave and sensible man—and I judge the plaintiff to be both—will put the episode behind him and get on with the job,' he said. The judge concluded by saying that he hoped that, having told his story and put his point of view to a sympathetic court, he would now lay to rest the ghosts of the past which had been haunting him, and they would trouble him no more.

Alas, it was not to be. Although initially accepting the judgment, Mr Doe took to brooding over what he still saw as a great wrong done to him by the psychiatrist who had ordered his involuntary admission and subsequently his treatment. One evening several years later, Mr Doe went to the psychiatrist's home, broke in and terrorised him for hours before being subdued by police and arrested. He was convicted and sentenced to imprisonment.

Boondies or Coondies?

Geoffrey Miller and I once opposed each other in an action for negligence.

The plaintiff, a young boy in Year 7 at Goomalling District School, was playing wars at lunchtime with other students. As part of the game, they were throwing small missiles of packed dried sand. Unfortunately, one of these hit the boy in the eye and he subsequently lost almost all vision. He sued the Department of Education for failing to maintain proper supervision. I appeared for the department.

The trial illustrated the linguistic differences between town and country. Both Geoff and I had been raised in Perth, and each of us separately had done what these boys had done. We called the missiles 'boondies'.

When Geoff questioned his young client, he asked if they had been chucking boondies at each other. I knew exactly what was meant. The boy, however, looked mystified.

Geoff repeated the question. By now Justice Jones was also interested.

Finally, the boy's face cleared. 'Aah,' he said. 'You mean coondies.'

The Great Newpark Jewellery Heist

It was a grey and rainy day in May 2004 when early-morning shoppers at the Newpark Shopping Centre in Girrawheen, a suburb of Perth, were startled by a loud crash, followed by the sound of breaking glass. Shortly after, the same shoppers were running for cover as a gun battle broke out between two armed and dangerous robbers wearing balaclavas and two security guards who happened to be in the shopping centre refilling an ATM. Eventually the robbers made their escape, leaving one of the guards wounded and bleeding.

This was a daring plan ruthlessly executed but brought undone by elements of stupidity. If not for the terror inflicted on innocent bystanders, it would have been a suitable plot for a Mack Sennett *Keystone Cops* film.

Three men, Bradley Noble, Johnny Piccolo and David Hintz, needed money and so conceived a plan to rob a jewellery store. The plan was that two of the men would break into the roof space of a shopping centre and make their way to the ceiling above a jewellery shop. Using a pinhole camera and monitor, they would observe when the owner arrived, took jewellery out of the safe and set it out in the display cabinets. They would then drop down through the ceiling, throw the jewellery into a bag, run through the shopping centre and make their escape in a stolen car driven by the third man, the getaway driver.

To overcome resistance, they armed themselves with a loaded shotgun and a pistol. Of course, at 9.30 am it was highly unlikely that there would be any opposition.

How wrong they were.

In the lead-up to the heist, mobile phones were purchased in a false name—James Clavell. The real James Clavell was a famous writer and author of a book entitled *Noble House*. The choice of name was not a coincidence.

To safely drop down through the ceiling required rope. This came from Noble's sister's house. Her former partner, Nick Martin, had been a removalist, she said, and left quantities of rope in her garage. A patch of blood on the rope was later matched to Noble's DNA.

The morning of 11 May 2004 was selected for the robbery. Things began to go wrong from the outset. The robbers needed to steal a car for the getaway. They found a Holden Commodore suitable for their needs and drove it away from where it was parked outside a house. The car was nearly out of petrol, however; the owner was planning to refuel in the morning. The lack of fuel soon became known to the robbers when the car coasted to a stop before they had gone very far at all.

No fuel. Late at night. What to do? Noble walked to the nearest twenty-four-hour service station (it was past 3 am) and borrowed a small silver can that only held four litres. He trudged out of sight of the CCTV cameras, returning on foot again for another four litres. He was to return once more, this time in a car that Hintz had hired a few days earlier.

Not an auspicious start.

Still, parts of the plan worked. Two robbers cut a hole in the roof and, as planned, lay quietly, waiting for dawn and the jewellery shop owner's arrival. The gang talked to each other using the mobile phones. Around 9 am, the store owner arrived and began laying out the stock into glass display cabinets.

At 9.40 am the robbers struck. Wearing dark clothing, balaclavas and gloves, they smashed through the ceiling with a loud crash and dropped to the floor. While the terrified store owner stood by, the two robbers began to break the glass cabinets and scoop the jewellery into a bag.

By chance, two security guards were refilling an ATM nearby. To protect the cash, each was armed with a pistol. Hearing the noise, they went to investigate. Robbery in progress.

One guard drew his firearm. 'Freeze,' he shouted.

The robbers did not freeze. Instead, they began to fire on the security guards, who returned fire in a running gun battle all the way to the front doors. Shoppers scattered and sought cover.

The robbers reached the getaway car, which began to accelerate away. As it did so, the front passenger, armed with a shotgun, saw the security guard emerging from the doors. Someone in the car said, 'You're gone.' The shotgun fired, wounding the security guard, who later had ten pellets removed from his body.

Satisfied that the guard was no longer a problem, the getaway driver slammed his foot on the accelerator and the stolen car lurched forward—straight into the back of a truck! With the getaway car now useless, the three men jumped out, leaving behind the bag with all the stolen jewellery.

One man approached a woman who was reversing out of a parking bay. He threatened her with a pistol. Her response? She wound the window up and drove away.

The other two had slightly more success. Approaching the driver of another car, they jumped inside, one in the front passenger seat and the other in the back seat. They soon discovered an unwelcome problem: the driver's four-year-old daughter was sitting in the front seat and the robber sat on her. They went some distance before the driver and his daughter were forced out of the car and walked slowly home in the pouring rain.

This being the 21st century, there was CCTV footage of the whole of the robbery and of the nocturnal visits to the service station. In a short time, the Newpark Shopping Centre was alive with police officers. Detectives soon had a lead on the suspects. Two days after the robbery, Piccolo and a female companion were stopped while driving in Mirrabooka. The pistol used in the robbery was found on the floor next to where Piccolo was sitting. Also found after a search of the car were two-way radios, communication scanners, gloves, screwdrivers and tinsnips. Data relating to mobile phone use linking the robbers to the crime was discovered. The three men were arrested and charged with aggravated armed robbery, stealing and attempted murder.

Almost exactly two years after the crimes, the three stood trial in Court No. 2 of the Supreme Court of Western Australia. The prosecution was undertaken by Mr Brent Meertens. I was the trial judge, sitting with a jury.

The prosecutor painted a persuasive picture for the jury, linking together the various circumstances. In Noble's case in particular, the evidence was entirely circumstantial.

To describe evidence as 'circumstantial' makes no judgement as to its strength. A case may be proved by direct evidence, such as a witness describing what was seen or heard. A case may be proved by an admission or confession. If the evidence is believed, a jury may be satisfied that the accused is guilty.

Circumstantial evidence involves an extra step. Facts are proved and an inference is drawn from those facts. If the only reasonable inference is that of guilt, then a jury may convict. However, there are three fundamental principles that govern most criminal trials, including this one.

Principle one is the presumption of innocence. Every citizen is presumed to be innocent of any charge made against them, unless and until the jury is satisfied that the presumption of innocence should no longer apply.

Principle two is the burden of proof. It is for the prosecution to prove the guilt of the accused. In cases where there is no issue about sanity, that burden never shifts from the prosecution. The companion principle is that an accused has no obligation to speak or assist the prosecution and is entitled to remain silent at all stages.

Principle three is the standard of proof. The prosecution must prove the guilt of an accused beyond reasonable doubt before a jury may convict.

Applying those principles to a case involving circumstantial evidence means that the prosecution must exclude all reasonable hypotheses consistent with innocence before a jury can convict. If there are two inferences available, one leading to guilt and the other not, then the proper verdict would be not guilty.

The trial ran for three weeks, and although the accused exercised their right not to give evidence, nevertheless some accused called witnesses.

The most dramatic of these was Chad John James, whom I had earlier sentenced for robbery in an unrelated matter. James initially declined to answer questions on the grounds that the answers may incriminate him. On the basis that he would get a certificate that any answers given in court would be inadmissible in criminal proceedings against him, I directed that he answer the questions. Mr James then gave evidence.

The prosecution had it all wrong, he said. The three men in the dock were not guilty. They had not been there at the Newpark Shopping Centre and had not committed the crime. Mr James and two companions, Frank Donaldson and Johnny Spitieri, had committed the robbery. The pistol? Oh yes, Frank had given that to James after the robbery. James had then given it to Piccolo as payment for a debt owed to the latter. That is why the police had found the pistol at Piccolo's feet in the car.

Frank would have loved to give evidence exonerating the three, but unfortunately he was dead.

Tracking Johnny Spitieri proved to be a bit of a problem as well.

Johnny Spitieri ... where had we heard that name? The year before, an Australian film had made it onto the screen. It was called *Gettin' Square*. The role of—wait for it—Johnny Spitieri was played by David Wenham. Curiously, the film featured a scene in which armed robbers broke through the ceiling of a bank, terrorising the customers.

It seemed a very improbable story to me, but I was not part of the jury. Only the jury could decide if the prosecution had proved its case against each of the accused beyond reasonable doubt.

In due course, the jury returned guilty verdicts on all charges against the three men, Hintz, Noble and Piccolo. They received identical sentences. For the crime of aggravated armed robbery, they were imprisoned for life. For the second crime of aggravated armed robbery involving the unfortunate father and his young daughter, eight years. For stealing the getaway vehicle, two years. For the attempted murder of the security officer, imprisonment for ten years.

If a person is convicted of aggravated armed robbery and sentenced to life imprisonment, they become eligible for parole in seven years. Whether parole is granted is another matter, of course. Piccolo and Hintz were not eligible for parole until they'd served ten years because of the sentence for attempted murder. In Noble's case I made a parole eligibility order allowing him to be considered for parole after eight years.

Piccolo and Hintz appealed against the sentences, but their appeals were dismissed. Noble appealed against his conviction on the basis that the verdict was unreasonable because there was not enough evidence to convict. His appeal was also dismissed and an application for special leave to appeal to the High Court was refused.

Hintz did not take well to prison life. Shortly after receiving the term of life imprisonment, he was sentenced to four years' imprisonment for trying to organise an escape, with accomplices who would supply arms and grenades and ram the accommodation block with a front-end loader. The plan was foiled when detailed codes and documents were discovered in one of the conspirator's cells.

A co-conspirator was Wayne Napier, who was serving a sentence of strict security life imprisonment with William Monaghan for wilfully murdering David Locke, whom they suspected of being a police informant in the Australian Nationalist Movement, an extreme white supremacist group led by Jack van Tongeren, later convicted of firebombing Chinese restaurants.

I had prosecuted Monaghan and Napier before Justice Murray and a jury in June 1990. They were defended by Geoffrey Miller QC and Brian Singleton QC. Despite their best advocacy, they were unable to overcome the effect of a confession. Videotaping records of interview was still in its infancy, but Monaghan's confession had been recorded.

Watching a killer calmly explain his motivations and actions is always chilling. In this case it was decisive.

The Yellow Rose of Texas

'The Yellow Rose of Texas' is an American folk song dating back to the early nineteenth century. It tells the story of a slave woman, Emily Morgan, who gave up her virtue by sleeping with Mexican general Santa Anna. While Santa Anna was distracted, Colonel Sam Houston's volunteer Texan Army charged the unprepared Mexican camp, winning the battle of San Jacinto in 1836.

The Yellow Rose of Texas is also a 417-ounce (11.8-kilogram) alluvial gold nugget in the shape of Texas, found by a lady fossicking by her campsite near Kalgoorlie while dinner was being cooked.

These origin stories have one thing in common: they are both false.

Emily Morgan was said to be a slave to Colonel Morgan, but no trace of a record can be found. There is no contemporary account of Santa Anna being seduced and losing the battle. The legend of Emily's apparent action of sleeping with the enemy came many years later.

The story of the nugget, by contrast, is of an ingenious crime involving no physical risk to anyone. In all my years, the Yellow Rose of Texas swindle stands out as one of the few inventive felonies.

The story begins in 1980 with three brothers and a friend. The brothers, Raymond, Brian and Peter Mickelberg, teamed up with Brian Pozzi to create a nugget and sell it in Las Vegas.

They went about the exercise very carefully. A gold nugget contains minerals other than gold. Research in a book on geology showed the approximate percentages of other minerals, such as silver. An atlas displaying a large map of Texas was used to make a tracing of the borders of that state. Gold worth $200,000 was purchased legitimately. A kiln was built in Ray's backyard. Other, smaller nuggets were first cast using the lost wax process to gain experience. Finally, the nugget was created. It was perfect. It looked like a genuine nugget that could withstand the closest scrutiny.

Now, how to create interest? Their mother, Peggy Mickelberg, was enlisted into the conspiracy. An elaborate story was prepared. The day of the reveal arrived.

On 25 July 1980, a Channel Seven television crew went to Jandakot airport to meet a small aeroplane flying in from Kalgoorlie. A little old lady with a mop of brown hair told a reporter she had found the nugget while out prospecting with her husband. She proudly posed while the cameramen took pictures and shot footage. Naturally, the story was a sensation. It was what dreams are made of.

More publicity was to come. The nugget was displayed in the lobby of a bank and a naming competition was held. Lots of people viewed the nugget, securely enclosed in a glass case. A visiting US sailor, noticing its resemblance to his home state, came up with the name 'Yellow Rose of Texas'. The plan was working well. A couple of businessmen paid $5000 as an option to purchase. Some smaller nuggets were sold to the Perth Mint to defray costs.

Then occurred one of those unfortunate coincidences of life. A month later, in September 1980, a genuine nugget, twice the size of the Yellow Rose of Texas, was discovered in Wedderburn, Victoria. That swamped the market for unusual nuggets. Disaster beckoned.

However, help was at hand. Alan Bond, at that time still a prominent Perth businessman, stepped in for what he said was the good of the state and purchased the nugget for $350,000. It was whisked away out of public view and into a bank vault.

There the story might have rested, with no one being any the wiser. However, in 1983 police officers searched Brian Pozzi's house on an unrelated matter and discovered a series of photographs detailing every step of the swindle. The plane carrying the little old lady and her husband had not flown from Kalgoorlie. Brian Mickelberg, who was the pilot, had earlier taken off from Jandakot, flown to a nearby airfield, then flown back once the TV cameras were in place. Peggy Mickelberg, wearing a brown wig, played the part of the little old lady prospector to perfection. It was ascertained that the US sailor had in fact been paid to suggest the name 'Yellow Rose of Texas'. Nothing was what it seemed.

Further enquiries were made by police. A disappointed Alan Bond was told he had paid well over the odds for his gold. In due time, all those involved were charged with conspiracy to defraud: that between 1 January 1980 and 6 November 1980 they conspired together to defraud members of the public by fabricating a gold nugget and pretending it was a genuine alluvial nugget for the purpose of its sale.

I was still recovering from a bout of hepatitis when briefed to prosecute before Judge Whelan and a jury in the District Court. At the outset, Ray Mickelberg and Brian Pozzi pleaded guilty. The trial of the other conspirators continued for three weeks and concluded with the conviction of Brian, Peter and Peggy. Malcolm Mickelberg, the husband and father, was acquitted.

Each was sentenced to a term of imprisonment, and their appeals against conviction and sentence were dismissed by the Court of Criminal Appeal.

*

Since the discovery of gold at Southern Cross, Western Australia, in 1888, there has been no shortage of fraud and shady dealings, not to mention murder.

In 1926, two members of the gold squad, Detective Inspector Walsh and Detective Sergeant Pittman, were murdered. The detectives had discovered an illegal mill used for stolen gold. They were shot and dismembered, then thrown down a disused mine shaft.

Suspicion fell on the licensee of the Cornwall Hotel, Evan Clarke, who confessed to being an accessory and nominated Phillip Treffene and William Coulter as the killers. After a trial in Supreme Court No. 2, at which Clarke turned King's evidence, Treffene and Coulter were found guilty of wilful murder. In October 1926 both men were hanged at Fremantle Prison.

Horatio Bottomley, an English swindler, made a fortune in floating companies and promoting shares in West Australian gold mining ventures, many of which never lived up to the hype and were eventually proved worthless. It did not stop speculators who were prey to Bottomley's blandishments and wild promises of gold waiting to be discovered. He was heard to murmur more than once that 'many a good mine has been ruined by digging a shaft'.

By contrast, the Yellow Rose of Texas nugget did not hurt anyone much, except Alan Bond's pocketbook, and was an elegant swindle.

Mugged by the Media

Veronica Stannard (not her real name) was on her way home from work at about 8 pm when she stopped at a set of traffic lights. The next few minutes were terrifying. While she was sitting quietly, waiting for the lights to change, Robert Lovell, high on Valium and booze, and armed with a screwdriver, forced his way into her car.

Fortunately, Veronica was able to jump out and run from the danger. Lovell shifted into the driver's seat and took off. Police were notified and Lovell was arrested a short time later, after getting petrol at a service station a few kilometres away.

The incident deeply affected Veronica, who wrote a heartfelt victim impact statement.

In common terms this was a carjacking. Lovell pleaded guilty to armed robbery and stealing a motor vehicle and came before me for sentence. Veronica attended the sentencing hearing. So did Lovell's partner and her mother.

Selecting the proper sentence was difficult. The crimes were serious and cowardly. Normally, a severe sentence would be called for. However, Lovell had a tragic background. Moreover, he had already taken positive steps to address his addictions. His partner, the mother of their baby, and her mother were prepared to stand by him.

By law, imprisonment is a sentence of last resort. A judge must consider all sentencing options and select an appropriate sentence that will both serve as a punishment and protect the community. The community is best protected, of course, if the offender can be rehabilitated and give up crime. I imposed an eighteen-month intensive supervision order so that Lovell would have a chance of living in the community, but with the threat of imprisonment hanging over him if he offended. Ordering him to stand down, I adjourned the court.

The *West Australian* newspaper headline the next day, 2 April 2009, read 'Carjack Victim's Anger as Judge Sets Thug Free'. A picture of an angry-looking Veronica standing in front of her car was captioned: 'Disappointed: [Veronica Stannard] says she is unhappy that the man who carjacked her vehicle was not jailed.'

For me, it was another day at the office. While I have utmost respect for the media's role in a robust democracy, a reporter does tend to ask the person most emotionally invested in the outcome to comment on the sentence passed by the person least emotionally involved. I was sorry that Veronica was angry. And so she was—but not at me, it turned out.

My associate Kate Black received a letter from Veronica, which told a very different story to that which had appeared in the newspaper.

Veronica had attended the sentencing hearing with her partner and left quite satisfied. She was a devout Christian. While she had arrived expecting Lovell to be gaoled, after hearing all the context of his past and his addiction she had changed her mind. She was not a vindictive person. She had spoken to Lovell's partner, saying she was satisfied and hoped he would take advantage of the opportunity.

When she read the newspaper article, Veronica was absolutely astounded as it was a complete misrepresentation of the facts and contained comments she had not made. The photographer had asked her to look angry, although she said she was not. She had believed it was a happy occasion and felt that Lovell's partner would regard her as a hypocrite and liar.

Now, there had occurred a glitch, which gave me the opportunity to assist Veronica. Lovell had not been released from custody because there was an outstanding charge of stealing petrol. Normally this could be dealt with in the Magistrates Court, but the parties thought it would be quicker and easier if I dealt with it.

On the hearing of these charges, Lovell pleaded guilty and was fined. I took the opportunity to correct the record by referring to Veronica's letter in the sentencing hearing. I was appalled at the newspaper's conduct, which had effectively re-victimised her.

The *West Australian* acknowledged its errors and printed a handsome apology on page three on 4 April: 'We were wrong. The newspaper acknowledges its article is incorrect and accepts that Veronica was neither unhappy nor angry. It regrets any distress caused to her.' The following Monday, the ABC's *Media Watch* described the newspaper as engaging in 'thoroughly old-fashioned faulty journalism'.

Few people would have found the courage to call out the errors. Veronica, having been physically mugged by Lovell and then metaphorically mugged by the newspaper, was one of those brave people.

The Early-Morning Coffee

Juanita Perez (not her real name) loved a cup of coffee first thing in the morning. Usually, she got it herself. But one morning in June 1983, she awoke to find her son had left a cup beside the bed. The coffee, however, was cold and tasted strangely bitter. After a mouthful she drank no more. And so she saved her life.

It was not her son who put the coffee by her bed. Its appearance was a mystery. Juanita lived with her three children and family dog in a northern suburb of Perth. She was divorced, though she had lived for a year with Ron Perry, whom she had met through an introduction agency. The relationship had not worked out and she had split from Ron and moved into a new home.

The day after she had sipped the coffee, she became violently ill. That capped a terrible week because, in addition, the family dog had died; they had buried him in the garden.

It was such an awful week that the following night she had a couple of girlfriends over and decided to get tipsy. Pouring herself a glass of white wine from a cask, she noticed that the wine was a strange pink colour. When she looked further, there appeared to be a gumlike substance in the bottom of the cask. Now alarmed, Juanita called the police.

The pink substance was analysed and found to be strychnine. Strychnine is a deadly poison used to kill rodents, and in Western Australia as a bait for rabbits and foxes. Possession is strictly con-trolled—but clearly not strictly enough. An alert detective had the dog exhumed. A post-mortem examination concluded that it had been poisoned with strychnine, perhaps as a test run.

Suspicion fell on ex-boyfriend Ron. Interviewed, he confessed to poisoning the dog. Then he'd broken into Juanita's house in dead of night and put the poison into the wine cask. As he was leaving, he saw the coffee pot, which gave him an idea. It was he who had put the poison-laced cup by Juanita's bedside while she was asleep.

Ron told police, 'If I could not have her, nobody else could.'

I was briefed for the prosecution. Henry Wallwork QC appeared for the defence. There was no dispute as to the facts. Mr Wallwork called evidence from a psychiatrist that Ron Perry was suffering from a depressive illness and was not responsible for his actions. The prosecution countered that the motive was not mental illness but spite.

The jury took three hours to convict Perry of housebreaking and attempted murder. Justice Brinsden sentenced him to a lengthy term of imprisonment for this egregious example of domestic violence.

The Great Brothel Robbery

Harry Olson (not his real name) was not the world's brightest crook. Although he had only been married for a few months, one night he was feeling decidedly frisky. He decided to visit a brothel in Hay Street, Perth.

This was in 1982, when $20 was worth something. The purchasing power within the brothel was $20 for fifteen minutes. Harry selected a young woman and they moved to a more discreet location—to wit, a bedroom. Fifteen minutes passed but Harry did not reappear.

After a grace period of a couple of minutes, the brothel madam knocked on the door. 'Your time has expired, you must leave,' she said.

Harry said, 'I'm just coming.' (I'm not making this up.)

Harry got dressed and departed. But he was not happy. He had not achieved satisfaction. In his mind, this was not a contract for a certain time period but for a completed service. After ruminating for a while, he wrapped a towel around his hand, held his finger out to pretend he had a gun, climbed back up the stairs and demanded money. The terrified brothel madam flung $20 at him and told him, not quite in these words, to depart immediately.

As Harry had driven his own car to the brothel, the make and number were observed and he was soon arrested. After he was charged with armed robbery and admitted to bail, kindly police officers drove him home to his in-law's house, where his young wife had fled on his apprehension earlier. It was nearly 5 am.

He was advised to tell his Yorkshire-born father-in-law the news first, and to take his advice as to how to break it to his wife. While the police officers sat awkwardly making small talk to the wife and mother, Harry took his father-in-law out the back.

On their return, remembering the advice to be subtle, Harry let his father-in-law do the talking: 'Silly young bugger's been up at knock shop.'

I prosecuted Harry, who was defended by Dusty Miller. One issue was whether Harry was armed. The brothel madam, in cross-examination, said that if it was a finger, it was a very long finger! The other issue was whether Harry was exercising an honest claim of right to the $20. The madam had said that Harry had demanded all the money in the place. Harry said he had only asked for his $20 back.

Harry was convicted of robbery but acquitted of the circumstance of aggravation that he was armed. Justice Olney fined Harry $3000.

The fate of his marriage is unknown.

Jackson Pollock and the Blue Polls

An early and controversial decision of the new Whitlam Labor government in 1973 was to purchase *Number 11, 1952*, an abstract painting by American artist Jackson Pollock.

The painting, soon to be known as *Blue Poles*, cost the Australian taxpayer $1.3 million, then a tidy sum. Today it is worth many times that amount. *Blue Poles* is on permanent display at the National Gallery of Australia, Canberra. Controversial at the time, today it is the gallery's most popular exhibit.

Jackson Pollock was an American artist who died at the age of forty-four in a car accident while heavily intoxicated. The technique he developed and used to create *Blue Poles* was to stretch a canvas on the floor, drip household paint onto it, then make brush strokes as the fancy took him. Every painting was a spontaneous discovery. Usually Pollock painted while inebriated. The idea that he would make preparatory studies for a major painting was ludicrous, and nobody could be possibly taken in by a suggestion that he had done so. Could they?

There was a young art dealer in Perth named Bohdan Ledwij, whose fine arts gallery boasted paintings by Australia's leading artists. A doctor, new to the art culture but keen to learn, was a prodigious buyer of paintings, all the while guided by Ledwij. Ledwij would lead him through the gallery murmuring, 'That Judy Cassab is yours ... I have just purchased a new Brett Whitely on your behalf ... You are very lucky I was able to buy a John Olsen ... This Leonard French is your latest acquisition.'

Unknown to Ledwij, the doctor kept a notebook in which he dutifully recorded each painting and its purchase price. In 1978 Ledwij announced that, from various sources, he had acquired nine studies for 'Blue Polls'. West Australian glitterati turned out at his gallery to 'ooh' and 'aah' over such a find in provincial Perth. A fawning piece in the Woman's Weekly added to the publicity. Ledwij made plans to display the studies in Sydney. A grand opening was planned. It never happened.

Experts who had watched the unfolding events—first with bemusement, then with anger—declared that the studies were fakes, and not very good ones at that. The bubble burst. The opening was cancelled. Ledwij promised to send the paintings to the United States for verification, but that was the last anyone heard of them. The experts pointed out the obvious: Pollock's improvisational style meant he never made studies.

His widow and estate administrator had never heard of these studies. Pollock had not used the name Blue Poles, let alone Blue Polls, to describe his work. By the time of this painting, Pollock had settled on a numbering convention. And Pollock painted on canvas, not on masonite.

Suspicion fell not only on Ledwij but on the doctor. He was able to establish his complete innocence in the fraud, partly by discovering that he had also been defrauded. The paintings—which Ledwij had told the doctor he had purchased and belonged to him, even though they were temporarily displayed in the gallery—were in fact on consignment. Ledwij had simply taken the money from the doctor.

That was not the only art deal. Ledwij had acquired a painting called The Sleeping Diana, said to be the work of the Flemish master Anthony van Dyck. Ledwij generously offered the painting as a donation to the Art Gallery of Western Australia when the money to purchase it had first been raised from other sources.

In the 1960s and early 1970s, Australia had a reputation as a cultural desert, something Gough Whitlam was determined to change on becoming prime minister in 1972. One of the measures taken by the federal government to cause the desert to bloom was to allow income tax deductions for paintings donated to federal and state art galleries. Of course, it took someone about five minutes to realise there was money to be made in this.

A painting would be purchased for $100,000. Through a series of round-robin cheque exchanges, during which no actual money changed hands, the painting would be bought and sold several times before landing back in the hands of the original buyer for $1 million. He received a certificate attesting to the purchase, less a small commission for the organiser. There was a time when the tiny art gallery on Norfolk Island was one of the largest galleries in the world! No doubt with fanfare and champagne, the proud donor would hand over his painting to the grateful gallery, pocketing a huge tax deduction.

There were some requirements for the gift, including that the donation was made to an approved art gallery. An approved art gallery must have climate control. The Art Gallery of Western Australia was then housed in what is now a renovated wing of Boola Bardip, the Museum of Western Australia, in Beaufort Street, Northbridge. It was not climate-controlled. The new art gallery, situated across a square, was so controlled, but the building was unfinished.

This brought the plan to an end. So Diana languished, sleeping through the fuss as the scheme unravelled. She was not painted by Van Dyck, but by another prolific artist: Anon.

Ledwij was charged with multiple counts of fraud involving the doctor and the Sleeping Diana. I was briefed to prosecute the committal hearing. A committal hearing is still available in some states. In Western Australia in 1979, it was a hearing before a magistrate, who decided whether the prosecution had produced enough evidence so that a jury might convict—what is known as a *prima facie* case. The committal was held in the Magistrates Court in Beaufort Street. Shortly after, the courts were closed for good and, in a minor irony, converted into offices for the art gallery.

Ledwij was committed for trial. At his arraignment in the District Court, Bohdan Ledwij pleaded guilty to various offences of fraud and was sentenced to six years' imprisonment, with a minimum of four years before parole eligibility. On his release, he became an artist.

I came away with an enhanced appreciation for modern Australian art.

———

Trucks, Trucks, Trucks

Dad was a director of Flower, Davies & Johnson, engineering merchants. The firm imported trains, cranes, trucks and buses, along with a host of other products such as Johnson outboard motors. It was always a treat when Dad took his sons to visit the firm's workshop in Leederville. Huge wooden crates would arrive to be unpacked and reveal a truck or bus ready for assembly. The trucks came from Britain and were manufactured by the Associated Equipment Company, universally known as AEC. Its triangular logo on the grille of an MTT bus or heavy-duty truck was a common sight in Western Australia during the 1950s and 1960s.

Being a city boy, apart from those early experiences, I knew nothing about trucks. So, in the way of things, I was the obvious choice for the prosecution in a series of conspiracy trials involving trucks.

It came about this way. William Charles Maizey was the affable manager of the truck division of a long-established motor vehicle sales company, Wentworth Motors. Maizey bore a remarkable resemblance to the American actor Ernest Borgnine, then well known for a long running TV series called *McHale's Navy*, about the adventures of the eponymously named skipper of a PT boat in the Pacific Ocean during World War II.

For some years, Maizey had conspired with others to defraud his employer. In simple terms, Maizey would buy a dud truck from his co-conspirator for an inflated price, and then sell or trade him a good truck for a low price.

Eventually, after much careful work by officers of the WA Police fraud squad and a young chartered accountant specially engaged for the task, police arrested Maizey and three others, charging him with conspiracy to defraud Wentworth Motors. There was not one conspiracy which they all joined, but three separate conspiracies, hence a need for three trials.

In 1978, still fairly new to the Crown and not yet thirty, I was briefed as junior counsel to F.J. (Jim) Whelan. Jim could properly be described as a character. An Englishman, he had seen service in Africa as a judge, hurriedly leaving Rhodesia with his family to prevent being murdered by a mob. He settled in Perth and, shortly after, joined the Crown as a senior prosecutor. With wit and humour, he could charm accused persons giving evidence into making admissions very much against their interests. Once, when Jim was cross-examining a female accused of murder and she was making admission after admission, the judge, Sir John Lavan, exclaimed to her: 'You don't have to agree with everything Mr Whelan says.'

Always fair, he lacked the killer instinct of Ron Davies, and the thoroughness of Michael Murray, but he was very effective. I liked appearing with Jim because I never quite knew what would happen next. Jim was appointed to the District Court in due course and served with distinction for many years with his friend and colleague David Charters, to whom I had been articled.

At the first trial, Maizey gave evidence that the money found in his bank account was not, as the Crown alleged, bribes paid from time to time, coincidentally after a truck sale to the other accused. Rather, he said, it was money paid over a period from the sale of a power boat he owned and kept at the Royal Perth Yacht Club.

Jim Whelan cross-examined on this point. Leading Maizey along in a jovial tone, Jim noted Maizey's appearance to Borgnine. This led to an enquiry: had people had ever called him Ernest? No? What about the character he played—what was his name? Ah yes, thank you for that—McHale. Yes, Maizey agreed, his friends did use that nickname.

Turning to the boat, Whelan asked what sort it was. A launch. Yes, quite big. And its name? *McHale*, the witness said.

Ha, very clever. And I suppose you had jokes about that too. When you sold it? What, 'McHale is for sale' maybe?

Quite right, Mr Whelan.

By now, all the jury members were smiling. I handed Jim a piece of paper. Jim asked it to be shown to the jury. It was an advertisement for the sale: a photo and 'McHale is for sale'. What is the date on the advertisement, he asked the witness.

Maizey suddenly stopped smiling. The advertisement was dated months after the money had gone into his account.

Maizey was on bail and so could leave the court at the end of the day. After the judge had adjourned the trial and as we were packing up, Maizey sauntered over. 'That was a low blow, Jim,' he said. Then he brightened. Patting his ample stomach, he announced, 'Off to feed the womb.' And, without malice, he departed.

Maizey and his co-conspirator were convicted. Maizey was sentenced to three years' imprisonment, with eighteen months to serve before parole.

At the second trial, two months after the first trial, Maizey did not give evidence and was again convicted. He received the same sentence, to be served cumulatively, but the Court of Criminal Appeal reduced the sentence to take account of a degree of double counting by the second judge.

Before the third trial, Maizey approached the Crown with an offer to turn Queen's evidence and testify for the prosecution. The offer was accepted.

It was decided that I would prosecute the third trial by myself. The accused was a man named Leopold Booy, who in the intervening years had relocated to Sydney. He had therefore briefed a Queen's Counsel from the New South Wales bar, Kevin Murray QC. Kevin was a barrister with a reputation for being a head kicker. Years later I crossed swords with him in the High Court in a case involving the death of two young men who had perished in the heat on a Kimberley cattle station.

There had been no committal on this occasion, and the Chief Crown Prosecutor, Michael Murray, had filed an indictment known as an *ex officio* indictment. Such an indictment—by virtue of office—is rare. Booy unsuccessfully challenged it.

The trial date was set, but a few days before it Kevin Murray withdrew from the case. Booy's solicitor managed to brief my old mentor, Paul Seaman QC, at very short notice. On the first day of trial, Paul asked for an adjournment to allow him some time to prepare the case. That was a reasonable request, and I did not oppose it. The judge was Frank Ackland, a rude and difficult judge at the best of times. He granted the adjournment—for one day!

The trial was hard-fought. Unlike the earlier trials, the defence made no admissions and required strict proof of every invoice and receipt. Maizey gave evidence but his unhappiness at ratting out his fellow conspirator was obvious. After ten days, the jury returned a verdict of guilty and Booy was sentenced to imprisonment.

The verdicts in all three cases were inevitable. The careful work of the young accountant and the charts he prepared were unanswerable. These were blatant frauds on Wentworth Motors. I came away from the trial with a wider knowledge of trucks than the AECs of my child-hood, and even today I can tell a Kenworth from a Mack.

Paths Cross

As in all walks of life, there are moments that can only be characterised as 'sliding doors'.

In 1979 a young man, Brough (not his real name), tried to evade police by hiding in the cabin of a vehicle in a builder's yard. When he was discovered, the police alleged he had tried to hit one of them, a detective named Hills (also not his real name), with a piece of wood. He was disarmed by Detective Sergeant Silich, whereupon, so it was alleged, he punched Hills in the mouth.

Silich and Hills were detectives attached to the Geraldton police. Silich was a stout man. His companion, Hills, was clever and disarming. I prosecuted several trials where they had been the investigating officers. They made an odd team.

I travelled to Geraldton to prosecute Brough for assaulting a police officer in the execution of his duty. The trial was held before Judge O'Connor, who was pleasant but out of his depth as a judge. Brough was defended by Ian Marshall, who in opening the defence to the jury said they would hear a different story. Far from being the assailant, Brough was viciously assaulted by the police.

And so the trial began. I called a doctor and five police officers. The trial lasted three days and ended with a conviction. There was uproar in court when the jury verdict was announced. The offender was aged twenty-seven, in regular employment and had no previous record. On behalf of the Crown, I conceded that imprisonment was not inevitable. However, the judge was having none of it. In sentencing Brough, the judge considered the 'monstrous lying account' given by the accused, who had attacked the integrity of police engaged in the trial. Brough was sentenced to imprisonment for twelve months, with a minimum of three months before parole.

Brough immediately appealed. Meanwhile, the case remained in the public eye. The Council for Civil Liberties and the opposition Labor Party called for an independent authority to handle complaints against police.

The Police Commissioner, Owen Leitch, disagreed. 'The present system is a good one,' he said. 'We maintain the discipline we deserve. Journalists look after their own. Doctors look after their own. Dentists look after their own.'

Another twenty-four years and a Royal Commission into the WA Police were to pass before the Corruption and Crime Commission was established, explicitly to deal with police misconduct. Thirty-five years after Mr Brough's trial, I became Corruption and Crime Commissioner.

An appeal against conviction to the Court of Criminal Appeal was unsuccessful but the sentence was reduced to three months. The judge had been wrong to consider the conduct of the defence.

Brough appealed to the High Court. For that, I was junior counsel, led by Kevin Parker QC. Brough was successful. The High Court unanimously quashed the conviction. The trial judge had made critical errors and seriously misdirected the jury. This was no doubt correct. Among other things, the judge told the jury that perjury was a crime and that, before concluding that the police officers were liars, they would have to be satisfied beyond reasonable doubt of that fact. This would completely have reversed the onus of proof, which the prosecution always carries.

I prosecuted other trials involving Hills and Silich. A woman visiting Geraldton complained she had been raped by a stranger on a popular beach. Hills interviewed a suspect, who denied he had been at the beach. Hills asked if he would mind rolling down the cuffs of his trousers. They were full of white sand. Halfway through the subsequent trial, the accused changed his plea to guilty and was sentenced by Justice Brinsden to a lengthy term of imprisonment.

Years later, Silich had risen to the rank of inspector when he was caught giving driver's licences to acquaintances. As DPP, I filed an indictment alleging ten counts of corruption, to which Silich pleaded guilty. He issued licences through the Kalbarri Police Station, but no driving test was ever done. He avoided prison because he had made no financial gain, but his police career was at an end.

Retired and living quietly in a Perth suburb, he and his wife were devastated when one of their sons died unexpectedly. They had another son, Vernon, who, like his father, was a heavy drinker. On the night they received the coroner's report into the death of his son, Bob, Silich and Vernon stayed up drinking whisky while Mrs Silich went to bed.

Sometime in the early hours of the morning, Vernon kicked his mother and father to death, then placed them next to the bed, arranging their bodies so they were holding hands. No motive for this double murder was ever apparent.

In 2010, Vernon faced trial for murder. I was the trial judge. Vernon was defended by Tom Percy QC, who called evidence that Vernon was a known somnambulist, a sleepwalker. Medical evidence showed it was possible that a person in that condition could unconsciously perform acts such as those alleged against Vernon. A person is not criminally responsible for an act that occurs independently of the exercise of their will, and Tom Percy argued that this was the case here. The prosecution disputed that Vernon had acted involuntarily.

Somnambulism is a genuine condition. In a famous Canadian case, *R v Parks*, the sleepwalker got out of bed, dressed and drove 23 kilometres to his parents-in-law's house, where he armed himself with a knife from the kitchen and proceeded to the bedroom, where he stabbed and killed one and severely injured another. He was acquitted by the jury and appeals by the prosecution were dismissed.

In the present case, the defence called a sleep specialist physician, while the prosecution called a psychiatrist. Following deliberation for four hours, the jury returned verdicts of guilty to murder. I sentenced Vernon to a mandatory term of life imprisonment and set a minimum term of fifteen years before parole could be considered.

Vernon appealed against his conviction and the DPP appealed against the sentence. The appeal against conviction was dismissed. There was a dispute as to the expertise of each witness, but the Court of Appeal held that both had expertise that could be given to the jury. The Court of Appeal upheld the appeal against the sentence and increased the minimum term of imprisonment before parole to nineteen years.

A Little Mistake

By the age of twenty-one, Jim Little (not his real name) was a seasoned career criminal. As a juvenile he had been convicted of burglary no less than eighteen times and was on parole. Then he switched to cutting tanks—opening safes with an acetylene torch. He briefly specialised in hotels: the Ascot Hotel, $10,000; another building, $8000; and on 29 August 1976, the Kwinana Hotel.

This last burglary was the one I prosecuted, with Brian Singleton defending. The trial took place in the District Court before Judge Pidgeon in the basement court, a cramped and cheerless place.

Jim was a south of the river boy. For those not from Perth, the city is bisected by the Swan River. Northerners would never think of moving south across the Narrows Bridge. Southerners look on the effete northerners with disdain. So Jim had likely never ventured north of the Swan River, unless to pursue his pecuniary ambitions as a burglar.

It was late on Sunday night when Jim and his accomplice broke into the Kwinana Hotel and cut open the safe. The weekend takings were all there, ready for banking the next day. The two burglars carried out nearly $10,000 and hid it throughout their car—in the glove box, in the boot, in the lining on the roof. Ten thousand dollars is a lot of money to hide. The two burglars set off north for a getaway—further north than either of them had ever been. They drove steadily, but shortly after dawn—possibly because the driver had fallen asleep—the car left the road between Karratha and Dampier and rolled over. Neither man was badly injured but ambulance and police attended.

Now, Jim had plenty of experience with police officers. Never having left the metropolitan area, he knew only that all police officers wore blue uniforms. Had he ventured earlier into the north of the state, he would have discovered that police officers dress in a khaki uniform, not blue. So when Jim, injured and waiting for help, handed a bag of cannabis he was carrying to a khaki-clad figure, he assumed it was an ambulance medic and gave instructions to 'hide it before the pigs get here'.

At the trial, Jim Little tried to explain away the origin of the money that was soon discovered about the car. Unfortunately for Jim, a lot of the banknotes from the weekend were still damp and smelled of beer. Jim was convicted and sentenced to three years' imprisonment without parole. An appeal against sentence was dismissed.

A Millennium Mistake

The world celebrated the start of the new millennium at one second past midnight on 1 January 2000. But the world was a year too early.

When a baby is born, it remains aged zero for its first year, until, at the beginning of the 366th day, it turns one. Put simply, the year 2000 was the last year of the twentieth century, not the first year of the twenty-first century.

The same millennial error by officials of the Reserve Bank of Australia nearly caused a miscarriage of justice.

In September 1988, members of the West Australian Police Drug Squad organised a sting operation to catch two brothers who were dealing in heroin and using others to sell the product. This was before the High Court case of *Ridgeway v The Queen (1995) CLR 19* restricted such operations. The plan was to try to buy drugs and see where the money went. A mainstay of law enforcement is always 'follow the money'. In this case, the advice was literal.

The drug squad obtained $3000 in cash, $50, $20, $10 notes. Officers recorded the serial number of each banknote. One $10 banknote stood out. It bore the serial number URF 300000. This was meaningful, because a note with such a number was valuable in the game of banknote poker. A detective committed it to memory.

Next day, the sting was on. An undercover police officer went for a ride in the car of a would-be heroin seller. A deal was done and $3000 was handed over to purchase four grams of heroin. The officer was let out of the car and the seller went to collect the goods. He drove to a house in Girrawheen, a suburb of Perth, where the two brothers lived. The house was under surveillance.

That afternoon, the Drug Squad raided the Girrawheen house and the seller's car. Inside the house, police found $2600 in cash. In a simultaneous raid on the seller's car, police located a quantity of heroin and, importantly, $405 in cash. The money from the house and car was seized and taken back to police headquarters.

Surprise, surprise. The serial numbers of the seized money matched the numbers noted down the day before. Among the notes was the $10 banknote with serial number URF 300000.

A police photographer was called in to record the notes before rushing off to take photographs at a retirement party for a senior officer. He used a camera that used rolls of film; all this happened before the advent of electronic cameras and smartphones. The negative would have to be developed before any use could be made of it. Unbeknown to the photographer at the time, his camera had a malfunction.

In due course, the brothers stood trial for selling a quantity of heroin to another and for possessing a quantity of heroin with intent to sell or supply it to another. The $3000 of cash found in the car and the home formed a vital part of the prosecution case. The brothers' evidence that the money found in their house had been left for expenses by their parents who were overseas was disbelieved. Each was convicted and sentenced to a term of imprisonment.

They appealed against their convictions on a number of grounds, only one of which is now relevant. That ground of appeal asserted that fresh evidence after the trial had come to hand which rendered the verdict unsafe, as it:

(i) Undermined the veracity of the prosecution case;

(ii) Indicated perjury and fabrication of evidence; and

(iii) Effectively removed the foundation of the prosecution case.

What was this explosive evidence?

After the conviction, lawyers then acting for the brothers made enquiries of the Reserve Bank of Australia seeking information about banknotes and serial numbers. Back came a response from a currency investigations officer and the manager of 'Graphic Reproduction and

Note Printing Australia', who had been employed in note printing for forty-three years. For twenty-three of those years he had been an expert, giving evidence in courts all over Australia. A very impressive résumé.

In his response, he advised that he had examined the records of the Reserve Bank and was able to say that the $10 note with serial number URF 300000 was produced at the note printing branch on 18 February 1988. It was consigned to the Reserve Bank in Brisbane on 16 June 1988. Banknote $10 URF 300000 was made available to the public on or after 15 November 1988.

This was a bombshell—if true. It meant that at least one banknote allegedly found in the brothers' possession on 30 September 1988 was not in circulation until two months later.

Such was the seriousness of the evidence and allegations of perjury levelled at the Drug Squad that I took charge of the appeal, leading Gail Archer.

I had my doubts about the evidence, notwithstanding the expert opinion. The officer who had photographed the banknotes following their seizure from the brothers showed me a negative image. The malfunction in his camera had caused a negative of the notes to be overlaid on the first negative from the retirement party. That party had incontrovertibly been held on 30 September 1988.

Between the filing of the appeal and its hearing, another Reserve Bank witness supplied a report based on the shipping details. As a result, the first expert was no longer prepared to assert with confidence that the note $10 URF 300000 had not been released until 15 November 1988. This partial change of heart caused legal aid to be withdrawn, so the brothers represented themselves on the appeal.

Because of this and the issues involved, I agreed that the state would fly the witnesses to Perth. At the hearing of the appeal, I called each witness to give evidence but asked no questions. This was done to allow the brothers to cross-examine each witness.

The expert witness had another surprise—this time for the brothers.

His evidence was that, a week before he'd flown to Perth, it had occurred to him—for the first time, apparently—that banknotes are printed in reverse order: that is, from the highest serial number down to lowest. Banknote $10 URF 300000 would not therefore appear in the series commencing 30 but in the series commencing 29. The result was that the banknote would not appear in substack 795, sent to Brisbane but not released until 15 November 1988. To confirm his theory, the expert watched a run of banknotes being printed.

How this had not occurred to him in forty-three years was left unexplained.

The brothers battled gamely on with their appeal but it was really all over bar the shouting. The Court of Appeal was scathing in its judgment. The history of this, wrote Justice Rowland, shows that the brothers had been on the receiving end of a most inept response from those responsible for keeping and understanding records relating to the identification and distribution of money from the Reserve Bank.

The court concluded that there was now no evidence to support a finding that banknote $10 URF 300000 was not in circulation on 29 September 1988. The appeal was dismissed and the brothers returned to prison to serve out the balance of their sentences. A miscarriage of justice was averted.

A final detail: I wrote to the Reserve Bank seeking reimbursement of the witnesses' expenses, given the circumstances. The Reserve Bank paid the bill.

PART FIVE
QUIRKY CASES

As I mentioned in the introduction, the case of *Presley v Geraghty* ignited in me a curiosity for interesting cases of an earlier time. I have written about these quirky cases for my own pleasure and in hope that others might find them interesting too. Part of the pleasure has been in researching the law and contemporary accounts where possible, often in newspapers or journals, sometimes in registries of births and deaths.

In this collection I have largely avoided criminal cases. There is little amusement in the misery and blighted lives that crime creates. But you will find within these cases a fascinating parade of characters.

The tales give an insight into the conditions of the times in which they occurred. Some show a young colony, eager to impose the rule of law, notwithstanding the wildness of an emerging society.

The tales were originally written for lawyers as a diversion, and many have been published in the Law Society of Western Australia's publication *Brief*. But they have a wider audience interested in little-known examples of social history.

The plight of a maid falsely accused of stealing by a reverend gentleman, of a terrified shop assistant, of a boy stolen from his parents are all part of our story. Some of the tales were written in anger, telling of the treatment of women who wished to marry, of the shameful imprisonment of an artist, of a pregnant woman treated as an invalid. The vicissitudes of students of law are reflected in one of the tales.

Many of the stories are included simply because I found the facts amusing. One can sense the annoyance of Mr Kidd at what he perceived to be high-handed treatment from the local magistrate, or the plight of the late-night traveller.

While some judges have perpetuated injustice while purporting to follow the law, most in these tales are doing their best to fulfil their judicial oath to do justice according to law, to all manner of people, without fear or favour, affection or ill will.

The Tale of the Bootleg Brewer

Long ago, in a city at the edge of the settled world, lived a man whose profession was making bootleg beer. For many years, the excise man had tried in vain to catch the bootlegger. Finally, success. The bootlegger was charged with being in possession of beer on which duty had not been paid. It was with quiet satisfaction that the excise man attended court, confident of victory. Alas, his hopes were dashed! After two days of evidence, the magistrate dismissed the prosecution.

Now, at this time there were in the city only two lawyers. If one was briefed for the prosecution, the other would be briefed for the defence. They shared one characteristic: both loathed the magistrate. The prosecutor needed little persuasion, then, to lodge an appeal in the Supreme Court on behalf of the excise man.

During the delay between the magistrate's decision and the appeal, an extraordinary event occurred. The good burghers of the town rebelled against the supposed tyranny of the governor and the cronyism of the entire Supreme Court—all one of him. It was suggested that they leave town on the next boat! And so they did.

Now there was a problem. There was no judge and cases were banking up.

Wise bureaucrats found an elegant solution. As it was not known how the turmoil would end, the appointment of a new judge might be precipitate. So a deputy judge was appointed.

Thus it was that the appeal came before the deputy judge. He was astonished at the faulty reasoning of the magistrate. Why, the evidence was overwhelming! The magistrate had got it wrong. The bootlegger was convicted and severely penalised.

So far, in this tale of events far away in time and place, nothing seems out of the ordinary. But as in all good tales, there is a twist. The erring magistrate and the righteous deputy judge were one and the same person! There the matter might have rested, but you will remember that the entire bar—both of them—hated the magistrate, and the deputy judge too for that matter.

The lawyer for the bootlegger forthwith appealed to the Highest Court in the Land, many miles away. As was the custom in those far-off days, the judges dressed magnificently in ornate apparel. Members of the bar dressed more humbly but still in a manner befitting their office.

All day the argument raged about whether the bootlegger in fact possessed duty-free beer. Of course not. The Highest Court in the Land was not concerned with such trifles. No, the important question for the court was simply stated: can you have a deputy judge when you don't have a judge? Less than a week later, the answer was known. 'No,' said three wise judges.

'Yes,' said two obviously not-so-wise judges.

Thus justice was served—and, back in the city far away, so was beer.

The Tale of the Alarming Affidavit

In 'The Tale of the Bootleg Brewer', we learned that the entire bar of the Northern Territory, both of them, loathed the magistrate and sometime deputy judge G.G. Hogan.

D. Roberts Esq. and R.I.D. Mallam Esq. were the only lawyers in Darwin in 1921. When one was briefed on one side of litigation, the other lawyer was briefed for the opponent. This arrangement continued harmoniously even after another lawyer joined the profession.

In 1921 the stipendiary magistrate and deputy judge (or so everyone thought at the time) was Major Gerald Hogan. Born in 1886 and trained as a solicitor, Hogan enlisted in the AIF in 1915 and saw service in Gallipoli, Egypt and France, being mentioned in despatches. Retiring as a major, he moved to the Northern Territory and became a magistrate.

For some reason, mutual antipathy developed between Roberts and Mallam on the one hand and Hogan on the other. Mallam complained that, in court, Hogan was rude and offensive.

It may be that Major Hogan was a little sensitive to criticism. What else could explain the extraordinary events that unfolded over the most minor matter when executors sought the assistance of the court in relation to the estate of the late Mr Goodya Singh?

The executors briefed Mr Mallam to make the application for advice to the court. Major Hogan had a temporary appointment as a judge while authorities found a suitable replacement. So he was the only available judicial officer.

When the matter first came before Judge Hogan (as he was then thought to be), probate had not yet been granted. The judge adjourned the case to 20 December 1920 for this to occur. When that day came, probate had still not been filed, and Mr Mallam sought a further adjournment, which the court granted to 17 January 1921. However, it did so while calling on Mr Mallam to show cause why he should not pay the costs of the adjournment personally.

Now, the dates are important. At that time, it was thought that Judge Hogan's temporary appointment would expire on 14 January 1921, and that there would then be a new judge to deal with the matter.

To show cause why he should not be personally liable for costs, Mr Mallam filed an affidavit on 23 December 1920. The contents of this affidavit alarmed the judge, who brought the matter back before him on 3 January 1921 (never mind the Christmas holidays) to deal with what he saw as contempt, if not perjury.

Mr Mallam was represented by Mr Roberts. In his affidavit, Mr Mallam deposed as to the difficulties of getting instructions by mail from his clients, who lived at Borroloola, a remote settlement on the McArthur River. These difficulties, Judge Hogan pointed out, had not been made known to the court at the earlier hearing. In fact, suggested the judge, the picture presented in Mr Mallam's affidavit was that of a solicitor worried by the difficulties of communication, and that any fault was that of the judge who selected the date. Judge Hogan was having none of it. He thought it was sinister that the affidavit also alluded to the forthcoming expiry of the judge's commission (it was extended).

The judge was firm in his conclusion: 'I am of opinion that the affidavit was made to deceive the court and would have deceived a court which had not a full knowledge of what had taken place.'

Alarming indeed. Difficult not to draw a distinction between such concealment of facts and perjury. What to do? The judge found the solicitor in contempt. He noted that there was no control over practitioners—no bar council or other help, not even strong public opinion. Judge Hogan decided that Mr Mallam was a distinct menace to the proper administration of justice in Darwin, and the public must be protected from him. He suspended Mr Mallam from practice for twelve months.

Mr Mallam was not the sort to take this lying down. During his first vacation in ten years, he dropped in at the High Court and obtained a stay, which therefore enabled him to argue *Presley v Geraghty*—the bootleg brewer—in front of Judge Hogan the next month, possibly to the latter's chagrin.

In due course, the High Court ruled that Hogan's appointment as deputy judge was a nullity and all decisions void. An ordinance retrospectively validated all the deputy judge's decisions except *Presley v Geraghty*—and Mr Mallam's suspension.

What became of the players in this little spectacle, which was played out in a hot and humid summer in Darwin without the benefit of air conditioning? Donald Roberts, who appeared for R.I.D. Mallam, was shortly thereafter appointed a Supreme Court judge, replacing Major Hogan. At thirty-two years of age, he remains the youngest ever appointment to a superior court in Australia. He retired due to ill health in 1928 and was replaced by R.I.D. Mallam. Roberrts did not pass away for another thirty years.

R.I.D. Mallam served for only five years before also retiring due to ill health. Described as an excellent judge, he was eccentric and witty, a dapper dresser in tropical suit and sunhat, carrying a walking stick and wearing a beard as a display of masculinity.

Perhaps someone high in government realised a circuit breaker was necessary to restore peace. In 1922 Major Hogan was promoted and transferred to German New Guinea (now part of Papua New Guinea) as Crown Law Officer. The *Territory* newspaper expressed its regrets at the loss of an impartial administrator who supplied the necessary courage and ability, and he had the good wishes of all fair-minded people.

His end was tragic. When the Japanese attacked Rabaul in January 1942, Major Hogan was captured and interned as a prisoner of war. On 1 July 1942, unaware that it was carrying prisoners to Japan, the submarine USS *Sturgeon* torpedoed the *Montevideo Maru*, which sank with the loss of more than 1000 lives, mostly Australian. Gerald George Hogan was among them. It is Australia's greatest maritime catastrophe.

The Tale of the Suicidal Shopkeeper

The nineteenth of October 1937 started like any other ordinary day for Ms Lucy Bunyan, a 23-year-old shop assistant working in Mr Jordan's Blacktown shop. It didn't finish that way, due to Mr Jordan's extraordinary behaviour.

It was a Friday evening, late-night shopping, so after tea Ms Bunyan returned to the store. On walking into Mr Jordan's office, she beheld a peculiar sight. Miss McGuinness, another employee, was talking to Mr Jordan when he picked up a revolver and extracted the cartridges. On the table was a bottle marked 'Poison'. Ms Bunyan left the room but couldn't help but overhear Mr Jordan say to Miss McGuinness that he was going to shoot someone.

Ms Bunyan came over all shaky and nervous, a condition amplified, she said, when shortly afterwards she heard a shot.

It was not Mr Jordan shooting himself—or at least not then—because when she later took the day's takings into his office, he tore up the pound notes and said he would not be there in the morning to mend them and have them banked. He told Ms Bunyan that 'we would hear of a death the next morning'. Ms Bunyan consulted a doctor the next day, who diagnosed 'neurasthenia' brought about by shock. This was then a fashionable diagnosis. She and Mr Jordan soon parted ways.

Mr Jordan, meanwhile, continued his erratic ways, possibly assisted by drink. One morning a few days later, he put some armour under his vest, shot himself (in the armour) and called the police. He said he would put 'the wind up the boys'—meaning his sons.

Whether or not he succeeded with his sons, he certainly frightened Ms Bunyan, who sued for damages for nervous shock. Justice Maxwell, who heard the case at first instance, held that there was no sufficient relationship between Ms Bunyan and Mr Jordan to create a legal duty towards her. She did not fear immediate personal injury. Ms Bunyan appealed the decision but fared no better in the Court of Appeal or the High Court. Every judge involved was, of course, male.

Although she lost at every level, the doughty H.V. 'Doc' Evatt, later leader of the Australian Labor Party but then a Justice of the High Court, would have allowed the claim.

Chief Justice John Latham adopted a robust view of the human condition: the acts of the defendant, taken together, could not be said to be calculated or likely to cause harm to any person, even his sons, if they were normal persons.

Justice George Rich made a snide comment about Ms Bunyan: 'It would be unkind, perhaps, to assume that both her claim and her condition were more readily attributable to the loss of her employment.' In fact, Sir George Rich illustrated a tendency towards sarcasm unbecoming in a High Court judge:

> [Bunyan's] counsel at the trial, however, may be congratulated on his success in manoeuvring into a position in which he was at liberty to disregard the pleadings and rely on any course of action which ingenuity might then or thereafter discover in the evidence which he was able to find.

As I have said, Doc Evatt was the sole dissentient. He wrote:

> Where a person, whether for malicious motives or those of self-display, wilfully alarms or terrifies another by the unlawful act of threatening to commit suicide, and that condition or alarm or terror causes physical illness, an action lies; and it is no answer to such an action for the defendant to set up either (a) that he was threatening to kill or injure himself, and no other person, or (b) that the plaintiff did not apprehend physical danger to himself, or (c) that many

persons, or a majority of persons, or even that especially formidable person 'the ordinary, normal human being' would not be alarmed or terrified, or have suffered illness as a result of the defendant's action.

And so Ms Bunyan's desire to sue her boss ended in failure. But that is not the end of the story.

Her solicitor was Mr Abram Landa, who, a few years later, acted for the unsuccessful appellant in another nervous shock case, *Chester v Waverly Municipal Council* (1939) 62 CLR 1. So incensed was he about the unfairness of the law, as he saw it, that he campaigned for a change in the law, and eventually was elected to the New South Wales parliament. In 1944, his efforts bore fruit. The *Law Reform (Miscellaneous Provisions) Act 1944* (NSW) provided: 'In any action for injury to the person caused after the commencement of this Act, the Plaintiff shall not be debarred from recovery damages merely because the injury complained of arose wholly or in part from mental or nervous shock.' Although that might have been little comfort to Ms Bunyan or Ms Chester, generations of future plaintiffs were better off.

As for Ms Bunyan, she appears to have recovered from the extraordinary events of 19 October 1937. In 1943 she married Mr Alfred Byrnes, and ultimately she outlived her husband, parents and sisters, passing away in 2000 at the age of eighty-seven.

Mr Jordan obviously overcame his suicidal impulses, living until 1950, when he died at the age of sixty-four.

The Tale of the Telephone Line

On 9 August 1901, eight months following the birth of the Common-wealth of Australia and its Constitution, Mr Robert Hannah was driving his horse and cab down Elizabeth Street, Sydney, when a broken overhead telephone wire snaked down and killed his horse, which overturned the cab and injured him severely.

In due course, Mr Hannah's action for negligence was heard by a jury. A difficulty about who exactly should be sued was resolved when Mr James Dalgano, Deputy Postmaster, consented to be the nominal defendant.

How did the accident happen? It appears that two workers were up a telephone pole when a wire snapped. Now, this wouldn't have been a great problem as the voltage in the wire was quite low. How-ever, on the way down it fell across a wire powering the trams that ran down Elizabeth Street and became electrified. When the cable finally made contact with the horse, it was electrocuted.

No one could really say why the wire snapped. It was only four years old. Wires could break for no reason. Still, the jury found that the defendant was negligent and awarded Mr Hubbard £200, a sig-nificant sum—in today's dollars it would buy a house. Mr Dalgano, who probably didn't care much as no one was blaming him personally, appealed to the Full Court of New South Wales.

The appeal was heard over two days and judgment delivered on 20 August 1903. Mr Dalgano's counsel, the unfortunately named Dr Sly, persuaded one judge that negligence had not been proved, but the other two judges upheld the jury's verdict, although not without some temporising. It was a case of 'you nearly won, Mr Dalgano—but not quite'. Mr Dalgano, probably thinking it was not his money anyway, sought and obtained leave to appeal to the High Court on 15 October 1903.

Now, the question as to whether there was any evidence of negligence on the part of the postmaster was one that had caused disagreement in the appeal court. Dr Sly wished to agitate it again in the High Court. He was opposed by a more appropriately named barrister, Wise KC.

In the event, a more interesting question came out of nowhere. Did the High Court have jurisdiction? Could the newly formed body have a proper role in this? The *Judiciary Act 1903* (Cth) was proclaimed and came into effect on 25 August 1903, five days after judgment had been given in the Full Court.

So, it was argued, the *Judiciary Act* was not retrospective, and Mr Dalgano had no vested right of further appeal following judgment. On the other hand, if the High Court gained its status and authority from the Constitution, there was nothing more to be said. It always had jurisdiction, even though it was an incorporeal body until 25 August 1903.

Faced with this conundrum on its very first day of sitting, the court acted decisively. It noted that the issue of its jurisdiction was an interesting question, the answer to which could wait for another day. Although leave to appeal had been granted, on second thoughts, there really wasn't much public interest in the facts, so the best thing, all in all, was to rescind the grant of leave.

That was that. Mr Dalgano retired shortly after. He died aged seventy-three on 8 February 1915, just weeks before thousands of young Australians would join him from the shores of Gallipoli. The constitutional question posed on 4 November 1903 is still, 122 years later, awaiting an answer.

The Tale of the Herbalist

Mr Jayasinga was many things—herbalist, phrenologist, palmist, masseur and confectioner. One thing he was not—a medical practitioner. So he was skating on thin ice when he examined the hands of a man who had a certain disease and told him he had a bad sickness. Fortunately for the man, Mr Jayasinga held a cure—herbal pills and liquids, with occasional vapour baths and massages. All for £25.

The authorities came to hear of the treatment—perhaps the patient thought it was unsuccessful—and Mr Jayasinga found himself before the Fremantle magistrate. Here he got a lucky break. The magistrate acquitted him, reading certain words in brackets in the *Medical Act* as being, well, in brackets.

Wrong, said the Full Court, quoting the well-seasoned Lord Esher: 'It is perfectly clear that in an Act of Parliament there are no such things as brackets any more than there are such things as stops.' Yes, I had trouble with that too.

Justice Burnside, the second judge, agreed with McMillan ACJ, although in doing so he uttered a *cri de coeur* that would not be out of place in the judgment of a modern Justice of Appeal: 'In the limited time at my disposal for considering matters which occupy the attention of this Court, I have come to the conclusion that the Magistrate erred in the opinion at which he arrived on the facts of this case.'

So Mr Jayasinga was sent back to the Magistrate's Court, which was under a direction to convict.

It is possible that Mr Jayasinga forsook his many occupations, or perhaps added another, because four years later he was prosecuted again in Fremantle—this time for pretending to tell fortunes. History does not record whether he predicted this fate.

The Tale of the Disaffected Law Students

Victoria University in Wellington, New Zealand, has an impressive honour roll of law graduates including a governor-general, a prime minister, four chief justices, five attorneys-general and seven solicitors-general. The author of the *Salmond on Torts* was a professor at Victoria before becoming a judge.

So it is little surprise that when Victoria's law students felt they were being hard done by, they would have the temerity to sue someone. Better still, they persuaded someone else to sue for them.

Now, I am sure that many of my colleagues in the law do as I do and drop off every night having read a few pages of *The Supreme Court Practice & Procedure*, better known as *The White Book*. (If you are too young to know what this is, feel free to turn to Google.) As the person said after watching a documentary on ship building, 'Riveting stuff.'

But I digress. In 1973, students at Victoria and other New Zealand law schools were required to take a subject known as Civil Procedure. Students studying the subject naturally needed to examine the statutes and rules that establish the procedures of the courts. However, the *Code of Procedure*—an assembly of all the procedural rules of the Supreme Court—was unobtainable from the Government Printer. The only alternative for the student who wanted their own copy was to purchase *Sim's Practice and Procedure* at the then considerable sum of $32.

The law students, through the student association, pleaded with the Government Printer and the law drafting office, but to no avail.

How unsatisfactory. As President McCarthy, in the Court of Appeal, noted in his judgment:

> It is of course obvious that a government should publish its own laws and make their texts available to its citizens. The Government accepts this is so and would wish to be able to comply with the requests of the students. But it says it is not in a position to do this.

In other words, 'Sorry, not sorry.'

Remarkably, the Government Printer acknowledged the problem in 1951, more than forty years after the *Judicature Act 1908* (NZ):

> The second and third schedules containing the 'Code of Civil Procedure in the Supreme Court' and the 'Rules of the Court of Appeal' respectively have been omitted on the ground that owing to the number of alterations made therein, it would be misleading to reprint them in their original form; and the reader is recommended to refer to 'Stout and Sim's Supreme Court Practice' and to subsequent Gazettes.

What an abrogation of responsibility, though one of which Messrs Stout and Sim probably approved.

In the judgment, one detects considerable sympathy by the judges for the plight of the students. It is probable they had encountered similar difficulties when at law school themselves:

> The need for students to have access to an up-to-date text of the code has become more pressing. Obviously, it is wrong that this need is not met. Every citizen should be able to obtain a copy of the rules of court at reasonable cost; a fortiori a student studying to become a lawyer.

The students had sought an order of mandamus to compel the Government Printer to update the civil procedure laws and rules. The judges unanimously held that a writ of mandamus could not issue. Perhaps if

the students had had access to an up-to-date copy of the civil procedure, they would have known this.

Postscript: Undeterred by a three–nil loss (four–nil if you count
the Chief Justice, who was the primary judge), the students sought
leave to appeal to the Privy Council. Leave was refused.

The Tale of the Pregnant Passenger

The SS *Kanowna*, built in 1902, marked a new era in the Australian coastal trade. It had 'superb' accommodation for 270 passengers and a cargo-carrying capacity of 7000 tons.

Commissioned by the owners for the Sydney–Perth route (stopping at Melbourne and Adelaide), it was a comfortable way to travel. It made eighty-six voyages to Fremantle, carrying over 11,000 passengers, before running aground off Wilsons Promontory and sinking in 1929. All that was in the future, though, when Mr De Pledge and his wife bought tickets for £15 for passage from Adelaide to Perth in December 1903.

When Mrs De Pledge went on board before the *Kanowna* sailed, a stewardess noticed that she was in an advanced state of pregnancy. The stewardess asked if it would be wise for Mrs De Pledge to travel, but Mrs De Pledge said that she would risk it. The baby was not due until late January or early February. The captain was informed.

Now, the contract of carriage provided that the captain could refuse to carry a passenger who was dangerously ill. The captain decided that the pregnant Mrs De Pledge met that definition and refused her passage. She and her husband disembarked at Port Adelaide before having gone anywhere, and for a time had trouble finding a hotel that would take them. Maybe difficulty finding accommodation in December is a common occurrence. There has been at least one other famous example.

In due course, on 5 February 1904 the world was deprived of another Sandgroper but delighted by the appearance of a new Croweater. The baby, christened Gwendoline Melina Victoria, would grow up, marry and live a long life, passing away in 1988.

Mr De Pledge sued the shipping company in the Adelaide local court, where he lost, the court deciding that the captain had executed his discretion honestly. Mr De Pledge was unhappy at the outcome and appealed to the Full Court of South Australia.

After a lengthy hearing, Justice Gordon found in favour of Mr De Pledge. He noted that, after their luggage was loaded and they had been shown their cabin, Mr and Mrs De Pledge went on shore again and walked about for a couple of hours until the time for sailing. 'It is remarkable ... that the woman should have walked the streets for two hours at the time if she was "dangerously ill",' he observed.

Justice Gordon was forthright about the evidence: 'In my opinion, there is not a tittle of evidence that the woman was ill at the time, much less dangerously ill.'

What a marvellous word—'tittle'. Maybe it will join the lexicon of modern judges.

Unfortunately for Mr and Mrs De Pledge, Justice Gordon's view did not find favour with the other judges.

Justice Boucaut avoided it altogether: 'I am not going to express any opinion as to whether the woman was dangerously ill, nor to discuss what degree of pregnancy would justify a ship's Captain in refusing to take a lady as a passenger.' Instead, Justice Boucaut fell back on the time-honoured formula that it was reasonably open for the local court to reach its decision, so that was that.

He also engaged in a bit of sophistry: 'In fairness to the plaintiff, with whom I sympathise, I will not say that I might not have come to a different conclusion on the evidence if I had been called on to decide the case.' After struggling with the double negative, I think the judge was telling Mr De Pledge, 'You nearly won, but not quite.' No doubt words of great comfort to Mr and Mrs De Pledge.

The Chief Justice, on the other hand, was as emphatic in his opinion as Justice Gordon was in his: 'There was ample [evidence] to justify the captain in coming to the conclusion that it would not have been safe for the woman to travel in that condition, and he was justified in refusing to take her.' Sir James Way's knowledge of the illness of pregnancy may have been even more vicarious than for males generally. He did not marry until he was sixty-two. His wife was forty-four and had an adult family.

Chief Justice Way then entered the world of medicine. Although agreeing that pregnancy is not in itself an illness, he contended that 'it is common knowledge that there are troubles and inconveniences to it. The dictionary definition of "ill" includes "causing pain, discomfort or inconvenience". These terms are all applicable to pregnancy or confinement.'

Some might say that the same could be said about a headache.

The Tale of the Amorous Gardener

Well, two tales, actually. Both pre-dated major reform of family laws in Australia and New Zealand.

Mr Ah Chuck, a market gardener, lived near Mr and Mrs Hedges and their family in Māngere, New Zealand. Presumably, when the vegetables were growing, he had some time on his hands. At all accounts, he often visited the Hedges household and was friendly with Mrs Hedges. Very friendly.

In February 1929, the Hedges welcomed a new addition to the family. But all was not sunshine and happiness. Six months after the birth, Mr Hedges instituted proceedings for divorce. The grounds? Adultery by Mrs Hedges with none other than Mr Ah Chuck. Mr Hedges was successful. A divorce was obtained.

Mrs Hedges was in a pickle. There was a child to raise. So action was taken against Mr Ah Chuck to pay maintenance.

Now, one might have thought that Mr Ah Chuck didn't have a legal leg to stand on. Several witnesses testified to the apparent closeness of Mr Ah Chuck and Mrs Hedges. The midwife and the attending doctor both said the baby looked part 'Mongolian'. And to top it off, Mrs Hedges testified that she had intercourse with Mr Ah Chuck on one occasion and that he was the father of her child.

Pretty overwhelming, one might think—and it had certainly been enough to obtain a divorce. But the law often moves in mysterious ways. Justice Herdman himself posed the issue:

Apart from the evidence of Mrs Hedges, I am invited to declare that because a Chinese neighbour was an occasional visitor to the house and appeared to be on intimate terms with Mrs Hedges and that because during wedlock a child is born to the woman which it is said exhibits certain physical characteristics that we associate with Mongolian people, I must decide that the presumption of legitimacy has been destroyed.

Well, yes, actually. However, the judge was more than equal to the task: 'I am not aware of any authority that goes to the length of deciding that the circumstances are sufficient to justify a finding of illegitimacy, and there is no accounting for the vagaries of nature.' So Mr Ah Chuck was spared the cost of providing maintenance for the child born as a result of his adulterous relationship. The result, though perfectly explicable to lawyers, would leave everyone else astonished at the unfairness of it.

Seventy years later, in another country, Mr Magill was not spared— at least for a time.

Mr Magill lived in Victoria with Mrs Magill. Mrs Magill had two children to another man while married but had persuaded her husband that they were his children. After their divorce, Mr Magill continued to pay child support until he learned the true facts. Then he sued his former wife for the little-used tort of deceit. He succeeded at first, then failed on appeal and in the High Court.

In the High Court, without any conscious attempt at irony, Mrs Magill's counsel argued that the appeal was misconceived. The High Court noted that the common law presumption of legitimacy was no more. (Sorry, Mrs Hedges, you were in the wrong time, wrong country.)

The court split on whether the tort of deceit could, on occasion, be a remedy for lies told by one partner to another. It might be. Then again, it might not be.

The Tale of the School that Disappeared

Woodbridge House is an integral part of West Australian history. Land at Guildford on the upper banks of the Swan River was cultivated by Captain James Stirling, the first governor of the colony. In 1883 Charles Harper purchased the land and built Woodbridge House, now a National Trust property. In 1895 he started a school for his family and other local children. The Church of England took over his enterprise, which continues today as Guildford Grammar School, an independent co-educational institution. In 1921 the Proprietary Schools of Western Australia Pty Ltd leased Woodbridge House, and this is when our tale begins.

Woodbridge House school was established by Cecil Clement Priestly, universally known as 'Pre', and his wife, Ruth. The boarding school, never more than thirty or forty boys and often run at a loss, was a preparatory school, readying boys for the Navy and secondary school scholarships.

During the depression, Mr Priestly kept the school going in the face of enormous difficulties, but no boy was sent home because his parents could not meet the fees. Mrs Priestly juggled the accounts. Sport was important, and Woodbridge had the only boys' hockey team. As a result, the team played against Presbyterian Ladies' College and Perth College. The annual father–son cricket matches had an extra twist: the fathers had to use pick handles instead of bats, with rather bewildering results.

Woodbridge school produced many leaders and scholars despite its small size. One was Francis Theodore Page Burt, known as 'Red' to all, and later Chief Justice and then Governor of Western Australia. Another was William Page Pidgeon, 'Bill', later a Supreme Court judge.

At some point, a small cloud, perhaps unnoticed at the time, flitted across the sunny school. The Crown became the freehold owner.

The school colour was red, and the classics were taught: Latin, French, arithmetic, algebra, geometry, English, history, geography, grammar and divinity.

The days stated at 7 am and concluded at 7.45 pm with prayers. Many of the boys slept on the verandah. Woodbridge was partly self-sufficient, and the boys were expected to help collecting eggs, milking cows and picking fruit—lots of it. As noted in the first edition of the *Phoenix*, the school magazine: 'Peaches raw, peaches in pie, peaches in jam, peaches stewed. Yes, we had them again this year. How horrible peach jam is and now it is figs! Even the pigs are going on strike.'

Woodbridge House school had been in existence for twenty years when an event of cataclysmic importance shattered the world. On 7 December 1941, a day that will live in infamy, Japan bombed Pearl Harbor. Australia declared war against the Empire of Japan the next day. By February 1942, the Imperial Japanese Army had advanced down the Malayan Peninsula. Singapore fell on 15 February 1942.

In Western Australia, preparations for war were frantic. Fremantle's significance as a port and submarine base was recognised. Clearly there would be an influx of servicemen and women who needed housing. Command centres were required.

In the middle of Fremantle, a graceful, large building that had been a lunatic asylum was now a women's home. It was also in need of repair. It would make a good headquarters building. Bureaucratic brains set to pondering and decided to transfer the elderly occupants to ... Woodbridge.

And so it was that, a week before the start of first term in 1942, Mr Priestly received a notice of eviction. It was not pleasant. Subsequently, Justice Dwyer described it:

I think I am justified in saying that re-entry was not made in a manner which should be imitated by the Crown or its servants in the future.

It may be that occasionally a letter was not couched in the politest of terms, but that is a habit which seems to have grown in public departments of recent years; courtesy in correspondence is seemingly now thought undesirable.

The school was closed, the furniture sold, the staff dismissed, the boys dispersed. The old women moved in as the boys moved out. Red Burt went to Guildford Grammar School. Bill Pidgeon followed Pre to Scotch College. Pre continued as a sports master at Scotch, passing away in 1955.

Mr and Mrs Priestly sued the Crown by way of the ancient remedy of Petition of Right. They were partially successful. The Crown's entry was wrongful, as the tenant was entitled to six months' notice, ending with the tenancy year. As the Crown's actions were taken in times of stress and its requirements were urgent, exemplary damages were not awarded.

The Priestleys—or, to be accurate, the Preparatory Schools Company Ltd—recovered damages for loss incurred on the sale of furniture and for compensation for staff. But Dwyer J found that any goodwill attached to Mr Priestly in person, not the company, and no damages were awarded for this, the principal aspect of the claim.

And so a school that had weathered good times and challenging times, led by a kindly man and his wife, just disappeared. The bright caps and red-ribboned straw boaters were never to be seen again.

The Tale of the Burning Bag

A typical January day dawned hot in busy Fremantle Harbour, where the SS *Panamanian* was loading flour for Ceylon. By morning knock-off, the temperature had climbed to 107 degrees Fahrenheit (43 degrees Celsius) in the shade. The lumpers or stevedores, better known as wharfies, climbed onto the deck for such relief from the heat as they could get. Cigarettes were passed around. Everyone rested for a while, drenched with sweat from working in the heat of the hold.

It was so hot that a piece of hessian, perhaps from a flourbag, was hung over a winch to keep it out of the sun. Perhaps the winch overheated and set the hessian smouldering. Or maybe one of the wharfies set it smouldering during smoko. However it happened, when Jim Durnin, one of the wharfies, saw the burning hessian bag, he became concerned.

First, he stamped on it. Still smouldering. What to do next? The *Panamanian* was of course surrounded by harbour water. Easy solution. Jim threw the smouldering hessian over the side to fizzle out safely. Or so he thought.

The day was 17 January 1945. As we read in 'The Tale of the School that Disappeared', Fremantle was strategically important after the fall of Singapore. By 1945, it was the largest submarine base in the southern hemisphere, sometimes hosting up to 20 submarines from the USA, Britain, and the Netherlands. Warships and merchant ships also called at the port in need of refuelling.

Submarines need fuel—dieseline, to be precise. Surface ships need furnace oil. Vessels were refuelled in the harbour. Pollution controls were not as effective as they might have been, and from time to time there was significant spillage of oil on the surface of the water, both dieseline and heavier furnace oil. Sometimes there might be only trace amounts, while at other times oil would pool around ships and wharves until tide or wind broke it up. The harbour and naval authorities knew this because a ship had caught fire following oil build-up a short time before.

Back to the *Panamanian*. To Mr Durnin's astonishment and apprehension, a twenty-foot sheet of flame shot skywards between the ship and the wharf, setting fire to the quay structure, the Panamanian and a submarine depot ship, HMS *Maidstone*, which was moved out of harm's way by two tugs.

The Navy and civilian fire services turned out to fight the conflagration. Black smoke from the doomed ship towered hundreds of feet skywards. When the fire was extinguished after three days and the smoke had cleared, a thousand feet of wharf had been badly damaged. The *Panamanian*'s wooden superstructure was burnt completely away, her hull blackened and blistered, her cargo destroyed. The officers and crew were left with only the clothes they stood in—all their money had burned away. One sailor, a New Zealand volunteer, died while fighting the fire.

HMS *Maidstone* was saved and went on to a distinguished career, until it was scrapped in 1978. The *Panamanian* was a total loss.

The owner of the *Panamanian* was the Eastern Asia Navigation Company Ltd, although it took the company some time to prove this in court. The company sued the Fremantle Harbour Trust Commissioners and the Commonwealth of Australia with a variety of causes of action. The loss to the company was enormous. The *Panamanian* was valued at £500,000—about $20 million today.

The trial took place over twenty-three days in 1949 before the Chief Justice of Western Australia, Sir John Dwyer. Alas, the company (or its insurers) was unsuccessful. A clause in the Harbour Trust regulations provided that all vessels moored along any wharf shall be at the sole risk of the owners and master.

The action against the Commonwealth, which had taken over large parts of the harbour, was also unsuccessful. It could not be established that the Commonwealth was responsible for dieseline being a hazard on the water.

An appeal was instituted direct to the High Court. These were the days before the Federal Court. The appeal hearing took nine days. The company fared no better.

What may perhaps made the pill more bitter to swallow was the judgment of Chief Justice Sir John Latham. He wrote that the company might have made a case that because the timber of the wharf at Berth 8, where the *Panamanian* lay, was impregnated with oil, the wharf was therefore in a dangerous condition, for which the Harbour Trust was responsible: it had a duty to keep the wharf in good repair. But, he added, no case that was made by the company founded on this theory.

Ouch.

A few reminders of Fremantle's wartime past remain if you look carefully enough. The part of the wharf which had been destroyed was replaced. Nothing remains of SS *Panamanian*. Mr Durnin died in 1977, long after the flames his inadvertent actions had caused that hot January day.

The Tale of the Prevaricating Witness

Dr Robert (Bob) Withers loved camellias and rhododendrons, going so far as to write a book about them: *Liliums in Australia*. He was very knowledgeable about the species and was recognised in 1995 when he was appointed a Member of the Order of Australia for services to horticulture. One of his creations was even featured on a stamp. When he died in 2005, aged eighty-two, he bequeathed his collection to the Royal Botanic Gardens in Melbourne.

All of which has nothing to do with the time he brushed with the law and ended up in gaol—briefly. It happened this way.

After serving as a private in World War II, Bob Withers qualified as a doctor in 1946 and commenced practice. Now, these were the days before breathalysers took all the fun out of defending drink drivers (thank you, Mr Bunning). In the absence of any scientific way of proving intoxication, witnesses were often called to give evidence of sobriety, or lack thereof. One evening, police asked Dr Withers to assess the sobriety of a suspected drunk driver. Dr Withers agreed and performed some tests.

In due course, Dr Withers was called as a witness for the defence. He said, 'I asked the defendant to walk up and down some steps I had in the surgery, which I consider he did in a satisfactory manner.' But there was a problem. In earlier evidence a witness said that the first time the defendant had walked up the steps, he had fallen. Naturally, the magistrate, sitting with two justices, asked: 'Tell me about the first time the defendant stumbled.'

Dr Withers answered, 'I did not feel it was a matter of importance.'

That seemed to have riled the whole bench. The magistrate said, 'I consider you have prevaricated in not disclosing the defendant failed to do the test satisfactorily on the first occasion and I propose to have you taken into custody to be dealt with.' And so he did.

But the magistrate had made several mistakes. The section in the *Justices Act* made wilful prevarication a contempt of court, not mere prevarication. Next, the magistrate gave Dr Withers no opportunity to answer the charge.

Dr Withers obtained an order nisi calling on the magistrate to justify the decision to commit him for contempt. The magistrate could not do so. Justice Martin entertained grave doubts that the evidence showed intentional—that is, wilful—evasion. He also had no difficulty in finding that the magistrate had failed to accord Dr Withers what we would today call procedural fairness. Dr Withers succeeded in having the contempt charge dismissed.

Dr Withers continued to practice medicine until 1989, though one suspects he was rather less willing to assist police in the future. After retirement he became a judge of camellias, no doubt fortified in that role by the knowledge that camellias can't prevaricate.

The Tale of the Interminable Divorce

The year was 1880 and Harriet Crayford wanted a husband. She had a baby born out of wedlock. As was common then, an unmarried mother was a social outcast and had great difficulty meeting her basic needs.

Working as a barmaid in a Christchurch hotel, Harriet was attracted by the name of the manager, Thomas Dorn. They were married in 1880. For a time, a witness described them as two doves devoted to each other. Later they were to become two devils.

The birth of a son increased the family but did not increase marital harmony. All was not well. They each drank—a lot. Moreover, Harriet complained that Thomas was cruel to her.

Thomas decided to leave his family behind and try his luck in Sydney. For two months Harriet had no money. Eventually, she travelled to Sydney with the children and the couple reunited at the White Hart Hotel, before Thomas was employed as a manager of the Charing Cross Hotel in Waverley.

The marriage did not prosper. Thomas continued his acts of cruelty: he threw a washing brush at Harriet, and on one occasion was seen threatening her with a carving knife.

Things came to a head in 1884. They had been arguing all day. At one stage they settled down and Harriet signed a paper promising to give up the drink. But that night trouble flared again. One witness described how windows were smashed and Harriet was in such fear that she jumped from the first-floor balcony, landing on a police sergeant.

The witness was both right and wrong. She did land on a police officer, but his rank was constable: Constable George Sergeant.

Harriet decided enough was enough and went to consult a solicitor, Mr Albert Nicholson, whom she knew because he was her husband's solicitor. Earlier that year, while licensee of the Victoria Hotel, Thomas had been prosecuted for allowing a table to be used for the apparently heinous crime of playing billiards after hours. Albert pointed out to the court that the charge had been laid under the *Billiards Act*, not the *Licencing Act*, and under the *Billiards Act* persons were allowed to play until midnight. Thomas was acquitted.

Albert evidently had a shaky grasp on what constitutes a conflict of interest, because he dropped Thomas as a client and immediately took instructions from Harriet. Their relationship quickly turned amorous.

Albert appeared for Harriet to apply for a decree of judicial separation on the grounds of cruelty and desertion. On 7 November 1884, a decree was granted by Justice Windeyer and Thomas was ordered to pay alimony for the children. Thus began what one newspaper later described as the interminable divorce.

While Harriet and Albert happily continued as lovers, Thomas took a darker path. He flatly refused to pay alimony or legal costs. When the unpaid alimony reached £13, Albert obtained a warrant of commitment for Thomas to be imprisoned unless he made payment. Even this threat did not persuade Thomas to pay the alimony he owed. Thomas was imprisoned in Darlinghurst Gaol for contempt of court.

After two years and four months, Justice Manning intervened. He understood Thomas might or might not be in gaol because of his obstinacy but it was time an inquiry was instituted. Noting that some people were imprisoned for non-payment of maintenance and served periods that should only be awarded for criminal cases, he ordered Thomas to be released.

Thomas had already commenced divorce proceedings against Harriet, naming Albert as a co-respondent and seeking £1000 damages against him.

Harriet and Albert argued before Justice Manning that the proceedings should be stayed until Thomas paid the costs and alimony he had so far refused to pay. The judge refused to stay proceedings. Harriet and Albert appealed. While the appeal was pending, Justice Manning refused to adjourn and instead settled the issues and the mode of trial. Justice Manning was not to be the trial judge.

In September 1887 the action was tried before Justice Stephen and a jury. It was a sensational trial over three days with lots of revelations. The jury accepted Thomas's evidence and ordered Albert to pay Thomas damages of £1000. Harriet's cross-petition on the grounds of cruelty was dismissed.

Harriet appealed. A few months later, the Full Court allowed Harriet's appeal and ordered a new trial because Thomas, not having paid alimony or costs, was in contempt and could not proceed until he had purged his contempt. Moreover, the issue of cruelty had been settled by the decree of judicial separation, granted years before by Justice Windeyer, so the jury had no power to find against Harriet on that point. To rub salt into the wound, Thomas was ordered to pay his wife's costs because she had no independent estate.

An issue in the first trial was whether Thomas had sexual intercourse with Harriet shortly before the trial commenced. Why was this important? Because that might amount to condonation of Harriet's adultery.

The trial judge had left the jury to consider whether sexual intercourse had taken place, and if it had, whether this amounted to adultery.

But the Full Court found this was an error. The Chief Justice held that sexual intercourse with full knowledge of the adultery necessarily constituted condonation. He said the husband who so acts in this dilemma either intends to forgive his wife or does not. If the former, that is an end to the matter. If the latter, it is opposed to public morality to permit him to assert non-forgiveness. 'To do so would be permitting him to treat his wife as if she was a prostitute, and a prostitute submitting as such to sexual intercourse with him, and this in the interests of public morals ought not be allowed,' said Justice

Windeyer. He was scathing of counsel's argument: 'The theory of a possible sexual intercourse without prejudice has only to be stated to be recognised in all its disgusting absurdity. I decline to entertain it for one moment and dismiss it from consideration as an insult to common sense and an outrage upon morals.'

A new trial never happened. Thomas declared bankruptcy. Harriet grew tired of the whole business, including Albert, described by a newspaper as a wicked-eyed little lawyer. She fled to Adelaide with the children and lived with her sister. It was left to her next solicitor, Mr Wilkinson, to apply for an order from the Full Court that he was entitled to payment of his costs.

By then the judges were tiring of Mr and Mrs Dorn, whom they strongly suspected of collusion, and made the order that allowed Mr Wilkinson to be paid finally for his work on behalf of Mrs Dorn.

And that could be the end of the story. But not quite.

When the dust had settled, Harriet returned to Sydney and resumed living with Thomas as man and wife. Thomas went back to his violent ways, and in November 1895 Harriet obtained an order nisi for divorce.

Albert was divorced in 1890. He had married Eugenie Nicholson in Brisbane in 1879. Apparently happy, they lived together for eighteen months. One morning Albert kissed Eugenie goodbye and set off for work. That was the last Eugenie saw of him for years. Instead of going to work, Albert caught the train to Townsville and later moved to Sydney, where he took up with a widow and had five children, still finding time for his dalliance with Harriet.

Albert did not defend the divorce but suggested he had left Eugenie because she had failed to follow through on a promise to abandon the Roman Catholic religion and become a Protestant. Eugenie denied this and won her divorce.

The Charing Cross Hotel, the scene of so much action and misery for the Dorns, continues to this day. It is now a gastro pub.

A Mouse's Tail: Mickey Mouse Goes to Court

In 1937, a manufacturer of radio sets wanted to market them under the names 'Mickey Mouse' and 'Minnie Mouse'. Walt Disney, inventor of both mice and the holder of a copyright in them, naturally opposed this course and won on all levels. Poor old Mickey, however, in winning, had to endure some judicial contempt.

Although the Chief Justice, Sir John Latham, thought Mickey and Minnie were two fantastic and amusing characters (a fan), Sir Owen Dixon described the grotesque forms and absurd antics of both (not a fan).

Sir George Rich had a bit each way, saying Disney had 'obtained great reputation or notoriety for the form and name of Mickey Mouse'. Sir George, perhaps mindful of a tendency for judicial ignorance, now thankfully long gone, thought it prudent to add, 'Minnie Mouse, his feminine counterpart'.

So Mickey, whose features appeared on everything from canned soups to cotton undershorts, from bridge scorers to boys' braces, triumphed.

I wonder what he would have thought of the New Zealand would-be politician who changed his name to 'Mickey Mouse' and campaigned on the slogan 'Put a mouse in the house'.

The Tale of the Boy Who Was Stolen

The Reverend John West was a formidable force for good in nine-teenth-century Australia.

Born in England in 1809, at the age of twenty he was ordained as a Congregational minister and sent to Launceston as a missionary with his young family. He helped found a newspaper, a school and a mechanics' institute, as well as being an active preacher. He even wrote a history of Tasmania. But his real passion was a campaign to abolish transportation to Tasmania. The movement spread to the mainland, and Reverend West was at the forefront.

In 1854 he accepted an invitation from his friend John Fairfax, a fellow abolitionist, to become editor of the *Sydney Morning Herald*. This enhanced, rather than diminished, his zeal for righteous causes.

And so he came to hear of the plight of Tommy, an Aboriginal boy. Discovering that Tommy was in the custody of a squatter, Alexander Collins, and sceptical of the circumstances, Reverend West applied for a writ of *habeas corpus*, calling on Mr Collins to produce Tommy to the court.

Habeas corpus ad subjudicendum is an ancient remedy dating from the reign of Henry II and is still available. It requires the person on whom the writ is served to produce the person being held in cus-tody to the court so that the legality of the custody can be ascertained. An application for a writ of *habeas corpus* is so serious that a court will set aside all other business to deal with it promptly.

Mr Collins complied with the writ and produced Tommy to the court. He told the court that Tommy was in his care with his father's consent and of his own free will. But he had told another story to a Mr Barber, who swore an affidavit. According to Mr Barber, Mr Collins said he had stolen Tommy from his parents and that he would never see his tribe again.

Chief Justice Stephen was scathing. In words that should have been emblazoned in every public institution:

> It might be admitted that the boy had been kindly treated but no end could justify an act such as was alleged to have been committed. It was a moral wrong—an outrage—an act of gross cruelty which no man of common feeling could hear described without an expression of strong indignation. It was not a light matter, but the infliction of an insufferable wrong ... These people were British subjects and if held responsible for crime on one hand, should be protected from outrage on the other.

Instead, those words were soon forgotten, and in due course governments across Australia began removing children from their parents, oft times by stealth.

Not until one of Australia's finest jurists, Sir Ronald Wilson, as President of the Human Rights and Equal Opportunity Commission, released a report titled *Bringing Them Home* in 1997, did the true effects of the program of removal enter the collective consciousness.

Sir Ronald was also a past president of the Uniting Church in Australia, a union of Protestant churches that included the Congregationalists. The Reverend John West would have been proud.

The Tale of the Trampled Tomatoes

Mr Kratochvil was a market gardener of Czech origins who had land skirting the shore of Lake Gnangara, in Perth's north. He grew melons, pumpkins and tomatoes—lots of them—on land that was enclosed by fences. On the other side of Lake Gnangara, Mr Dall and his son kept cows and a young Holstein bull. It was that bull which was the cause of the trouble to follow.

On 1 January 1955, Mr and Mrs Kratochvil took a short break away from the market garden. The bull decided he would celebrate the new year by leading about fifteen cows around the lake, through the fence and into the market garden, whereupon they trampled the tomatoes and mashed the melons. Mr Kratochvil's loss was severe. In a few short hours, the results of months of hard work were ruined.

Mr Babra, a neighbour of Mr Kratochvil, tried to chase the cattle out, but the bull made to attack him so he wisely withdrew. The next morning Mr Kratochvil and his wife arrived about 7 am and tried to chase the cattle out, but the bull got fractious and they had to take shelter. 'The bull added insult to injury by chasing me and my pal when we tried to remove the cattle,' Mr Kratochvil was reported as saying.

In due course, young Mr Dall offered a paltry sum in compensation and offered to buy more plants for Mr Kratochvil at a time when it would have been useless to replant. Maybe he didn't realise the steaks were high. And so, later in the year (things were quicker in those days), Justice Wolff heard Mr Kratochvil's claim for damages.

Under the *Cattle Trespass Fencing and Impounding Act 1882*, there was an obligation on Mr Kratochvil to have a sufficient fence. Indeed, his property was surrounded by a fence that continued into Gnangara Lake for about thirty metres, the lake forming a further barrier. What is 'sufficient'? Well, nothing if the breed and strain of cattle are particularly mischievous.

Justice Wolff didn't focus only on Mr Kratochvil's fence. He examined the Dalls' obligation and was scathing:

> Their fences were useless, and despite the habit of this type of cattle, they let them roam at large without a herdsman. They have been repeatedly warned by the local authority not to let them stray, but their philosophy seems to be that it is other people's duty to keep them out not theirs to keep them in.

Mr Kratochvil recovered damages for all of his 3950 tomato plants and his crops of watermelons, rock melons and pumpkins.

In 1955 Perth's population was 360,000. It is now nearly three million. Lake Gnangara is no longer a rural setting. The city has surrounded it. What became of the fractious Holstein bull is not recorded.

The Tale of the Unfortunate Letter

The whole trouble occurred through a question asked by a magistrate which would have been better not asked at all.

Mr Albert Amos Kidd fought with honour during the Great War, had been awarded the Military Cross and shaken the hand of His Majesty King George. After the war, he returned to his trade in Western Australia's mid-western Gascoyne District as a soft drink maker. He was much respected in the region, and so he was much aggrieved by the question posed while he was defending an action in the Carnarvon Local Court.

As a former military man, Mr Kidd's first, though regrettable, impulse was to return fire. This he did in the form of a letter to the magistrate, Fergus Finbar Horgan, written during an adjournment:

> F.F. Horgan, Esq.
> Dear Sir,
>
> I did not think that I would live to be so mortified as I was to-day in your Court. Publicly accused of being a party capable of sinking to the depths of so sordid a crime as bribery—against a decrepit woman—to obviate payment of a paltry 20 pounds. When His Majesty King George gripped my hand and decorated me with the Military Cross, I did not think it would ever be my dolour to meet one of His Servants capable of so base an act as to prostitute our Dear Emblem—the Scales of Justice. Prematurely judged. British Law is founded on facts fortunately, when administered unbiasedly.

To-morrow I have to defend my most priceless possession—my good name—and I will defend it while I have breath in my body.

I am, Sir, yours faithfully.

A.A. Kidd, Lieut. M.C.

The magistrate was unimpressed at the letter, to put it mildly. He fined Mr Kidd £10 for contempt of court. Mr Kidd was not pleased, and it took some time before he was taken to the cells, where he remained until the fine was paid some hours later. The magistrate also banned the letter from publication.

Mr Kidd was not going to take this lying down. His honour was at stake, or so he believed. He posted a copy of the letter in a public place in Carnarvon.

If the magistrate was angry before, he was incandescent now. Mr Kidd was hauled before the court and, after further insults from Mr Kidd, the magistrate sentenced him to fourteen days' imprisonment for contempt of court.

But as the Full Court decided, the magistrate had made an error. The sentence imposed was for two offences, not one. As Justice Draper put it, 'The Magistrate unfortunately, fortunately perhaps for Mr Kidd, took the wrong procedure.'

The court agreed on the result but, as sometimes happens, got there by different routes.

The Chief Justice thought the publication was not in the face of the court. If a magistrate is to commit a person for contempt of court immediately, the magistrate must have personally witnessed the contempt. In other words, the contempt must be in the face of the court. As the display of the letter had not occurred in the court, the magistrate had no jurisdiction and there was no contempt.

Justice Draper thought it was contempt but the wrong procedure had been used.

Justice Rooth thought he would wait until the question arose before opining as to whether it was contempt.

Mr Kidd resumed a more peaceful life in Carnarvon, manufacturing aerated waters. Six years later, he and his wife took a holiday in the south. On 20 May 1938, his many friends were pleased to learn that, after four weeks of serious illness, Mr Kidd was now convalescent and well on the road to recovery. Unfortunately, that recovery was short-lived and he died on 27 July 1938.

As for Magistrate Horgan, he had only been in Carnarvon for a short time. However, he was busy with a Gilbertian Poo Bah list of duties as Acting Stipendiary Magistrate for the Gascoyne District, Magistrate of the Carnarvon Local Court, Chairman of the Gascoyne Licensing Court, Warden of the Ashburton and Gascoyne Goldfields, Treasury Paymaster and Clerk of Courts.

F.F. Horgan returned to Perth in 1929 to take up the position as Special Magistrate to the Children's Court, where he served faithfully for many years. He lived to nearly 100, dying at the age of ninety-seven in 1965.

The Tale of the Pub with No Gents'

Jimmy Smith may seem an unprepossessing name. Joynton Smith sounds far grander, as Mr Smith was known after he added the extra name. Born in 1858 in England, eldest of twelve children, he shipped as a cabin boy to Australia, here to make his fortune and reputation. He passed away in 1943 as Sir James Joynton Smith, a pillar of society and a force in promoting rugby. Joynton Park in inner-south Sydney bears his name.

After working at various occupations, he leased the Imperial Arcade Hotel in 1896. Renamed the Arcadia Hotel, it became the foundation of his second fortune (he had gambled away the first). The residential hotel became very popular. Situated by the Imperial Arcade running between Pitt and Castlereagh streets, Sydney, it was also a popular bar, though Smith himself was a teetotaller.

One hot afternoon, Mr Mountnay stopped at the Arcadia Hotel bar for a few drinks. After a while, nature being what it is, he asked the barmaid, 'Show me where the lavatory is,' to which she replied, 'Go through them two doors, cross the arcade and there you will find it.' It appears that the hotel did not have its own conveniences but used those in the adjacent arcade.

Mr Mountnay, no doubt hurrying a little, went through a door marked Hotel Arcadia and down an ill-lit passage. He came to a dark entrance and, thinking relief was at hand, turned in. Alas, it was not the promised urinal but an uncovered lift shaft, down which

Mr Mountnay fell, severely injuring himself. He sued the owner of the Arcadia Hotel and recovered £300 in damages.

Joynton Smith appealed to the Full Court. The three judges who heard the appeal must have been imbued with Victorian decency to the extent that they denied Mr Mountnay his damages. At issue was whether the brief words spoken by the barmaid were admissible in evidence.

Justice Owen: 'It seems to me that it would be a monstrous thing to suppose it was any part of the duty of a girl who was employed in the bar of a hotel to serve customers with drink to point out to those customers where the lavatory for men was.'

Justice Pring: 'It is contended that the evidence is admissible on the ground of authority on the part of the barmaid to direct male customers to the places of convenience. I decline altogether to lay down a law which would lead to such indecency.'

Maybe their honours had never been caught short. Perhaps they had never been in the front bar of a hotel.

Mr Mountnay appealed to the High Court, where he had success. Sir Samuel Griffith, Chief Justice, in delivering judgment, was scornful of judicial sensitivities: 'I can see nothing unseemly in asking the only person on the spot representing the proprietor where the place was that the proprietor was bound to provide for the convenience of his customers.' So Mr Mountnay kept his award of damages.

The Arcadia Hotel continued to provide comforts, if not conveniences.

In September 1909, Mr Henry Cox from Woy Woy and his wife were guests at the hotel. Arising early one morning, Mr Cox was thirsty. A bottle of water was handy, so he poured himself a glass. It was to be his last. He immediately turned pale and died.

This is not good publicity for a hotel. Poisoning customers is somewhat worse than directing them to fall down a lift well. However, the hotel was not to blame. A young Polish visitor, Stanislaus Dyktor, had been experimenting with electroplating in his room and had rather carelessly left a bottle containing cyanide of potassium in his room, assuming the maid would dispose of it.

Things moved more quickly than today, and three months later Mr Dyktor stood trial for manslaughter. He was swiftly acquitted. Justice Tucker said he agreed with the verdict of the jury but warned Mr Dyktor in future to be very careful in dealing with chemicals or other matters of the nature of which you know nothing.

Smith sold his interest in the Arcadia Hotel and later was a co-founder of the popular paper *Smith's Weekly*. Knighted in 1920, he was a Lord Mayor of Sydney and a member of the New South Wales Legislative Council. After his death in 1943, the fight over his estate lasted for six years, one of the most expensive pieces of litigation of its time.

The Arcadia Hotel and the Imperial Arcade were demolished in 1961.

The Tale of the Defamed Drover

When stuck behind a slow-moving and smelly semitrailer full of cattle or sheep, instead of fuming about the live animal trade, pro and con, why not calm yourself by retreating to a gentler time when animals were droved, not driven?

Even though the vast majority have always been city dwellers, there is a part of us, like A.B. 'Banjo' Paterson, who still 'fancy that I'd like to change with Clancy, like to take a turn at droving where the seasons come and go'. This brings us to the tale of the defamed drover.

Mr Blood was a drover by trade and was engaged by Mr Matheson to drive a large flock of sheep from Quorn, in South Australia, to Leigh Creek, 220 kilometres to the north. As Matheson's sheep were being driven through Hawker, about 60 kilometres from Quorn, some sheep belonging to a local butcher named Leopold got mixed with them.

The boy who shepherded Leopold's sheep swore Mr Blood tried to prevent this mixing, and after it happened tried to get Leopold's sheep out of the big flock. In this he failed, and all the sheep were driven away together. Leopold, when he was told of the occurrence, made no effort to recover his sheep. Mr Blood said that only five strange sheep got mixed with his at Hawker; he told Matheson this and delivered that number directly as he reached his destination. Three of Matheson's sheep were left at Hawker, lost there when the mixing took place.

Now, of course, Mr Blood could not really tell one sheep from another—have you ever tried?—so he continued on his journey with the butcher's sheep hidden in his flock.

Worse was to come. Two lambs owned by the local constable, Barlow by name, went missing also. One turned up in Mr Blood's flock when he set camp at Mern Merna, just outside Hawker. Constable Barlow, incensed by the loss of his lambs, no doubt fattening nicely, wrote to Mr Matheson:

> On the 18th and 19th, a flock of sheep passed through Hawker; I believe they were your property. Anyhow, the drover left them here, and probably did the same elsewhere; and to make the count right, he has got away with a few belonging to different owners. I suppose he knew there would be little chance of your noticing it at the count.

To this letter Matheson replied, asking for further information and saying that he had told Mr Blood that he would never employ him again if the charges were found to be correct.

Constable Barlow replied: 'Mrs Grundy says that some of the pick and shovel men not a hundred miles off the railway line had some cheap mutton lately.' The same letter asserted: 'Neither do I care to express my opinion on paper as to the honesty of your drover.'

Now, drovers might sometimes write letters 'with a thumbnail dipped in tar' but they are as fearsome in protecting their reputation as any other folk. This even though the enlargement of a herd while driving through towns and across paddocks was not exactly unknown. So it was that Mr Blood, the drover, sued Mr Barlow, the constable, for libel. The matter was tried by a magistrate and justices, who found in favour of Constable Barlow. But Mr Blood appealed against the decision.

In the Full Court, Gordon J found for Mr Blood. Constable Barlow had pleaded that he acted within the scope of his duty as a constable. Gordon J would have none of it: 'But the privilege does not extend to defamatory expressions wholly unwarranted by the circumstances which have come to the knowledge of the officer; and if such expressions are used the law imputes malice and the privilege is gone.'

The laws of defamation are complex and confusing, even to experienced practitioners in the field. Contemporary judgment databases are replete with the difficulties of mounting a coherent plea of defamation. Things then do not seem to have changed much in 100 years.

Constable Barlow (or his lawyer) had not raised a plea of justification. Therefore the magistrate erred in his directions to the justices because the truth of the libel was not in issue. So the Full Court decided Mr Blood was entitled to damages for the loss of character and of employment which he had clearly suffered.

One hopes that, after a while, 'as the stock are slowly stringing, Blood rides behind them singing, for the drover's life has pleasures that the townsfolk never know'.

The Tale of Pannikin to Prison

For much of the twentieth century there were few middle-class homes that did not have a print of ghost gums or blue-grey hills hanging on the wall. The artist was Albert Namatjira, a Western Arrernte man from Hermannsburg.

Greatly admired in his day, he was patronisingly accorded what might be described as 'honorary white status'. In 1957 he was awarded British subjecthood and Australian citizenship, which carried with them freedom from restrictions on purchasing or possessing alcohol. It would be another ten years before a referendum changed the Constitution to enable Australia's Indigenous peoples to exercise such rights as they had including citizenship. Alas, too late for Mr Namatjira—as was the postage stamp issued in his honour in 1968.

As an honorary white citizen, Mr Namatjira was allowed to buy alcohol. However, his adult children and many of his friends were still wards of the state. Selling or giving alcohol to a ward was forbidden under the Northern Territory Licensing Ordinance.

In 1957, Mr Namatjira, his wife and their large family were living just out of Hermannsburg, then a Lutheran mission west of Alice Springs. He was supporting up to 600 people through the proceeds of his art.

On 26 August 1958, Mr Namatjira was travelling home in a taxi, accompanied by another artist, Mr Henoch Raberaba, an adult ward of the state. Mr Namatjira had with him a bottle of rum. Mr Raberaba asked for a drink. Mr Namatjira responded that he could not do so. It was against the law. However, he could give Mr Raberaba a pannikin.

Now, for you city types, a pannikin is an enamel-coated metal drinking mug, without which no bushman would be properly equipped. In what else can you drink billy tea? Having lent Mr Raberaba his pannikin, Mr Namatjira called on the driver to stop, whereupon Mr Namatjira got out of the taxi for a while. This happened several times on the journey.

Mr Namatjira did not see what happened, but it is easy to guess. Each time Mr Namatjira got out, Mr Raberaba helped himself to a generous slug of rum, courtesy of the pannikin. This mild ruse was quickly discovered, and Mr Namatjira was arrested and charged with supplying liquor to a ward. On 7 October 1958 he was convicted after a trial in the Alice Springs Magistrates Court and sentenced to six months' hard labour. He immediately appealed against both his conviction and sentence before Justice Kriewaldt.

Martin Chemnitz Kriewaldt was, like Mr Namatjira, a Lutheran. He was the sole judge in the Northern Territory for almost the whole of the 1950s. Respected as a benchmark of fairness and justice, he tried to be fair and merciful, although he displayed the condescension typical of many of his generation. An example appears in the judgment:

> [E]ven before I came to the Territory, I was an admirer of the art of the Appellant [Namatjira]. Two pictures by one of his sons have graced the walls of my living room for some years. All my life the duty of Christians towards heathens and the duty of the more fortunate towards the less fortunate have been impressed on me.

Mr Namatjira was represented by the highly respected Maurice Ashkenazy QC, who ingeniously argued several constitutional and interpretation grounds of appeal, which the judge easily dispatched. Perhaps Mr Ashkenazy recognised that, on the facts, it was an open and shut case against Mr Namatjira, and so it proved.

He had slightly more success on the sentence. The judge considered as mitigation that all his life Mr Namatjira had habitually shared his belongings with his friends, making it more difficult, though not impossible, for him to resist Mr Raberaba than it would be for a person not similarly accustomed to share. (Remember the 600 people he was supporting.) The sentence was reduced to three months. An application for special leave to the High Court was unsuccessful.

Within two years, both Albert Namatjira, fifty-eight, and Martin Kriewaldt, sixty, passed away.

The episode is best summed up by the author, journalist and activist Len Fox:

> Here is a man, who with his glowing art,
> Gave us the beauty of our country's heart;
> Here is a man whose skin was coloured brown
> And so we spurned his gifts and trod him down.
> Here is a man whom we said with love
> We make you equal under heaven abo
> And now as final proof we love him well
> The key turns slowly in his prison cell.

The Tale of the Lawyer Who Leaped

Despite being the middle of summer, Saturday, 13 January 1951 was a blustery day—too blustery for yachts to return safely to Fremantle from Rottnest Island, off the coast of Perth.

Colville Parslow, whose lugger *Alanna* was moored at Rottnest in Thompsons Bay, was in a pickle. He was a part owner of the yacht but had to be back in Perth for business. Leaving a somewhat inexperienced crew with a promise to meet them at Fremantle the next day to help with derigging, he caught the ferry back to Perth.

The next day the wind dropped, and on the return journey the *Alanna* was becalmed. What's more, the engine failed. By lunchtime the *Alanna* was drifting near a reef a few miles south-east of Rottnest.

Col was concerned about his friends and the lugger. Being an aviator, Col had no difficulty in persuading a fellow pilot, George Bailey, to fly Col as his passenger to Rottnest in a Tiger Moth, a sturdy biplane. They took off about 12.45 pm.

And so the stage was set for the calamity which followed.

Colville Oliver Parslow was thirty-six. A West Australian, he had graduated from university with a law degree and completed articles in Perth before spending time working with T.J. Hughes, famous as (among other things) the gadfly who nearly brought down the government in the great constitutional case of *Clydesdale v Hughes*.

Perhaps because it was difficult to pursue his love of sailing in Boulder, in Western Australia's landlocked goldfields, Col moved back to Perth. He seems to have lived an adventurous life. In December

1938 Col and his friends were sailing to Rockingham when they hit a sandbank and capsized. This necessitated a swim to Woodman Point, over a mile away, and earned him a rebuke from the water police to take more care.

Although Col enlisted in the Army in 1941 and was discharged in 1943, he appears to have continued in legal practice. After he enlisted, Col appeared for a husband who gave evidence that his wife was in the habit of entertaining soldiers at her home. When court adjourned, the man's son followed the husband into the street and began to shove him, before Col intervened by stepping between them. Things calmed down, but after Col moved away the son called after him, 'I hope the next time you go yachting, the boat capsizes and you drown.'

In 1942 Col married Madeline McAdam, known as Mollie, in Fremantle. By 1951 he had his own practice in Mount Street and was known as 'the Flying Lawyer' because he used air travel a great deal for work. He was a member of the Air Pilots Association and an experienced aviator.

And now we return to Sunday, 14 January 1951.

A Tiger Moth has an open cockpit for pilot and another open cockpit for a passenger. Col was dressed in blue overalls, a scarf and a flying helmet. After taking off, Bailey flew from Maylands Aerodrome to Rottnest. There was no sign of the *Alanna*, so they headed back to Fremantle, then took a zigzag course at 500 feet—about 150 metres—to Rottnest again. The sea was calm and crystal clear. The *Alanna* was spotted slowly drifting towards a reef.

Col became agitated because he considered the crew inexperienced, even though a competent yachtsman had joined the boat in his place. He discussed the possibility of jumping from the plane with Bailey, who told him not to be foolish. Bailey then busied himself for a few minutes, preoccupied with the lugger. When he looked forward again, Col was in a crouched position on the lower wing. Mr Bailey shouted at him.

Colville Parslow rolled off the wing and to his doom. Turning slowly in the air, and out of control, he hit the water. His downward passage was observed by Bailey, and by all on board the *Alanna*. They immediately launched a dinghy but nothing could be done. Col had slipped beneath the waves. Despite an intensive search by water police, his body was never found.

When George Bailey returned to Maylands Aerodrome, he found in the front cockpit the overalls Col had been wearing, neatly folded, as well as his scarf, helmet and shoes.

Poor Mollie. She was now a widow. Although it was quite clear what had happened, the common law required seven years to pass before death was presumed. Mollie applied to the Supreme Court for leave to file an affidavit setting out the circumstances of Col's disappearance. Fortunately, Justice Walker was sympathetic and on 21 April 1951 ordered that Mollie could prove death by affidavit.

Everyone should make a will, especially solicitors. But had Col gone to the trouble of executing a will, written on parchment, sealed with wax and tied with pink ribbon? Well, not exactly. He had executed a short will, duly attested by two witnesses, leaving everything to Mollie. The will that Justice Walker admitted to probate on 30 April 1951 was written on the flyleaf of a book entitled *A Book of Ships and Seamen*.

Mollie lived until 2011 and never remarried. Perhaps she took comfort from the poem Col wrote on the other side of the flyleaf:

> Nor time nor space the aircraft knows
> When sweeping us apart;
> But hour by mile my longing grows
> To be with you, dear heart.

The Tale of the Missing Brooch that Wasn't

In nineteenth-century Victoria, the Reverend Charles Clark was a well-known Baptist minister. He had made a fortune lecturing throughout the colonies and preached to overflowing congregations. Described as an exceedingly kind and pleasant man who dressed nicely and gesticulated gracefully, he might also have been, as this tale unfolds, a man inclined to act with haste.

Being genteel Victorians and living close to the Fitzroy Gardens in Melbourne, Reverend Clark and his wife employed a servant, Bridget Langan. On 20 July 1869 Bridget was sent upstairs to get a handkerchief. She took her time about it but eventually she came down and gave it to Mrs Clark, who then left with her husband for an engagement.

Later that night, on their return, Mrs Clark went to her jewellery drawer—of which she had the only key—and discovered that a valuable diamond brooch was missing. Detectives were sent for immediately and, at the request of Reverend Clark, took Ms Langan into custody for stealing the brooch.

On the way through the Fitzroy Gardens to the watch-house, Reverend Clark asserted that Ms Langan had said, 'If you look in the cupboard you will find the brooch.' She also said, 'You will get back your brooch but who will give me back my character?' His offer that they return to home immediately was rejected by Ms Langan, so they continued to the watch-house, where she was imprisoned. To Reverend Clark, that was tantamount to a confession.

He must have been perturbed when later his wife found the brooch in the same drawer, albeit in a different place.

It may be that Mrs Clark was feeling remorse over her husband's hastiness in accusing Ms Langan, because she had to leave the police court the next day because of her feelings for poor Ms Langan.

The charges against Ms Langan were abandoned, and in due course she took legal action against Reverend Clark for malicious prosecution and false imprisonment. She failed in her first action as the jury found there was a reasonable suspicion she was guilty. Therefore the prosecution was not malicious. However, she recovered £75 damages for false imprisonment.

The trial judge told the jury to ignore the Fitzroy Gardens conversation when considering false imprisonment. Was he right to do so? 'Yes,' said the Full Court when dismissing Reverend Clark's appeal. The imprisonment commenced when Ms Langan was given into the charge of the detective at the house, and Reverend Clark's state of mind had to be judged then, not later. The judges expressed some doubt during argument as to whether the words spoken amounted to knowledge of a felony in any event!

Reverend Clark fared no better on his damages appeal. To show that ingeniousness is not confined to the modern era of advocacy, Reverend Clark's counsel argued that as she was taken through the Fitzroy Gardens at night, not much damage was done to her character and nominal damages only should have been awarded.

Chief Justice Stawell would have none of it. 'There is injury to the character of a person even suspected, an important matter to a servant.' (To Ms Langan, this comment must have seemed like a Stawell gift.[8])

So virtue triumphed and the wealthy Reverend Clark was a little bit less wealthy for a time.

---

8 The Stawell Gift is Australia's oldest short-distance running race, held annually in Stawell, Victoria. The town was named after the Chief Justice.

The Tale of the Tardy Coroner

In 1903, on his retirement as a police magistrate and coroner after for-ty-three years, William Caswell was described as 'courteous in manner, merciful to the deserving and hater of all sham'. The many admiring speeches did not mention 'punctual'. He had served across New South Wales. For twenty-five years he had been the magistrate and coroner in Moruya, a picturesque town on the coast south of Batemans Bay. His time in Moruya was not uniformly happy, though, and at one stage he found himself having to answer charges that seemed to stem from a religious disagreement.

Perhaps his stress from those unfortunate proceedings coloured his judgment in what was to come. Whatever it was, his tardiness con-tributed to what a judge later described as a very unwise proceeding.

In 1877 it was the practice of the coroner to sit with a jury. Mr Collier, who lived some distance from Moruya, was summonsed for jury service at 9 am. This time arrived and passed. No coroner. Mr Collier became more irritated. Finally, at 10 am, the coroner arrived.

Mr Collier was not amused. He spoke to his fellow jurors loudly enough for Mr Caswell to hear. 'It is hard to be summoned for 9 o'clock. Caswell could not attend because he had not his cows milked and had to supply the stores with butter before he could attend to his business.' To emphasise the point, Mr Collier repeated those words several times, and concluded by saying, 'I am not a toady and get no favours.' Poor Coroner Caswell. Mr Collier had not finished with him. At the conclu-sion of the proceedings, while Mr Caswell was making his way back to his buggy, Mr Collier, from the deck of a boat bearing him home, screeched, 'I defy you!'

That did it. Coroner Caswell caused Mr Collier to be charged under the *Vagrancy Act* with unlawfully using insulting behaviour towards Mr Caswell whereby a breach of the peace might have been occasioned. Mr Collier was fined £3 or one month in gaol.

But were the words insulting? That was the question for the Full Court when Mr Collier appealed against his conviction. 'No,' said three judges.

Justice Hargrave thought that the 'toady' reference might bring Mr Caswell up to heat, but more was needed. While hooting might be insulting, screeching was not.

Justice Fawcett was scathing about the coroner. Mr Collier, in his opinion, was justified in making the observation that he had. No doubt Mr Caswell was irritated at being found at fault with the discharge of his duty, but the words were amply justified by his conduct.

Justice Manning, who called the proceedings 'very unwise', also thought Mr Caswell was in the wrong for having kept the jury waiting for an hour.

Mr Caswell moved shortly thereafter to Goulburn, where he served faithfully to general acclaim for the next quarter-century. In due course, the person who had caused him so much grief with the original charges against the coroner (which were dismissed) welcomed him back to Moruya as a friend.

Finally, a point to note. If a magistrate or coroner unreasonably keeps you waiting, don't, whatever you do, hoot. Screech instead.

The Tale of the Late-Night Traveller

Many of us have experienced frustration at being in transit through airports. There are few places to sleep and the wait seems interminable. It is often late at night. But at least you are unlikely to be ejected from the airport before your plane is scheduled to depart, and there is usually a place to get a beer or a meal. Picture, then, the plight of Mr Shair Mahomet.

In 1901, he needed to travel from Nulla Nulla, a small railway siding near Moorine Rock, to Yellowdine, out of Southern Cross in Western Australia. Mr Mahomet decided to go by train. Only five years before, the Eastern Goldfields line had been extended to Kalgoorlie and the line went right through Nulla Nulla, so this was an obvious choice. Besides, it was a long journey by horse, mule or camel. As it turned out, the journey was not so convenient.

Yellowdine was a small siding, and it was necessary for Mr Mahomet to change trains in Southern Cross. The train pulled in at Southern Cross late in the evening: it was 10.45 pm. The train to Yellowdine was not due to depart until 3.40 am. What to do? Well, fortunately there was a waiting room by the platform, so Mr Mahomet ensconced himself within to pass the time until he could travel on.

Mr Mahomet was probably the only passenger at such a late hour and the stationmaster might have been longing for home and bed. But he couldn't leave without locking up, and he couldn't do that while Mr Mahomet was sitting peacefully in the waiting room.

The stationmaster ordered Mr Mahomet to leave the waiting room. Whether Mr Mahomet waited on the dark and lonely streets or somewhere else was of no concern to him. After all, Southern Cross was a boom town with ten hotels and inns.

Mr Mahomet didn't think this was quite fair. Besides, he was comfortable where he was. So he told the stationmaster where to go (or something like that).

Well, the stationmaster, who was now probably very tired as well as angry, had had enough. He caused Mr Mahomet to be arrested and lodged in the police lock-up. I suppose Mr Mahomet did get some shelter that night—though not much sleep.

The next day, the magistrate was not impressed by the actions of the stationmaster. He ordered that Mr Mahomet be freed immediately. Mr Mahomet did as all good people should and consulted a solicitor, Mr N.K. Ewing, who sued the Commissioner of the Railways for malicious arrest and false imprisonment.

In the early skirmish, Justice Parker thought Mr Mahomet might have had a rough deal, but he didn't have a legal leg to stand on. However, on appeal, the Full Court disagreed. Mr Mahomet had a through ticket from Nulla Nulla to Yellowdine and therefore had to wait at Southern Cross for a change of trains. The Commissioner had no right to revoke his licence to be in the waiting room without cause. The Full Court ordered that Mr Mahomet's legal action could proceed after all.

History does not record what the ultimate outcome was, but the Commissioner would have been wise to settle.

The Tale of the Prohibited Passenger

In the mid-1970s Dirk Schuiling was a young Dutch entomology student with an adventurous streak. After eight months working in the South Celebes, he spent time touring Indonesia before the fancy took him to visit Papua New Guinea. Being aware that some paperwork might be needed, Dirk made his way to Jayapura, in Papua, to seek out the Papua New Guinean consulate. There was not one. However, a helpful Indonesian official came to his aid and advised Dirk that a permit was unnecessary so long as he held an onward air ticket. Helpful—but wrong.

Dirk purchased an onward air ticket from Port Moresby to Australia and on 1 June 1977 boarded an Air Niugini flight for Wekak, in Papua New Guinea. The smiling flight attendant, with nary a glance at Dirk's documentation or enquiry as to a permit, showed him to his seat and the plane took off.

The flight was not direct to Wewak but stopped in Vanimo on the way. All passengers were ordered to disembark so their papers might be checked. Dirk's turn soon came. The first document to be inspected was his vaccination certificate. Uh-oh. His cholera vaccination was overdue. Consternation among officials. Arrangements were made to send him to the hospital. Dirk told them he had not received a permit yet, but no one paid much attention. The health matter was more urgent.

At the hospital, a doctor administered the cholera vaccination, and for good measure gave him two drops of polio vaccine as well. Then he asked about Dirk's permit. No permit? No problem—I will ring the police to issue you with one, he was told.

In due course Dirk accompanied the police back to the station and told them his story. The response—Dirk was arrested and placed in the cells overnight. Chief Inspector Alphonse Krau charged Dirk with being a prohibited immigrant.

The next morning Dirk appeared in court before the local magistrate and was sentenced to three months' imprisonment with hard labour at the Boram Correctional Institution. As the institution was in Wewak, Dirk had finally reached his destination, but his adventure had turned into a nightmare. He contacted the Acting Public Solicitor, and nineteen days later an appeal was listed urgently before Justice Kearney.

The judge was scathing. Although the conviction was proper in law, the prosecution should never have been brought. While Dirk was a prohibited immigrant, he was not a surreptitious border-hopper, crossing by stealth in the night, or by forged documents, or by trickery, or by evading an officer. Nor had he attempted any of those things. He was simply an international traveller caught up in one of the many entanglements of modern travel. He had acted honestly throughout, if exhibiting some of the fecklessness of youth.

The judge singled out Air Niugini for special criticism. Had a check been carried out in Jayapura, Dirk would never have been allowed to board the aircraft and none of this trouble would have occurred. Dirk should have been treated with courtesy and consideration until the tangle had been unravelled.

Justice Kearney reduced the sentence to nineteen days, the time Dirk had already spent in prison, and so he was released from imprisonment. In due course, all was sorted out and Dirk left Papua New Guinea.

Dirk Schuiling completed a master's degree and is now a respected scientist.

Chief Inspector Alphonse Krau, who laid the charge, retired from the police after a life of community service and was awarded an MBE. In 2013, while trying to break up a fight, he was brutally murdered.

Sir John Kearney, a judge of the Supreme Court of Papua New Guinea from 1976 to 1982, was appointed a judge of the Northern Territory Supreme Court in 1982 and served with distinction until 1999. He was awarded a CBE in 1976 and made a Knight Bachelor in 1982.

At Kearney's farewell from the bench in 1999, he was described as 'patient, detached, courteous and fair'. But on one occasion in June 1977 his detachment gave way to palpable anger at the injustice occasioned to an innocent young traveller.

The Tale of the Student in a Bind

In November 1948, five-year-old Rita arrived in Fremantle with her parents, leaving wet and war-weary England behind them.

Little Rita grew up with ambitions to be a teacher. Her mum was a homemaker and her dad was a carter. Money was tight. Rita and her father did what was then common: in return for an education in teaching, Rita entered into a bond, with her dad as guarantor. In 1961, Rita enrolled at Graylands Teachers College, then a collection of ramshackle buildings, boiling in summer and freezing in winter.

Graylands was established in the 1950s as a temporary facility to deal with the demand for teachers in a baby-booming state. Rita was one of a large cohort of females—they outnumbered men by five to one. This imbalance was necessary, as we shall see.

In 1962 Rita continued her studies and was part of the production team for *Miss Hook of Holland*, a student musical. Then, in June, she found to her surprise that she was pregnant. Rita and her boyfriend wished to regularise the situation by marriage, and the sooner the better. And therein lay the problem—and the reason for the great disparity in student numbers. Training lots of women students was necessary because they had the pesky habit of getting married, at a time when married women were not nearly as welcome in the workforce as they are today.

Australian public services had a marriage bar. A woman employed in public service was required to resign when she married. Obviously, the males who led politics, the public service and the judiciary knew far better than women what a woman could not do. Those men clearly thought that a woman would be quite unable to multitask her spousal and family duties with a career.

Back to Rita. Typical woman—she wanted it all: marriage, completion of studies, a career in teaching. Mr Biggins, the acting principal at Graylands, soon put her right. Rita was told that she could continue and complete her course notwithstanding that she was pregnant, but that if she intended to marry she would have to resign.

Read that again. Yes, it is still as stupid as the first time.

Left with little choice, Rita signed the letter of resignation that Mr Biggins had drafted.

Now arose the question of the bond. Rita and her father would have to pay it back. It was more than £250. The conditions, especially about marriage, were very restrictive. In fact, the bond was so one-sided that it was surprising it was written on both sides of the paper. Rita and her dad resisted the claim. The Minister for Education sued.

There was then, and is now, a rule of public policy that covenants in restraint of trade or marriage are illegal. But, as with most things in the law, there is some wriggle room, as Justice Virtue deployed in his judgment. A restraint is not necessarily illegal if it is *reasonable*. Noting (and quoting Lord Davey) that public policy is always an unsafe and treacherous ground for legal decision, the judge concluded that the public policy rule could be tested on the basis of reasonableness. Then he hit his straps:

> It is clear from the regulations that the policy of the Department is opposed to the appointment of married women as permanent teachers and there is nothing against public policy in this. Probably the reverse because in the ordinary way it would no doubt more often than not be for the benefit of the community that a married woman should be free to devote herself to her ordinary domestic duties and to the bringing up of her family rather than that she should be offered any particular inducement to engage in full time employment.

Nor did the judge think it wrong to offer some slight discouragement to marriage until a woman was in her early twenties.

The argument that Rita was an infant when she entered into the contract fared no better. The contract was for her benefit and was binding. The upshot was that in 1965 Rita and her father lost this battle—by about four years.

Two years later, the Holt government ended the marriage ban for the Commonwealth Public Service. The states followed. Four years on, in 1969, the Education Department admitted five married women to study at the Claremont and Graylands teachers' colleges. In 1984 the *Equal Opportunity Act* made it illegal to discriminate against a person on the grounds of marital status or pregnancy.

And Rita? She married, lived happily and in due course qualified as and became a primary school teacher.

The Tale of the Parsimonious Pearler

There once was a young man named Holmes who decided to make his fortune collecting pearls and shell out of Onslow, Western Australia.

Pearling was a dangerous and difficult trade, though it could pay well. Our pearler engaged an experienced diver for the valuable pearl shell, Mr Ah Mat Siam. For a time the pearler and his diver worked amiably together, but one day they fell out.

Holmes sued Mr Siam in the Onslow Magistrates Court for taking pearl shells. It ended badly for the pearler. He lost. Dr Thorp, the resident magistrate, did not believe him and rejected his evidence, finding in favour of Mr Siam.

Now, this was a problem. Mr Holmes had other actions to pursue in court. The pearler came up with a crafty solution. In every other legal action, he subpoenaed a particular witness—the magistrate, Dr Thorp. But Dr Thorp proved equal to the task. He continued to sit in judgment on the actions brought by the pearler, undeterred by this transparent device.

Throughout their squabble, Mr Siam had not been paid by the parsimonious pearler. Mr Siam was no lawyer, nor did he hire one, instead utilising the provisions of a new piece of remedial legislation, the *Pearling Act 1912*.

On 9 October 1914, Mr Siam's claim for £24/18/6 for wages, eighteen shillings for sustenance and £10 in lieu of notice came on for hearing before two judicial officers, as required under the *Pearling Act*. Dr Thorp presided with a justice of the peace.

It is difficult to escape the conclusion that a degree of animosity may have crept into the relations between the bench and the pearler. Mr Holmes suffered from a speech defect. Accordingly, he asked for an agent to assist him in court, articulating his defence. The pearler's request was refused. However, Mr Siam had no similar difficulty in persuading the bench to allow the Onslow wharfinger, Mr Morgan, to prosecute the case on his behalf.

More was to come. The newfangled *Evidence Act* had come into force just eight years before and allowed the plaintiff to call the defendant to give evidence. And this is just what Mr Siam did. Mr Holmes indignantly refused. The bench was not amused and immediately committed the pearler to prison for twenty-four hours for contempt of court.

Tempers must have cooled somewhat, because after about ten minutes Dr Thorp went to the police station, where the pearler was confined, and withdrew the contempt charges. The pearler came back to court and the case continued.

Now the pearler admitted that he owed Mr Siam some £2/3/4, but that was all after he had deducted the cost of pearl shells misappropriated by Mr Siam. The trouble was that the magistrate had ruled against the pearler on this very point in the earlier proceedings.

Undeterred, the pearler now played his trump card—yet again. He called the magistrate to give evidence. This time, the magistrate did not disappoint. He descended from the bench, leaving the justice of the peace in charge, demanded and received one guinea—the sum required to be proffered to a witness under subpoena—and took the oath.

He was examined by the pearler. When that concluded, with the majesty that only a resident magistrate can exude, he ascended again to the seat of judgment. The parsimonious pearler lost. Badly.

Eventually the whole messy business landed in the Full Court on 18 August 1915. All day the court heard arguments from two leading counsel of the time. At the end, in the words of the *Daily News* for that day: 'In fact it was too much for their Honours to settle off hand, so they decided to take time to talk it over and give their judgment later.' A week later, the court spoke. It may have been all right for the magistrate to go into the witness box, but it was definitely not okay for him to return to the bench.

Among other things, the magistrate had made an order for witnesses to remain out of court. So he had disobeyed his own order. There was no one to rule on the admissibility of the evidence. If he refused to answer a question, could he compel himself to answer? And if he did not, could he commit himself for contempt? The pearler had a victory.

History does not record whether Mr Siam was ever eventually paid, but perhaps there is a clue to the answer. On the day the argument was held in the Full Court, 18 August 1915, Mr Holmes quietly enlisted in the Army and did not return to civilian life until 1919.

Both the pearler and the diver lived long lives. Mr Siam stayed in Onslow as a fisherman and died in 1955, at the age of eighty-four. Mr Horace Lister Holmes—for that was the pearler's full name—married in 1928, moved to Claremont in 1936 and died in 1974, at the age of eighty-three.

The pearling industry in Onslow collapsed soon after the events in this tale, moving north to the more plentiful waters near Broome.

The Tale of the Biased Beak

As we read in 'The Tale of the Bootleg Brewer', the Northern Territory was a pretty wild place in the early twentieth century. The region was full of surprises, and sometimes strange things happened. Maybe they still do.

Charles Barnett Story served with distinction with the AIF in France in World War I, rising to the rank of colonel. In October 1922 he was appointed Government Secretary Northern Territory Service. As Government Secretary, Story was responsible for every public officer in the Territory. Three years later, his services were dispensed with and he ran unsuccessfully for parliament as a member of the NT Representatives League. When he died in 1941, still in service as Commandant of the Bonegilla army base, he was accorded a funeral with full military honours.

Arthur Quelch claimed to have been educated at Sandhurst, and that his father was a King's Counsel. He served in the Boer War, including at the Siege of Ladysmith, in World War I and in the Punjab as an officer in the Dragoons. He travelled through Russia with the author H.G. Wells and explored Africa with the adventurer General Sir Harry Maclean. Oh, and he was a British spy as well. If any of this was true, it would have been quite a comedown in 1924 for Mr Quelch to find himself working as a wharfie and winchman in Darwin. In 1935 Quelch contracted Hansen's disease and saw out his days in the Channel Islands leprosarium, declining offers to move back to society. He is buried there.

The paths of these two men from completely different back-
grounds were destined to cross once, in an altercation that reached the
High Court. It happened this way.

Colonel Story lived in accommodation provided in a house called
'Aspendale', colloquially known as the 'Mud Hut' or, as Mr Mallam,
defending, described it, the 'Dud Hut'. In any event, one Sunday in
May at about 8 am, Colonel Story set off to walk to church. Opposite
the police inspector's house, Mr Quelch accosted Colonel Story, seizing
his left arm and shouting, 'Are you going to fight me?' Shortly afterwards, it was on.

Surprisingly for Mr Quelch, Colonel Story won hands down. Mr
Quelch was arrested looking somewhat worse for the experience.
Mr Quelch gave a different version in court on his trial for assault, but
the Special Magistrate, Mr Playford, did not accept his evidence and
he was convicted of assault.

On behalf of Mr Quelch, Mr Mallam quickly appealed to the
Supreme Court, whose only judge was Mallam's old sparring partner,
now Justice Roberts. There were several grounds of appeal that were
unsuccessful, but one ground proved a winner.

Mr Playford was not only a special magistrate but also Director
of Lands and Mines. In that latter capacity, his superior officer, to
whom he was accountable, was ... Colonel Story. Justice Roberts was
satisfied that Mr Playford was not, in fact, biased. However, continued
the judge, there was a real likelihood that the magistrate would have
a leaning towards Colonel Story because of the connection, and, perhaps unconsciously, tend to believe him in a case where everything
might turn on credibility. Because of the real likelihood of bias, the
judge determined that the conviction was without jurisdiction and
substituted a verdict of acquittal.

So Mr Quelch was acquitted on what some lay persons might
regard as a technicality. Certainly Colonel Story thought so, because
he engaged an eminent King's Counsel, Sir Edward Mitchell, to apply
for leave to appeal before the High Court.

It did not go well. After Sir Edward had been arguing for some time,
the acting Chief Justice, Justice Isaacs, said: 'We have a very strong

opinion about it, Sir Edward. We do not of course wish to curtail your argument in any way.'

Sir Edward ran up the white flag. 'Quite right and kind that you should give me an indication. I have no chance.'

The argument was probably over much earlier, when Justice Stark remarked that in his opinion Justice Roberts was right in every particular in his law.

It was many years before the High Court introduced time limits and lights. Maybe they didn't ever need them.

The Tale of the Naughty Neighers

It might come as a surprise to younger readers that in some capital cities in Australia, well into the 1950s, milk was delivered house to house by 'milkos' who used horses for transport. The same was true in Melbourne, where our tale is set.

Mr Hubbard senior started a dairy in 1902 in Hampton, a southern suburb. By 1955, he had long retired and handed over to his son Patrick, who had big plans.

In September 1950 a group of milk retailers, carriers and dairy farmers had formed a public company, Southern Dairies Ltd, to supply pasteurised milk in metal-capped bottles, the first milk-selling organisation to combine in this way. Patrick was the general manager and the Hubbards were substantial shareholders.

Horses had been used and stabled at the dairy since the 1920s, although not continuously. From 1952, though, horses began to be kept overnight at the dairy—not in nice clean stables but in tumble-down accommodation. And so the flies multiplied. And the smell. And the noise.

Finally, Mr Munro, who lived next door, had had enough. He approached the Sandringham Municipal Council, the Department of Agriculture, even the RSPCA, all to no avail. Finally, he did what the judge said he should have done in the first place and sued for nuisance in the Supreme Court. The trial, before Justice Sholl, took eight days.

At the heart of Mr Munro's complaint was the fact that the noise kept him awake at night. Now, to many, the occasional broken night's sleep is a price to be paid for living in a modern vibrant city. But not to the law. Justice Sholl quoted the Master of the Rolls, Sir Wilfred Greene, from a case in 1937:

> I certainly protest against the idea that if persons, for their own profit and convenience, choose to destroy even one night's rest of their neighbours, they are doing something which is excusable. To say that the loss of one or two night's rest is one of those trivial matters in respect of which the law will take no notice appears to me to be quite a misconception.

Perhaps Sir Wilfred occasionally suffered from insomnia.

At this point in the judgment, the defendant's lawyers probably realised they had backed a loser. Mr Munro obtained an injunction and damages. He no doubt slept well in his bed that night, and for many nights thereafter.

By 1955, the days of horse-drawn milk floats were numbered. In the course of his judgment, Justice Sholl gave milkos some free advice. After pointing out that the delivery of milk by electric or motor vehicles could be on the way, he continued: 'The general improvement in living and social standards in this country which is very estimable in itself is likely to cause a necessary acceleration in that progress which milk distributors would be wise to recognise.'

Southern Dairies Ltd fell into liquidation fifteen years later.

The Tale of the Trickster Tippler

What do a bottle of Napoleon brandy and a huge storm have in common? Read on and you shall see.

At the end of a hard day's work outside in the heat, most Australians like to kick back with a beer or two, or maybe a soothing Scotch. Well, Golgie Kelly had been working hard and thought he was entitled to a drink. That sense of entitlement earned him nine months in the slammer.

You see, the day Golgie was working was not just any day, it was a couple of days after Christmas Day. And not just any old Christmas Day, but Christmas Day in 1974, in Darwin. That was when Cyclone Tracy struck in all its fury, killing seventy-one people and causing $837 million worth of damage. More than 70 per cent of Darwin's buildings were destroyed.

The federal government swung into crisis mode and sent Major General Alan Stretton to take charge. The Governor-General, Sir John Kerr, declared a state of emergency and invested General Stretton with full powers. Federal public servants, including police officers, flew into Darwin to help with the relief effort. Even the local gaols were emptied as prisoners joined in the clean-up in difficult conditions and sweltering heat.

And so we return to Golgie, who was one such prisoner.

At day's end, feeling in need of a tipple, Golgie approached Mr Lionel Fernandez at the Casuarina High School, which was being used as an evacuation centre. Golgie told Mr Fernandez that he was Sergeant

Detective Walker of the Commonwealth Police and that he was here to requisition all liquor and spirits at the school. Mr Fernandez, who was perhaps somewhat credulous, believed Golgie, who departed with a bottle of whisky and a bottle of Napoleon brandy, value $12.

Golgie Kelly was soon apprehended and charged with impersonating a police officer and obtaining property by false pretences.

He appeared before the chief magistrate on 30 December 1974. Darwin was still in chaos, though order was slowly being restored and repairs made. But the majesty of justice continued unaffected. The chief magistrate took a serious view of the offence, perhaps worried about looting and lawlessness, and sentenced Kelly to nine months' imprisonment. And that might well have been that—but not exactly.

Major General Stretton was told of the facts and the sentence. He immediately strode into the courthouse, sent his compliments to the chief magistrate and declared the court closed. The magistrate, who was hearing another case at the time, looked surprised and adjourned that case to speak with General Stretton. Subsequently, both men met with Chief Justice Forster, following which General Stretton apologised for his actions—proving once again that the pen really is mightier than the sword. The general had bluffed that his powers extended to the judiciary (the martial sword). The magistrate called his bluff (the peaceful pen).

Back we go to Golgie Kelly, who instituted an appeal with Ian Barker as his counsel. Persuasive though he was, the appeal judge would have none of it.

At a time when police from other parts of Australia were being flown into Darwin, at a time when some were in clothes that did not really identify them as police officers, it was surely important to discourage persons from seeking personal gain or advantage by passing themselves off as persons vested with police power and authority.

Nor did Mr Barker's argument—that Kelly's action had been a childlike ruse and that the whole transaction had a faintly absurd tint—find any traction. Despite the drama Mr Kelly's sentence had created, with accounts published throughout the world, he remained in prison to finish his term.

And the world moved on. The Chief Magistrate, Mr David McCann, left the Northern Territory shortly thereafter and settled in Western Australia, becoming a magistrate and, in due course, coroner. On his retirement in 1996, the Attorney-General, Peter Foss, paid tribute to McCann's dedication to Western Australia's coronial service and to the teaching role he played in the development of the Australian Coroners' Society.

Mr McCann contributed, perhaps unintentionally, to the development of the concept of procedural fairness as the respondent in *Annetts v McCann* (1990) 170 CLR 596.

The Appeal Judge, James Muirhead AC KStJ QC, encountered Mr Barker again when Mr Barker QC prosecuted the case of *The Queen v Alice Lynne Chamberlain*, the details of which are as well known as Cyclone Tracy. Muirhead relocated to Perth and became a Royal Commissioner into Aboriginal Deaths in Custody, later returning to the Northern Territory for a time as Administrator.

Nothing can be found as to what became of Golgie Kelly, notwithstanding his moment of world fame.

The Tale of the Famous Button Seller

There once lived a man who seemed to make a living selling buttons at shows because there was good dough in it. But the forces of law and order suspected all was not as it appeared.

The button seller was well-dressed and respectful and seemed to have money sufficient for his needs. However, it was his companions who caught the eyes of the authorities. They were fellow showmen whom he met in public places by day.

Now, it may seem hard to believe, but less than seventy years ago certain behaviour could lead to a person being deemed an idle and disorderly person, a rogue and vagabond or, worst of all, an incorrigible rogue. Moreover, the law had provisions for preventative justice. A person threatening to commit a breach of the peace was required to give sureties, as was a person found to be of evil fame.

The authorities argued that the button seller was a person of evil fame because of his association with convicted and suspected persons.

So it was that, one fine day, the button seller appeared before Alan Bateman, resident magistrate. The magistrate found the charge proved and ordered the button seller to provide sureties. Thus, the button seller who, until that day, was merely a seller of wares at sideshows, became famous in an evil sort of way. Resisting the urge to simply 'button it up', he decided to appeal to the Full Court.

The leading judgment was given by Mr Justice Virtue. What a marvellous name for a judge in a case such as this. Until I became a law student, I thought that Justice was his given name and he was a man who combined not one, but two excellent moral qualities.

The judge noted that police had the button seller under observation for six months and on no occasion had he done anything wrong. All the police had noted was that the button seller frequented hotel bars and billiard saloons at country and district shows and, in the daytime, was sometimes seen in the company of convicted or suspicious persons.

The learned judge had trouble with the meaning of 'evil fame'. It was not found in standard or legal dictionaries as a phrase of specialised meaning, and nor were they words in common use. The judge went back in time to the reign of Edward III for assistance. Skipping a few centuries, Justice Virtue then enlisted that trusty helpmate William Blackstone:

> [I]t is held that a man may be bound to his good behaviour for causes of scandal, contra bonos mores, as well as contra pacem ... Thus also a justice may bind over all night-walkers; eavesdroppers; such as keep suspicious company, or are reported to be pilferers or robbers; such as sleep in the day and wake in the night; common drunkards; whore-masters; cheats; idle vagabonds; and other persons whose misbehaviour may reasonably bring them within the general words of the statute, as persons not of good fame; an expression, it must be owned, of so great a latitude, as leaves much to be determined by the discretion of the magistrate himself.

If those who sleep in the day and wake in the night were targeted for strong police action, scarcely a university student would be safe.

The Full Court held that the evidence fell far short of establishing that the button seller was famous, let alone infamous. If this evidence was the best they could do, the Full Court effectively told the police to 'zip it'.

The button seller continued his itinerant life, hawking his wares throughout the south-west of Australia and, presumably, playing billiards and talking with whomever he pleased.

The Tale of the Superior Shamrock Whiskey

This is a story of Irish whiskey. You can tell that because of the 'e'.

In the nineteenth century, the Irish added the 'e' to differentiate themselves from what they viewed as the inferior Scottish whisky. (The Scots, of course, have a different version.) Anyway, this is about Irish whiskey with an e, and—lest there be any doubt—Shamrock Whiskey.

The families of Kirker and Greer were both whiskey blenders and merchants who merged their businesses in the middle of the nineteenth century. One of their products was Shamrock Whiskey, advertisements for which appeared in *The Bulletin*, a Sydney paper, as early as 1883.

In 1886, Kirker, Greer & Co. became one of the founders of the Irish Distillery Ltd at Connswater, in Belfast. It became one of the largest distilleries in the world: at its peak, it distilled over two million gallons of whiskey a year. One of its products was, of course, Shamrock Whiskey.

Now, Kirker, Greer & Co. exported two kinds of Shamrock Whiskey to Australia. Seven-eighths of their product was bottled by them in Belfast and sold in Sydney for five shillings a bottle. But one-eighth was cask whiskey, judged slightly inferior. This was bottled by others in Sydney and sold for four shillings and sixpence.

One bottler of the cask whiskey was Benjamin Neville Mayman, known as Neville. He arrived in Sydney as a young man of twenty-five to manage a weighing machine company but soon became a publican.

He married in 1896 and was a keen amateur thespian. In 1898, he purchased the Brighton Hotel in Oxford Street and spent £3000 on improvements, converting it into what was described as one of the handsomest and most striking hostelries in the city. Although he was chair of the Benevolent Society, his benevolence didn't prevent him from accusing the Salvation Army of creating a nuisance in Oxford and Riley streets with their band.

By 1900, Neville was a wealthy man. Part of his wealth came from selling whiskey—to be precise, Shamrock Whiskey he had bottled in Australia. Now, his bottles and labels looked identical to the Kirker, Greer & Co. product. He even added representations of medals the bottled Shamrock Whiskey had won, though his cask whiskey had not.

In 1901, Kirker, Greer & Co took legal action before the Chief Judge in Equity for an injunction, alleging that Neville was passing the cask whiskey off as their own Shamrock Whiskey, which they asserted was slightly superior. An odd stance to take, perhaps, as Kirker, Greer & Co. had allowed others to use identical bottles and labels—albeit without the medals.

But was the bottled Shamrock Whiskey in fact superior to the cask Shamrock Whiskey? Well, the trial went for five days on this very point, and the judge must have felt like a snifter himself after some of the 'expert' evidence.

A Mr Adams considered the bottled whiskey superior, but he was an interested party. Mr Adams claimed to be an expert until three years before, when he injured his mouth, and his tasting capacity could not be then tested at trial.

Mr Forbes considered the bottled whiskey superior, but did not profess to be an expert whiskey taster. Moreover, he was also what lawyers call an 'interested party' in that he was an employee of one of the litigants.

Mr Kerr was an expert and thought the bottled whiskey was superior, but he had a heavy cold during the trial and his tasting capacity could not be tested.

Mr Collum was a Kirker, Greer & Co. expert witness and considered the bottled whiskey superior, but when he retired into the associate's room and the two whiskies were supplied to him in glasses without his knowing which was which, he pronounced the cask whiskey bottled by Neville to be a nice, palatable whiskey, and the plaintiff's bottled whiskey to be coarse and rank. (The solicitors must have paid his fees as an expert witness with gritted teeth.)

Neville himself gave evidence that there was no difference between the two, but he was also an interested party.

Mr Bourke, the manager of Robert's bottle department, said he could not tell the difference between the two, but he was not an expert.

Justice Simpson decided that, overall, the bottled whiskey was slightly superior. If Neville had not included the medals, it would have been a different story, but that tipped the balance in favour of an injunction preventing him from selling his cask whiskey as Shamrock Whiskey.

Two years later, Neville sold the Brighton Hotel to buy the Liverpool Arms. He prospered and later sold the Liverpool Arms for a considerable profit. With his wife, Florence, and their daughter, Neville travelled to Europe, where they all pursued acting careers.

Sometime after Florence's death in 1925, Neville returned to Australia and ran a private hotel for many years, passing away in 1941 at the age of seventy-four. Fate was not as kind to Kirker, Greer and Co. On 4 April 1918, Kirker, Greer & Co. (Australasia) Ltd was ordered to be wound up.

In the early 1920s, the Irish Distillery Ltd was sold but it could not survive the *Volstead Act* in the United States, as Prohibition took away the ability of the large Irish diaspora there to access Irish whiskey. In 1929 the distillery was closed. The Connswater site is now a retail park.

If this little tale has given you a thirst, do not despair. In 2007 the name Kirker Greer was reborn as an independent brand owner and distributor. Among their products is Shamrock Whiskey.

The Tale of the Lost Invitation

It started with an invitation which a maid forgot to give to the lady of the house.

Dr William Russ Pugh was a doctor in Launceston in 1842. He had a large practice and his expertise in other areas was recognised by the 2000 or so residents of the northern city of Van Diemen's Land. But Dr Pugh was distracted by a looming crisis, which may have caused him to lose perspective.

Mr Lewis William Gilles, a former naval officer, was the manager of a bank called Archer, Gilles & Co., later to merge and become the ANZ Bank. He was in severe financial distress, having lost £400 in a banking transaction. Perhaps his circumstances caused him to overreact.

Both Pugh and Gilles were members of the Launceston Club, a club established for gentlemen. In early June 1842, Mr and Mrs Gilles held an evening party and ball. Invitations were sent out through the post, including one for Dr and Mrs Pugh. When the invitation arrived, the maid paid two pence for its receipt but forgot to give it to Mrs Pugh. Being unaware of the invitation, Dr and Mrs Pugh did not respond or attend the ball.

Their absence annoyed Mrs Gilles, who told people so, one of whom told Dr Pugh. He wrote to Mr Gilles saying Mrs Pugh was in ignorance of the invitation, and that it was not delivered to any member of the household. This latter statement was, of course, wrong.

There the matter should have rested, but human nature being what it is when people feel slighted, it did not. Mr Gilles tracked down the letter and discovered that it had been delivered by the post office and paid for. Mr Gilles considered that Dr Pugh's actions were unbecoming, and he complained to the Launceston Club's committee that Dr Pugh had behaved in an ungentlemanly manner.

When Dr Pugh heard of the complaint, and checked that it was true, to say that he was furious would be an understatement. In dead of night, with a companion, he called on Mr Gilles and demanded satisfaction—a duel.

Mr Gilles sensibly demurred on the grounds that they should wait for the committee's decision. In the meantime, he consulted two soldiers, who both told him there were no grounds for a duel. Captain Stewart further advised that Dr Pugh was not entitled to challenge, as he was guilty of tergiversation (equivocation, prevarication—but you already knew this word, of course).

Later that day, the committee decided Mr Gilles' complaint was unfounded. However, the committee had overstepped its mandate and had no right to do so. Under the rules, the question had to be put to a meeting of members. Had it been, the result might have been different. When Dr Pugh had earlier tried to have Mr Gilles removed from the club, he had been resoundingly defeated.

But for the time being Dr Pugh was exonerated. He was not one to be gracious in victory. He posted a notice in bold letters on the club's door, where everyone could see it:

> Mr Lewis William Gilles having instituted charges against me derogatory to my character which he failed to substantiate and having refused to afford me satisfaction, I hereby proclaim him a COWARD and a LIAR.
> WR Pugh
> July 8, 1842.

Two things happened in consequence. The members of the Launceston Club were so riven in their loyalties that many resigned, and the club dissolved. It would be forty years before a new club was founded.

The second thing was that Mr Gilles sued for libel. The trial was held in the new courthouse on 6 October 1842 before Chief Justice Pedder and a jury of twelve. The libel was admitted, so the only question was the quantum of damages. Mr Gilles sought £2000, which might have alleviated his financial circumstances as it was an eye-watering sum.

The jury were having none of it. After deliberating only a few minutes, they returned to court and announced a verdict in favour of the plaintiff for damages in the sum of one farthing, the smallest coin in the realm. They added that each party should bear their own costs. No doubt the jury felt there was fault on both sides and the whole thing was a waste of everyone's time.

Mr Gilles left Launceston in 1844 for Adelaide, where he helped his brother manage the Glen Osmond lead and silver mine for a time, then he joined the public service in Victoria and serving for fourteen years as a magistrate in Warrnambool. He retired back to Glen Osmond and died in 1884 at the age of eighty-eight.

Dr Pugh was a popular doctor in Launceston and a man of many accomplishments. He was yet to face a further action against him, where he ... but that is a tale for the next quirky case.

The Tale of the Jealous Doctor

As observed, Dr Pugh was a popular and well-respected doctor in Launceston. In early November 1841, Mr Thomas Williams, a merchant, was taken ill. The family physician, Dr De Dassell, was summoned and called in other doctors for consultation, including Dr Pugh. Mr Williams had a strangulated hernia. An operation had to be performed immediately or Mr Williams would surely die. Even with a successful operation, death was probable. All the doctors agreed that Dr Pugh was the best person with the skills. The patient consented.

Dr Pugh advised Mr Williams' friends to get him to make a will. The operation was difficult. It took place at 4 am. At the conclusion, the patient was relieved and slept well. Alas, relief was temporary. A couple of days later, the symptoms returned. Dr Pugh and the other doctors told Mr Williams there was no hope. He died the next day.

It must have been a grim time. There was no anaesthetic. Indeed, not until 1847 was the first operation in Australia conducted under anaesthetic. As it happened, the surgeon who performed that operation was Dr Pugh, who thus maintains a place in the pantheon of anaesthesiology.

Naturally, there was a post-mortem. All the doctors who had been at the operation were present. All except one were satisfied that the operation performed by Dr Pugh was not the cause of death. The dissentient was Dr De Dassell. However, he was a silent dissentient at the time. He did not make his feelings about the operation known to anyone, either during or immediately after the operation. Nor did he voice them at the post-mortem.

Mr Williams was consigned to his grave, and there the matter rested for months.

In June 1842 there came to Launceston town Burton George Haygath MD, a young man looking to establish himself as a doctor. He and Dr De Dassell soon met, and the latter told him that the operation had been badly performed by Dr Pugh, who had caused the patient's death. Dr Haygath was most interested, although at the time of the operation he had been 25,000 kilometres away.

With only the word of Dr De Dassell to go on, on 22 August 1842 Dr Haygath swore out a private information charging Dr Pugh with manslaughter. Why? As counsel for Dr Pugh subsequently put it: 'This either shows an extreme instance of philanthropy, in leaving his own country to come here to do good, or you must impute it to a very different feeling towards a man he could never have known.'

A magistrate, Mr Breton, conducted a hearing. Dr Pugh attended with counsel. Dr Haygath conducted the case himself. The hearing lasted twelve hours until midnight. In Mr Breton's opinion, Dr Haygath's manner was very improper, both in addressing the bench and in examining witnesses. His manner appeared very malignant both against Dr Pugh and the other doctors. The magistrate dismissed the case.

Now, we know from 'The Tale of the Lost Invitation' that Dr Pugh was not one to let bygones be bygones, or to be magnanimous in victory. Not at all. He sued Dr Haygath for malicious prosecution before Chief Justice Pedder and a jury.

Poor Dr Haygath. His star witness was to be Dr De Dassell. But each time his name was called, there was no response. He never appeared. On the other hand, other doctors did give evidence. Dr Gaunt said an operation on Mr Williams had been agreed after the usual remedies had proven unsuccessful—warm bath, bleeding, tobacco injection and so on. The operation was competently performed.

The Chief Justice summed up for the jury both the law and the facts, concluding by saying that he thought there was not a tittle of ground on which the defendant had to rest his case. The jury were out for fifteen minutes before returning a verdict in favour of Dr Pugh and awarding him damages of £250.

The *Medical Gazette* was forthright about Dr Haygath:

> If the motives of that individual were in reality good, the conscious-ness of his error, and the weight of his disgrace, must, we apprehend, fill him with regret; if his intentions were otherwise, the just severity of the law and the fiat of society must ere this have rendered his punishment sufficiently weighty.

Dr Haygath went to gaol and seems to have disappeared from history.

Dr Pugh continued his medical practice and was also active in other areas. He assisted Count Paul Strzelecki in the chemical analysis of coal and minerals. He helped coroners in matters of poisoning. He was a founding member of what became the Tasmanian Society. It was his interest in chemistry that led to his use of ether as an anaesthetic in 1847. He died in 1895 at the age of eighty-nine.

The Tale of the Naughty Comic Books

As all good stories begin, once upon a time, more than sixty years ago, Australian girls were at risk of becoming lured into immorality and misfortune. Not by evil and manipulative men, but by comics with such salacious and enticing titles as *Real Love* and *Darling Romance*.

To deal with 'this great menace in our midst', Queensland established the Objectionable Literature Board. Whether the literature or the board was objectionable is open to interpretation. Almost immediately it struck, banning a host of comic books, targeting, it must be said, a group we would today call 'teenagers'.

Clearly these books were dangerous. The matron of a Salvation Army Industrial Home for Girls had known girls to read the books from cover to cover, over and over again. She claimed girls accustomed to reading these books were found to be excited and unbalanced in the presence of males, but their behaviour improved when deprived of the books in question. If that were not enough, a psychiatrist testified that the books constituted a danger to emotional, rather than intellectual, interests.

The board banned the books. The publishers appealed to the Supreme Court. Alas, no succour there, although Sir Mostyn Hanger was on their side. The majority prevailed.

However, the determined publishers did not let the matter rest. After all, the comic books were popular (and profitable). So it was that after three elderly gentlemen in Queensland had considered the content of *Love Experiences* and *Popular Romances*, to name two more, novels written expressly for teenage girls, five elderly gentlemen of the High Court would decide on the literary merits of the publications.

The result was a cliffhanger, so to speak: 3–2.

First, the three disposed of any idea that the works might be regarded as literature in the same league as *Pride and Prejudice* or *Wuthering Heights*. 'What they contain is an affront to the intelligence of the reader … The stories are extremely silly, the letter press is stupid, the drawings are artless and crude and situations are absurd.' Tell us what you really think, your Honours! But the three reminded themselves that they were not concerned with the damage done to the intellect or, for that matter, the eyesight of the readers.

To modern readers accustomed to judges who voraciously devour every document before an appeal commences, it may come as a surprise that the court did not actually read the books until after hearing the argument as to why they were obscene.

Then the three were surprised. When they turned to the publications, their actual character proved quite unexpected: 'The theme of nearly all is love, courtship and marriage, virtue never falters and right triumphs. Matrimony is the proper end and if you are not told that happiness ensues, it is the constant assumption.' This latter observation of course denotes that the books were obviously works of fiction.

The three found that the pages contained nothing prurient, lewd or licentious: 'There are adventures, short lived because of the size of the book, bad men, sometimes wealthy, but the heroine always escapes by the aid of the strong embracing arms of a good young man on whom fortune is yet to smile.'

So what was the fuss all about? It appears that the books were illustrated. The eyes of the heroine were drawn with lids either drooping or unduly raised, and her lips, though drawn in black and white, were obviously rosy as only lipstick could make them. 'There is too an evident though crude attempt to infuse the subject with glamour, in the modern technical sense of the term.' Technical glamour. Of course.

Obviously, though, at least one of the three judges was a fan of Robbie Burns, who used the word 'glamour' in a less modern way.

Or maybe they were just pedantic. It appears that all the heroine did physically in any of the comic books was embrace and kiss. That might have been enough for the majority of the Court of Appeal to find obscenity, but not for the three.

What of the minority? Sir Edward McTiernan was sixty-four. He had married less than ten years before and had no children. He described the books as 'consecutive drawings in panels of young persons in postures of enthusiastic affection, often kissing and fondling and indulging in absurd slang and erotic patter: The motif is an accent on sex.' You can see where this is going.

'All of the books are calculated to excite the amorous passions of adolescents and immature persons and to infect those who are sweethearts with brutish standards of behaviour unworthy of the custom of courtship and the institution of marriage.' Justice Webb was no less forthright. He was satisfied that reading the books would engender a desire to seek similar experience and stimulate immoral sexual behaviour.

And so virtue either triumphed or was defeated, according to your personal point of view and the girls of Australia were free to read comic book romances to their hearts' content.

All the judges, sad to say, have passed on, so leaving an unanswerable question: what would each one make of Mills & Boon (which publishes 100 books a month), Tinder, *The Bachelor*, *Married at First Sight* ...?

The Tale of the Persistent Customs Officer

One of the first pieces of legislation passed by the new Commonwealth parliament in 1901 was the *Immigration Act*, which would remain in force for nearly sixty years. Its aim was to limit non-white immigration, particularly Asian immigration, and preserve the predominance of the British within Australia.

A would-be immigrant was given a dictation test: they would be required to write out fifty words in any European (or, later, a prescribed) language dictated by an immigration officer. The test was usually given in English but could also be in another language.

Some of the dictation tests were difficult to emote, even if the test was in English:

> If the land is ploughed when wet the furrows may, and in all probability will, wear a more finished appearance, and will be more pleasant to the eye, but land so ploughed will be more inclined to become set or baked, and when in this state will not produce a maximum yield.

An alternative:

> It is only in the south that any training in his profession is undertaken by the fetish man: in all other parts of the region the office devolves on its holder in quite an accidental manner: the distinction is thrust upon some native whose fortune has in some way distinguished him from his fellows.

If a would-be immigrant managed to write what was dictated as one of these alternatives, there were other options for the customs officer. The immigrant could be given a test in any European language—perhaps the Italian weather report.

Although the High Court was generally sympathetic to the principles behind the *Immigration Act*, there were some limits on the breadth of languages that could be employed.

Mr Egon Erwin Kisch was a Hungarian agitator—by which it was meant he was anti-fascist. In the 1930s, when appeasement was all the rage, he was regarded as a troublemaker. Mr Kisch was fluent in English and several European languages, but the customs officer thought he was more than equal to the task of denying entry and gave Mr Kisch a dictation test in Gaelic (of which the customs officer himself had only a rudimentary knowledge). This was too much even for the High Court, which ruled that Gaelic was not a European language under the *Immigration Act*.

All that happened in 1934, and the story of Mr Kisch is well known.[9] Let's begin our tale.

Mr Ah On, an Asian man subject to the *Immigration Act*, seems to have been a shadowy figure. He claimed to be forty-two or forty-three years old but was more likely twenty-five to twenty-seven years old. He said he was a gardener in Australia for twenty-eight years but his hands, which he declined to submit to medical examination, presented no appearance of any hard work.

For many years he avoided the authorities, but on 15 October 1925 he was found in Osborne Park, a suburb of Perth. He failed the dictation test. The question then arose as to whether he had entered the Commonwealth more than three years before failing to pass the dictation test. If he had, he was home safe. Mr Ah On called evidence before the magistrate to show that he had been in Australia for more than three years, but to no avail. The magistrate convicted Mr Ah On.

All was not over. Mr Ah On appealed to the Supreme Court and on 14 December 1925 he succeeded, although Justice Northmore

---

9 For example, see *Our Man K* by Nicholas P. Hasluck (Penguin, 1999).

dissented. The appeal was allowed on the basis that the magistrate erred in failing to take account of the evidence of Mr Ah On's witnesses. And so Mr Ah On walked free.

But not for long. Within a few months, the customs officer, an indefatigable Mr Williamson, located Mr Ah On again in Perth and gave him another dictation test. Again, Mr Ah On failed. The magistrate dismissed the charge, and Mr Williamson no doubt thought that another appeal to the Full Court would likely end in another loss. So it was that Mr Ah On's case reached the High Court directly on 22 November 1926.

There the customs officer had a win. The court, by majority, allowed the appeal and entered a conviction. An issue was the constitutional question whether the *Immigration Act* was ultra vires, or beyond the constitutional power of the federal parliament. Although Knox CJ and Duffy J thought it was, the other judges disagreed. Justice Isaacs stated the case plainly: on the court's decision 'depends the power of the National Government to give any effective force to what is known as the white-Australia policy or to any policy of controlling undesirable immigration'.

Justice Isaacs did not think much of Mr Ah On, who, in his eyes, was a Chinese immigrant who 'in all moral probability—he alone being able to confirm or dispel it, surreptitiously foisted himself on this community, successfully eluding observation for some years and eventually has unquestionably perjured himself wholesale in the witness box to escape the consequences'.

The court held that various averment provisions within the *Immigration Act* were valid and so Mr Ah On was convicted. The consequence was deportation.

Did he go quietly? Not a bit of it.

On 30 June 1928, the *Mirror* newspaper reported:

> It was learned in Perth this morning that Ah On, the elusive China man [sic] had been arrested in Melbourne under the name of Lu Chin. Ah On was the principal figure in the celebrated deportation case that went from Perth through successive courts to the High Court

of Australia, the China man being finally convicted. That was many months ago and Ah On has, until now, eluded his pursuers. He will be deported from the country.

And so ended the story of Mr Ah On in Australia—but it is not quite the end of this tale. On 4 March 1927, the Assistant Secretary of the Home and Territories Department, S.J. Quinlan, wrote to the Collector of Customs in Fremantle under the heading 'Directions to be observed in connection with the application of the dictation test'. He noted:

> See method of application—various court cases have been lost through evidence being furnished that the test had not been correctly applied. The main point to remember is that, although a language may be chosen with which the immigrant is not acquainted, the test should be applied in such a way that he would be afforded a reasonable opportunity to write the passage out if he were literate and knew the language.

So continued the circular:

> Pencil and paper should be handed to the person to be tested and it should be clearly explained to him what he is required to do and, if necessary, an interpreter should be employed to explain the requirement. [The irony of this sentence seems to have been lost on the Assistant Secretary.] The whole passage should be read over once to indicate what the passage is, and then repeated more slowly as the actual test, a few words at a time right to the end of the passage, whether the pertinent person attempts to write or not.

If there was any doubt that the dictation test was to preserve the White Australia policy, the last instruction would settle it:

> If the officer has good reason to believe that the person tested could write in English, a passage of not less than 50 words in some other European language may be selected. If an officer is not available

to read the passage correctly in the language chosen, a person acquainted with the language may be authorised in writing by an officer to dictate the passage.

The *Immigration Act* was repealed in 1958. The *Racial Discrimination Act* came into force in 1975.

Of course, Mr Ah On and his brushes with the law were long ago, and we live in much more enlightened times. No one now would suggest that applicants for a visa should take an English language test—would they?

The Tale of the Shattered Skiff

Agnes Irving was the apple of her father's eye. Clark Irving was a successful merchant and grazier in the rich Armidale region of New South Wales in the mid-nineteenth century. Among his many achievements, he was a founder of the Clarence and Richmond River Steam Navigation Company and a member of the New South Wales parliament.

Now, one thing essential to a steam navigation company is a steamship. In 1862 Mr Irving travelled to England to oversee and take delivery of a paddle steamer—one 203 feet long and displacing 440 tons. He was away so long that his seat in parliament was vacated (he was re-elected), but on 28 November 1862, the *Agnes Irving*, as he had named it, arrived in Brisbane and was almost immediately set to work trading along the coast and up the inland rivers.

A ship needs a captain, and the *Agnes Irving* had many, but the one who features in this tale is Captain Frederick Bracegirdle. Born in Surrey in 1831, on his death in 1916 he was described as one of the oldest and most distinguished ship masters of Sydney. (As a small digression: his son Leighton Bracegirdle had a distinguished naval career, retiring as a rear admiral after serving for many years as official secretary to the Governor-General.)

Frederick doesn't seem to have been the type of man you could call Fred. After many years sailing the seven seas, in 1869—perhaps seeking a more domestic life—he joined the Clarence and Richmond River Steam Navigation Company. When he retired fifteen years later,

Captain Bracegirdle had completed 658 voyages to the northern rivers. It was on one of these voyages that the skiff shattered.

It happened this way. Bill Arkins had charge of Mr Streather's light skiff and tied it to Ross's wharf, next to the main wharf at Grafton, while he went for his dinner. On his return, seeing the *Agnes Irving* approaching, he moved the skiff and moored it between a punt, or lighter, and the shore.

The *Agnes Irving*, under the command of Captain Bracegirdle, was affected by the ebbing tide, and instead of coming neatly alongside it slewed and steamed straight into the punt, crushing it against the skiff, which 'broke into atoms'.

At the subsequent trial in the District Court at Grafton, Mr McKenzie, an eyewitness, told the jury that in his opinion if the skiff had not been there, nothing would have happened! Captain Bracegirdle, who was in command, said that as far as he was concerned, the punt was at fault. He often had to move the punt, and no one who knew anything about boats would leave it there. (A man of firm opinions, one surmises.) He continued: even if he had not stopped at the wharf and had gone straight past, the wash from the *Agnes Irving* would have driven the punt against the skiff anyway.

The jury decided the steam company was liable for the damage to the skiff. The company appealed to the Full Court. Captain Bracegirdle's evidence did not find favour. In the court's decision, it was quite lawful for the plaintiff to put his boat there, and the defendant had no right to expect it to go out of the way of their steamer. The court held that there was sufficient evidence of negligence to put before a jury.

And so, presumably, Mr Streather got a new skiff. The *Agnes Irving* continued in service for another two years, until just after Christmas it was wrecked at the mouth of the McKay River. Captain Bracegirdle was not aboard. No lives were lost. Divers can still explore what remains of the paddle steamer.

After leaving the Clarence and Richmond Rivers Company, Captain Bracegirdle served as assistant harbour master in Sydney for twenty years.

The Tale of the Short-Changed Surveyor

One morning long ago, someone woke up with a bright idea. The British Army in India needed horses, but there were difficulties in breeding them there. Australia had plenty of land. Why not breed horses in Australia and ship them to India? And so the Western Australia Land Company was formed in Britain. Subscribers included Sir James Stirling, a former Governor of Western Australia, and Elizabeth Fry, prison reformer.

Where would the venture be established? The new convict-free settlement based on the Swan River. What to call it? Seems obvious, really. The combination of the names of the two countries: Australind.

The venture proceeded apace. Subscriptions were sought for prospective settlers. Plans were displayed, showing a thriving township with churches, gardens, shops. These were premature to say the least, because there was nothing even surveyed yet, let alone built. In January 1841, the Reverend John Smithies described the venture as 'one of the greatest puffs that there has been for some time'. He urged his fellow Methodists not to join.

To build a town, first you need a surveyor. And here we truly begin.

James Gardner Austin, an architect and engineer, was engaged by Australind as a surveyor at £400 per annum. With his wife and two sons, Robert and James, accompanied by other members of the surveying party, he arrived in Western Australia on the schooner *Island Lady* in December 1840. They soon set about mapping the 103,000 acres of land the company had acquired. The work was long and hard, but his team were loyal.

In March 1841, the first group of settlers arrived. The appointed leader, or Chief Commissioner, was Marshall Waller Clifton. Austin was already busy with his party of surveyors, including Robert. Austin's men would later give evidence of his hard work and competence. However, relations between Austin and Clifton soon soured. On 3 August 1841, Mr Austin was fired.

After pointing out that he had wanted the directors to remove Austin for a while, Clifton came to the point in his dismissal letter: 'You have conducted yourself in a disobedient and disrespectful manner to me, your superior and on this day acted in a most disrespectful insulting manner to me in the presence of several of the workmen and labourers.' Austin was terminated with immediate effect and directed to return all unused rations and equipment.

Clifton reported to the directors in London immediately and received a prompt response. Well, 'prompt' is perhaps a relative term. Mail was carried by sailing ship to and from England. Email was some distance in the future; sea mail was the go. On 23 April 1842 the directors responded to Clifton's letter of 5 August 1841, noting that Austin's behaviour had been highly reprehensible, and that Clifton had shown greater forbearance than he deserved.

But events had moved on. Austin had issued a writ against Clifton, claiming six months' wages—£200—for wrongful dismissal. The action was heard before Civil Commissioner Mackie in the Civil Court on 7 December 1841 (a propitious date 100 years later).

The defendant took a technical point first. There was no evidence that the signature on the letter of appointment was that of Mr Buckton, a company official. After some argument and evidence, the commissioner accepted the evidence of the appointment.

The only other point raised was that the defendant should be the company, not Clifton personally. The commissioner intimated a ruling at law that the defendant was liable, whereupon Mr Scholes, appearing for Clifton, indicated that no defence would be offered. Judgment was duly entered for Austin, so, in time-honoured fashion, Mr Scholes asserted he would appeal to the Governor in Council, and Mr Nash, for Austin, responded that his client was being harassed by that threat, and if Clifton did appeal, Austin would appeal to the Privy Council in London.

Clifton does not appear to have been the forgiving kind. A few weeks after the judgment, he wrote: 'The increase of population in this neighbourhood, and with it the occasion and inclination to go to law frequently, seem to me to call for some means of trying civil causes in the district.'

Alas, despite everyone's best efforts, the project failed. The company ran out of funds, as its increasingly despairing letters in response to Clifton's requests attest. By 1843, most of the settlers had taken up other land in the colony more conducive to farming and horse breeding. The township that had been so carefully surveyed was never built.

What happened to the participants? Clifton stayed in the colony, prospered and went into politics. In 1851, Austin senior was appointed Superintendent of Works for the colony, resigning in 1853 to return to England. He was succeeded by Richard Roach Jewell. Robert Austin became a surveyor, and mapped the Murchison Gascoyne district, he and his party nearly dying of thirst in the process.

And Australind? One hundred and fifty years on, it has become a thriving settlement as an outlier to its one-time rival, Bunbury. When driving down the Forrest Highway, turn off at the scenic drive that leads you to the Leschenault Estuary. By its banks you will find a memorial with an etched diagram of the town that might have been.

The Tale of the Troublesome Tractor

In 1904, Mr Holt first tested his steam-powered track-type tractor in Stockton, California. World War I brought track vehicles to prominence, and they were ideal for farming and road works. By the 1920s, a Cletrac track-type tractor was the one to have. The Cletrac Model F was a revolutionary crawler designed for cultivating and other row-crop duties.

'Cletrac Model F is the tractor farmers everywhere have been waiting for since the beginning of the tractor industry,' ads proclaimed. 'A tractor that actually replaces the horse and mule, that will do all the work on the average farm and yet sells at a price the average farmer can afford to pay.'

This tale is about Cletrac tractors in Western Australia, where widely differing views as to their reliability were discussed and litigated. Cletrac tractors were distributed and sold by Messrs Drummond and Dvoretsky, motor vehicle dealers of 42 William Street, Perth.

In 1922 the *Motorist and Wheelman* magazine was anxious to secure firsthand information about the modern tractors working under Australian conditions and dispatched a representative on a tour with Mr Dvoretsky on 24 May 1922. He reported:

> On this first occasion, I had seen the Cletrac in action, I was considerably surprised at its ease of control and the small space it required for turning. Being on the road, the tractor required a supply of fuel to take it the eight-mile journey to the scene of future labours. The

Cletrac made good work with an eight-disk shearer after 180 points of rain. The gentleman in charge of Mr Clements' property, Mr Hamon, arrived on the scene.

To allow Mr Hamon to observe the Cletrac's principles of operation, the writer took charge of the sulky which had conveyed him to the siding, and for about two miles along the road Mr Hamon watched the mechanic on his job. The wheel was then handed over, and without the least difficulty Mr Hamon drove the machine for the remaining six miles to the homestead.

The *Great Southern Herald* of Katanning also sang the praises of the Cletrac tractor on 13 December 1922:

> F.W. Maine has received word from Messrs Drummond and Dvoretsky that they last week received an order from the Peel estate group settlement, for four Cletrac tractors W model for immediate delivery. This speaks volumes as to the merits of this tractor. The first Cletrac received was sold to the Peel estate nine months ago where it has been working continuously at heavy de-scrub, ploughing, drainage and log hauling. Giving no trouble whatever and the account for spares has amounted to just under £5. The tracks were in perfectly good order and show little or no signs of wear.

The *Southwest Times*, in Bunbury, reported on 14 October 1924:

> Last week a demonstration was given by Mr Dvoretsky of Drummond and Dvoretsky, when with Mr C.A.W. Trigwell's Cletrac and a road plough, several chains of road were ploughed in remarkably quick time and according to reports to the entire satisfaction of the large gathering of spectators.

It was said that the Cletrac tractor was as capable of efficiently and economically doing the work of eight horses in hauling a harvester or a seven-furrow plough. It may have been these advertisements and articles, or perhaps the gentle blandishments of Mr Dvoretsky, that persuaded the Sykes to purchase a Cletrac tractor for the considerable sum of £466/11/7. The Sykes farm was at Pithara, just south of Dalwallinu.

The tractor was delivered to the farm on about 11 September 1923. Mr Barnes, an experienced mechanic employed by Drummond and Dvoretsky, was engaged to drive the beast. Sadly, things began to go wrong. First the rivets, then the rings on the rear sprocket became loose and had to be re-bolted. Then the machine shed its bowels into the oil sump, in which small pieces of white metal had been found and subsequently a set screw. Mr Barnes tried to fix it again.

The letters between the Sykes and Drummond show a continuing manifestation of problems, including an intent by Mr Drummond to blame 'unskilful usage was the cause of the troubles'. This argument at trial was given short shrift by Justice Burnside:

> In my judgment the vendors of agricultural machinery for use by the farming community are not entitled to claim immunity on the ground of the want of mechanical skill on the part of the farmer. It is common knowledge that the very recommendation upon which sales are affected is that no special knowledge or machinery is required to operate this class of machine. Their very simplicity is their highest attraction. It is very doubtful whether any such machines would be sold if only skilled mechanics had to be employed to use them.

Justice Burnside may have had in mind an article in *Farm Implements and Tractors* showing an eleven-year-old boy driving a Cletrac. His photograph was captioned 'An experienced hand'. The journal noted: 'During the past season, he took care of 40 acres of oranges on rocky bench land without damaging a single tree and saved his father upwards of 1,000 pounds in labour alone.'

The Cletrac tractor was the subject of other legal actions. Messrs Drummond and Dvoretsky sued Mr Hester and Son, who were orchardists in Bridgetown, for failing to purchase a second-hand tractor or pay for the freight.

Mr Keening, for the plaintiff, conceded that the tractor was delivered in bad condition but contended that the plaintiff had lost no time in replacing worn parts. To do this, new castings had been ordered from Perth, but some had been defective and broken down immediately. Mr Dvoretsky had therefore obtained others from his own farm. In the meantime, the tractor had done all the cultivating that was necessary in the defendant's orchard while waiting for the parts to arrive.

The court, however, found in favour of Mr Hester.

Mr McKenny, described as a farmer of Kojonup, also had a Cletrac tractor. He was unhappy with it. He offered Mr Barnes a fiver if he could make the tractor go for two hours. However, the tractor 'went bung' after running for three-quarters of an hour. Mr McKenny required the tractor for the purpose of fulfilling contracts into which he had entered for sinking dams. He said, 'It is of no use to him whatever it will not work. It is not a machine that can economically work a dam, sinking or farming.' Judgment was given, again, against Messrs Drummond and Dvoretsky.

The *Sunday Times* on 6 July 1924 reported on Mr Barnes' new enthusiasm:

> [T]he first privately owned aeroplane in the State is the 110hp Sea Cone, recently purchased by Mr F.J. Barnes, who proposes utilising it for business purposes in the eastern Wheatbelt. Mr Barnes was until recently, connected with the firm of Drummond and Dvoretsky in Perth but is now located in Kwulyn.

Maybe his tribulations with Cletrac tractors caused him to seek solace in the skies.

Messrs Drummond and Dvoretsky seem to have survived the litigious tangle. On 19 February 1930, the *Daily News* reported: 'Mr Dvoretsky of Messrs Drummond and Dvoretsky, the Agents for Cletrac tractors, will combine business and pleasure on a trip to Sydney.'

Gradually, track vehicles lost favour to tractors with tyres, which were more versatile and easier to fit among the seed rows. After World

War II, track vehicles regained some popularity as West Australians cleared a million acres a year to open land for farming. Much bushland was cleared by stringing a chain between two former tanks.

Such is progress. The impact of tracks on our soil remains in the degradation of marginal land and the effect on the climate.

The Tale of the Burning Bus

A lady crossed her legs.

From this inconsequential movement, like the proverbial butterfly fluttering its wings and causing a hurricane on the other side of the world, the dogged owner of a bus company and the respected owner of a leather goods manufacturer came face to face in a courtroom before Justice Abbott of the Supreme Court of South Australia.

It happened on 3 September 1945. War had ended. Ray McGuire finished his schooner at the Windsor Castle Hotel, near Victoria Square in Adelaide, and took a seat on a Choat Bus Company Fageol bus for his homeward journey to Aldgate, in the Adelaide Hills.

McGuire was a wild lad in his youth, having several brushes with the law, but by 1945 had settled into the trade of boot repairer. He carried three parcels with him. Two contained boots and the third a quantity of rubber strips, shoe-repairing nails and finishing ink. Oh, and a quart tin of Demon Sole Cement.

He walked down the aisle to the back of the bus, and there he sat in the centre of the long bench seat. Putting two parcels by his feet and the third containing the bits and pieces on his lap, he made himself comfortable and began to read the evening paper.

But not for long. As the bus grew more crowded, passengers began filling the bench seat. A young lady sat down next to McGuire. Trying for a more comfortable position, she crossed her legs. Unfortunately, in so doing, she bumped McGuire and the third package fell from his knees.

What a mess. The lid of the tin of Demon Sole Cement came off, spilling its contents over the floor. McGuire did his best to clean up, using his newspaper to mop the sticky mess. He managed to soak up most of the liquid. Other passengers, once keen to sit at the back, now moved forward to other seats. Windows were opened to let out the smell. The bus continued its journey, leaving McGuire in a puddle of misery and Demon Sole Cement.

About 6.20 pm, the bus had wheezed its way up past Eagle Mountain on the hill to Stirling. Here McGuire planned to alight. He also had another light in mind. He put a cigarette in his mouth—and struck a match.

'Before I got near the cigarette, there was enough fire to light 10,000 cigarettes,' he said later. 'The flame had a sputtering shooting effect ... my trousers were burnt and singed up to the knee.'

The bus stopped immediately and the few remaining passengers quickly evacuated. Gathering buckets of water and bags, they tried desperately to put out the fire. To no avail. Perhaps they should have tried sand to smother it, as Justice Abbott, in an impressive display of hindsight, later suggested.

Although McGuire claimed to have made some scatterbrained attempt to put out the fire, the driver's evidence was that he, the driver, was the last to leave the bus, which, according to Justice Abbott, relieved the occasion of any fancied resemblance to the exploit of Casabianca ('The boy stood on the burning deck, whence all but he had fled ...').

Now, actions for product liability had received a boost ever since a mischievous snail climbed into a bottle of beer in Paisley, Scotland. Mr Choat, whose bus it was, consulted lawyers including a future Chief Justice of South Australia, Dr Bray. They recommended suing in tort for a dangerous and defective product. An action was launched against Julius Cohn & Co., a leather goods manufacturer run by the founder's son Jack.

Julius Cohn & Co. purchased Ajax Cement in five-gallon tins, which the firm sold in quart tins as Demon Sole Cement. The Ajax tins were marked 'Highly Inflammable—Flash point 60'. The Demon Sole Cement tins bore no such warning.

The trial ran for eight days and judgment was delivered on Christmas Eve, 1947. It was not an early Christmas present for Mr Choat, who lost. Justice Abbott found no negligence on the part of Julius Cohn & Co. He found that Demon Sole Cement would not burn even if a lighted taper was held to it. However, it would blaze merrily if lit by a match.

In reaching this conclusion, he conducted experiments with an expert. He also had a view of a boot factory, where employees dropped burning cigarette ends and matches without any fear, despite the constant smell. Justice Abbott rejected any notion that the tin lid was defective.

So Mr Choat lost both his bus and his lawsuit.

Founded with his wife, Ruth, in 1927 to provide a service between Mount Barker and Adelaide, Mr Choat's bus company had grown even through the Depression years. A backward step was taken in 1935, when he was sent to gaol for defrauding the state revenue by forging tickets, but by 1945 the business was well established and had a dozen buses (less of course one Fageol).

When he died in 1970, Mr Choat was still in the family business. He was survived by Ruth, five children, seventeen grandchildren and one great-grandson. The Choat Bus Company was taken over by the Transport Authority later in the 1970s.

Julius Cohn & Co., founded in 1899, was taken over by a larger leather goods company in the early 1950s. Jack Cohn stayed on for a time.

In 1950, McGuire was drinking with a mate with his rifle leaning up against the bar. While he went on an errand, his mate stole it. Perhaps he should have used some Demon Sole Cement to fasten it to the floor.

A Tale of Boys and Sugar

It was the grimmest of times. In dead of night, armed men would steal into houses and kidnap men and boys. They would be herded onto ships and sent across the seas to work as indentured slaves on cotton plantations. Many died from the gruelling work, which was twelve hours a day, from sunrise to sunset. Boys, some as young as twelve, quickly succumbed to the heat and disease. The plantation owners, jealous of their profits, fought measures to bring the trade under control. There was talk of secession.

No, dear reader, we're not talking about the Deep South of the United States but the Far North of Queensland, Australia. In 1869 the *Leeds Mercury* condemned Queensland as a slaveholding country like a second Carolina.

As time passed, cotton plantations gave way to sugarcane plantations. The trade in men and boys remained. The 'blackbirders', as they were called, continued to bring in labourers from Pacific islands, tempting them with lies or using force.

Legislation was brought in to regulate the labour and provide some measure of protection for the Pacific islanders, sometimes called *kanakas*.

The *Polynesian Labourers Act 1868* was an attempt to regulate the human trade. It was largely unsuccessful due to constitutional restraints. It had no application beyond the Queensland border. In 1972 the British parliament passed the *Pacific Islanders Protection Act*, which had greater success.

The *Polynesian Labourers Act* was more effective domestically. It provided for inspections and imposed fines for breaches. The union movement pressed for prosecution of employers who breached the act. Liberal-minded public servants such as Richard Bingham Sheridan were sympathetic to the plight of the indentured workers. Even so, they were often treated like slaves and rented out to other plantation owners.

On 27 January 1877, Mr Sheridan, a Polynesian inspector, visited Charleville Station, managed by Mr Henry Paul, and spoke with the owner, Mr Arthur Paul. It was soon established that four youths and boys, Bambumbo, Bebbee, Horse and Nearlanley, had been lent to Charleville Station from another business, Corser & Co., for £14 a week, but no labour transfer document could be found. Mr Henry Paul thought £14 was too dear, as the boys were too young for the price. He was under the impression that his brother was only paying Corser & Co. four shillings a week. Henry Paul thought the whole transaction was most improper and would soon be remedied. The boys had been ten months on the other plantation and had no clothes issued to them.

Arthur Paul was charged with failing to report to the local magistrate as to any transfer of labour from Corser & Co. to Charleville Station.

On 8 February 1877 the charge came before the Maryborough police magistrate, Henry Reginald Buttenshaw. He is recorded as having been born at sea off the island of Tristan da Cunha. Mr Buttenshaw had started as a clerk of courts but by 1877 had been a police magistrate for many years. He seems to have been popular and humane. When he left Roma for Maryborough in December 1872, the inhabitants of Roma presented him with a testimonial consisting of a claret jug and silver salver.

The defendant pleaded not guilty. The first witness was the inspector, Mr Sheridan. It was the next witness who caused the trouble.

Mr Buttenshaw left the bench and entered the witness box, deposing that no report had been made to him respecting the employment of any Polynesians. While this evidence was being given, the bench was occupied by F. Bryant Esquire JP. He had not been present for Mr Sheridan's evidence.

After taking evidence from Mr Henry Paul on behalf of the defendant, the magistrate convicted Arthur Paul, who was fined £10 for each labourer. That is over $11,000 in today's money.

Notice of appeal was promptly given, and on 13 March 1877 the In Banco, or Full Court, consisting of Cockle CJ and Justices Lutwiche and Lilley, unanimously allowed the appeal on the simple ground that the magistrate had not been present throughout the hearing. Nor had Mr Bryant. (In this, the court anticipated the result in 'The Tale of the Parsimonious Pearler' by nearly forty years.)

The judicial disapproval does not seem to have hurt Mr Buttenshaw's career. In 1880 he was appointed as an assistant immigration agent and inspector of Polynesians at Maryborough. Mr Sheridan had by then retired to pursue a political career as an ally of Samuel Griffiths.

Mr Buttenshaw noted publicly that 'it is dishonourable to the colony that the lives of Kanakas should be so wasted'.

In a parliamentary debate on the Pacific Islanders Labourers Bill on 29 October 1880, the age of the labourers was discussed. It was noted that the present age of sixteen years had failed, as more boys had been brought to the colony and put to fieldwork: 'It was no doubt a fact that lads were torn from their homes before their physical power was developed.' Mr Buttenshaw informed parliament that the low age at which boys were introduced to labour increased the death rate.

The bill passed into law and included compulsory healthcare. A hospital for the care of Pacific islanders (one of four) was built at Tirana, not far from Maryborough. The hospital and adjacent cemetery are now heritage-listed.

Mr Buttenshaw left Maryborough in 1886 to become a relieving magistrate, before passing away in Cooktown on 17 October 1888.

North Queensland continued to fight controls over the Pacific islander trade until the newly established Commonwealth parliament passed the *Pacific Islanders Labourers Act 1901*. Enacted in part to further the White Australia policy, it nevertheless ended the human trafficking of Pacific islanders.

But not before North Queensland threatened to secede above the 22nd parallel over the abolition of Pacific islander labour. Might Australia's history have taken a different turn and followed the United States into civil war over slavery?

The Tale of the Bag of Money

It was the time of the Great Depression. Thousands were out of work. The Depression hit governments hard as well: New Zealand was forced to limit the export of silver money, especially to Australia, where it commanded a premium. Naturally the temptation to smuggle was alluring. And so begins our story.

Sam Willey, a rigger by trade, was lucky. He found work as a boatswain on SS *Paiko*, a cargo and passenger ship, part of a fleet owned by the New Zealand Shipping Co. A boatswain is responsible for rigging, equipment and general maintenance. The boatswain is effectively chief of the deck crew.

In 1933, the *Paiko* left Newport News, Virginia, for Melbourne, calling at Dunedin, New Zealand. She carried cargo but no passengers. On 18 August 1933 she left Dunedin. Three days later, Mr Willey was carrying out a routine inspection when something in the forepeak caught his eye. There was a tarpaulin where no tarpaulin should be. He lifted a flap to discover a vegetable bag. Inside the bag were English silver coins totalling £355 and five shillings. The boatswain was an honest man. He immediately reported his find to the captain, who took the bag and put it in the ship's safe until they reached port. On arrival in Melbourne, the captain reported the find to the Controller of Customs, Mr Maurice Synan.

Mr Synan had joined the Victorian customs service in 1898, the year of Mr Willey's birth. He transferred to the Commonwealth customs service on Federation, and had enjoyed a distinguished career.

He decided that the bag of money would be forfeited to the Common-wealth. The shipping company, the government of New Zealand and Mr Willey all lodged claims to the money, but after a time the others withdrew, leaving only Mr Willey to pursue his claim.

This was a matter of federal jurisdiction. There was no Federal Court of Australia, so Mr Willey lodged his claim in the High Court. Matters proceeded at a leisurely pace, and it wasn't until 30 October 1936 that the action was heard before Justice Starke.

By this time, two events of significance had occurred. First, Mr Willey, who had been living in Leichhardt, New South Wales, returned to England with his new wife. Of course there were no video facilities back then such as Zoom or Teams, and returning in person was too expensive, so Mr Willey was unable to give evidence at the hearing. This was to prove decisive.

The second event was that Mr Synan, after watching a cricket match, suffered a heart attack and died on 8 January 1936. He was sixty.

Unusually, then, neither party was present to hear Justice Starke, after a short hearing, dismiss Mr Willey's claim. Even though Mr Willey had told the captain he found the bag of money, and the captain had told the customs officers, that evidence was inadmissible. There was no direct evidence that Mr Willey had actually found the bag.

Mr Willey fared no better on the appeal, which was heard by the High Court in February 1937. Mr Willey had a supporter. Justice Evatt, always one for the underdog, would have allowed the appeal. But the other judges would not. Justice Dixon noted that the bag of money was not lost. It was stored where the owner or agent could fetch it. Justice Rich had no doubt that the silver was anything but lost. The embarrassment to the owner had proved sufficient to prevent him from coming forward and claiming the bag. That did not give Mr Willey possession, and anyway the evidence was inadmissible.

So the matter ended. The Commonwealth was enriched by £355 and five shillings. The honest boatswain, Mr Willey, lived in London for the rest of his days, passing away in 1976 at the age of seventy-seven.

On 18 May 1941, en route from Albany, Western Australia, to Freetown, Sierra Leone, the *Paiko* was torpedoed off the coast of Liberia by German U-boat 107, with the loss of ten lives.

In the course of his judgment, Justice Rich noted that 'the Commonwealth have the advantage of coming within the apothegm *Beati possidentes*,[10] which, if it is not a legal maxim, embodies a legal truth'. To which might be added another legal truth: *Nunquam inter imperium et sacculum pecuniae.*[11]

---

10 'Blessed are the possessors'.

11 'Never get between the government and a bag of money'.

The Tale of the Ditch

Douglas Stuart Wylie may have been a little overprotective of his rubber plantation near the village of Sangara, east of Kokoda, Papua New Guinea. But then again, maybe he had good reason. Over the years, the Sangara Rubber Plantation Ltd had survived many challenges. Formed in 1935 after failure first of a cocoa plantation, then of a sugar plantation, it nestled in a valley between Kokoda to the west and Mount Lamington to the east. Sangara was a small village, home to the Orokavia people.

After switching to rubber trees, the company appointed Aubrey Eric Simpson as a manager. He was a colourful character. In 1932 he and another man were charged with assault and acquitted after the chief prosecution witness said neither of the accused should be in the dock. The jury said they had heard enough evidence and returned a verdict of not guilty without leaving the court. Mr Simpson also was cleared of a charge of false pretences in 1933 by jury verdict.

Unfortunately, personal matters began to intrude into his working life as manager, and on 18 November 1941 Mr Simpson literally blew his brains out with a shotgun in Adelaide.

D.S. Wylie, an accountant who had tended to the company since its cocoa days, then became manager as well as secretary. Three weeks later, the Imperial Japanese Navy bombed Pearl Harbor and Australia was at war with Japan.

The Japanese in due course invaded Papua New Guinea. On 28 July 1942, D.S. Wylie, by then in Sydney, described what we now know as the Kokoda Track. He said that only a narrow path, which in some places winds steeply around the sides of precipitous mountains, is available to the Japanese in their progress from Awala to Kokoda. By then the Japanese had pushed through to Sangara and occupied the plantation. The war years were brutal to the plantation workers.

After the war, D.S. Wylie took back control of the plantation and set about recommencing production. In 1947 an enterprising salesman purported to sell off pieces of the plantation. A prosecution for false pretences ended in an acquittal, despite D.S. Wylie's evidence.

Then came 21 January 1951. Mount Lamington, long thought to be dormant, exploded. Due to the topography, the rubber plantation and its neighbours were largely undamaged, but the pyroclastic flow killed nearly 3000 people, including most of the population of Sangara. As Papua New Guinea was under Australian control at the time, it is the largest civilian tragedy in Australian history.

In 1956, D.S. Wylie survived an attempt to remove him as manager by dissident shareholders, described contemptuously as Pitt Street farmers.

And at last we come to 1957. By now D.S. Wylie had moved from Sydney to Papua New Guinea and lived on the plantation as manager. His next-door neighbour, L.W. Stevens, owned a plantation called Enbaubo.

L.W. Stevens had survived the Mount Lamington explosion, though his Jeep had not. By 1957 he had acquired another Jeep, which he used to drive into Popondetta, a nearby town/ He sometimes gave a lift to friends of his who worked on D.S. Wylie's Sangara Plantation.

L.W. Stevens' house was close to the plantation's boundaries, and for some time he would drive through the Sangara Plantation (it was unfenced) to get to the government road. Until 7 September 1957. On that day, L.W. Stevens drove along the Sangara Plantation Road until he came to a barricade with a sign reading 'No admittance'. D.W. Wylie was entertaining visitors at his house a short distance away. L.W. Stevens asked him to remove the barricade. No dice.

During the next week, L.W. Stevens cleared a track from the boundary to the Sangara Plantation Road. The cleared track ended at the boundary, where tyre tracks had guided the way through the Sangara Plantation to the government road.

On 14 September, L.W. Stevens drove with some friends to Popondetta. As lawyers would say, his licence to drive through the Sangara Plantation had been revoked. He was a trespasser but he drove through anyway.

As soon as L.W. Stevens had gone, D.S. Wylie sprung to action. He gathered up his wife and a couple of workers and headed to where the track entered his plantation. Carefully, he supervised the building of a ditch across the tyre marks that he knew L.W. Stevens would follow. The ditch was twelve feet long, three feet wide and three feet (about a metre) deep. Then D.S. Wylie ordered that the ditch be covered with leaves so that it was invisible. The trap was set.

It was 2 am when L.W. Stevens set off to drive his friends back to their homes. In his Jeep. Off he went down the newly cleared track to the boundary. Without stopping, he followed the tyre marks. It was a dark night. Bang. The Jeep fell into the pit. L.W. Stevens was injured. His friends, though shaken, were not. The Jeep was significantly damaged.

D.S. Wylie had got his message across well and truly. No admittance to the Sangara Plantation. No short cuts.

No doubt he was, for a time, pleased at his effort. The trap had worked perfectly and had caught the Jeep. There would be no more trespassing onto Sangara property by his erstwhile friend. However, L.W. Stevens sued D.S. Wylie in the Supreme Court of Papua New Guinea.

The judge held that L.W. Stevens was a trespasser and entitled to no separate duty of care. But deliberately setting a trap by digging a ditch where D.S. Wylie knew that his neighbour would come was beyond the pale. D.S. Wylie was not entitled to create a retributive danger. L.W. Stevens recovered damages for his minor injuries and for the repair of his Jeep.

Despite D.S. Wylie's best efforts, the Sangara Rubber Plantation was wound up in 1962.

Acknowledgements

The collection of quirky cases contained in this book could not have been written until there was general access to judgments from years gone by.

The Australian Law Information Institute—Austlii—has as its purpose improving access to justice through access to legal information. Established jointly in 1995 by the law schools of the University of Technology Sydney and the University of New South Wales, it is an invaluable resource, aggregating publicly available legal information from the earliest days of colonial settlement to current judgments from the High Court and courts and tribunals throughout the Commonwealth.

With a little effort, much background can be found on Trove, a website operated by the National Library of Australia. The National Library of New Zealand provides a similar comprehensive service. Newspaper accounts at the time give context to some of the cases and insights into the people involved.

The Battye Library contains microfiche copies of West Australian newspapers. These are invaluable if you already know where to look. Unfortunately, there are no search facilities.

I acknowledge and thank the custodians of these invaluable sources.

My special thanks go to those long-departed jurists who endeavoured faithfully, sometimes in difficult circumstances. Their judgments are often as fresh and learned as those given today—though considerably shorter.

In the memoir that precedes the quirky cases, I have relied mainly on my own recollections. As judges know better than most, memory may be a false guide. Where possible, I have supported my memory by reference to contemporary accounts published in newspapers and judgments, particularly from appeal courts.

'The Tale of the Bootleg Brewer' was adapted from *Presley v Geraghty* [1921] 29 CLR 154.

'The Tale of the Alarming Affidavit' was adapted from *Re Estate of Singh* [1921] NTJ 4.

'The Tale of the Suicidal Shopkeeper' was adapted from *Bunyan v Jordan* (1937) 57 CLR 1.

'The Tale of the Telephone Line' was adapted from *Dalgano v Hannah* (1903) 3 SR NSW 494; *Dalgano v Hannah* (1903) 1CLR 1.

'The Tale of the Herbalist' was adapted from *Stephens v Jayasinga* (1913) 15 WALR 55.

'The Tale of the Disaffected Law Students' was adapted from *Victoria University of Wellington Students Association v Shearer* (1974) 2 NZLR; *Victoria University of Wellington Students Association v Shearer* CA 31/73.

'The Tale of the Pregnant Passenger' was adapted from *De Pledge v Australasian United Steam Navigation Company Ltd* (1904) SALR

'The Tale of the Amorous Gardener' was adapted from *Magill v Magill* [2003] HCA 51, 226 CLR 551; *Ah Chuck v Needham* (1931) NZLR 559.

'The Tale of the School that Disappeared' was adapted from *The Proprietary Schools of Western Australia Ltd v The Crown* (1944) 46 WALP 37). Grateful acknowledgment to the Battye Library and 'A brief history of Woodbridge House School, East Guildford 1921–1941'.

'The Tale of the Burning Bag' was adapted from *Eastern Asia Navigation Company Ltd v Fremantle Harbour Trust Commissioners and The Commonwealth of Australia* (1949) 51 WALR 94; *Eastern Asia Navigation Company Ltd v Fremantle Harbour Trust Commissioners* (1951) 83 CLR 353.

'The Tale of the Prevaricating Witness' was adapted from *Morriss v Withers* (1954) VLR 100.

'The Tale of the Interminable Divorce' was adapted from *Dorn v Dorn and Nicholson* 9LR (NSW) D1; *Dorn v Dorn and Nicholson* 8LR (NSW) D2; *Dorn v Dorn and Nicholson* 9LR (NSW) D17; *Dorn v Dorn and Nicholson* 9LR (NSW) D7; newspaper articles in Trove.

'A Mouse Tail: Mickey Mouse Goes to Court' was adapted from *Radio Corporation Pty Ltd v Disney* (1937) 57 CLR 448.

'The Tale of the Boy Who Was Stolen' was adapted from *Ex Parte West* [1861] NSWLeggeSC 32.

'The Tale of the Trampled Tomatoes' was adapted from *Kratochvil v Dall* (1956) 57 WALR 55.

'The Tale of the Unfortunate Letter' was adapted from *Kidd v Horgan* (1930) 32 WAR 117.

'The Tale of the Pub with No Gents' was adapted from *Mountnay v Smith* (1903) 3 SR (NSW) 688; *Mountnay v Smith* (1904) 1 CLR 146; *R v Dyktor* 7 December 1909.

'The Tale of the Defamed Drover' was adapted from *Blood v Barlow* (1907) SACR 136; 'Clancy of the Overflow' (1889), A.B. Paterson.

'The Tale of Pannikin to Prison' was adapted from *Namatjira v Raabe* (1958) NTJ 608.

'The Tale of the Lawyer Who Leaped' was adapted from *In the Will of Colville Oliver Parslow* (Walker J 31 April 1951) and various articles in the *West Australian*.

'The Tale of the Missing Brooch that Wasn't' was adapted from *Langan v Clark* (1889) VLR 252.

'The Tale of the Tardy Coroner' was adapted from *Ex p. Collier* (1877) NSW Knox R 513.

'The Tale of the Late-Night Traveller' was adapted from *Shair Mahomet v The Commissioner of Railways* (1902) 5 WALR 107.

'The Tale of the Prohibited Passenger' was adapted from *Schuiling v Krau* (1977) PNGLR 176.

'The Tale of the Student in a Bind' was adapted from *Minister for Education v Moreschini* [1965] WASC 40.

'The Tale of the Parsimonious Pearler' was adapted from *Ah Mat Siam v Holmes* (1915) 17 WAR 197.

'The Tale of the Biased Beak' was adapted from *Story v Quelch* [1924] NTJ 46.

'The Tale of the Naughty Neighers' was adapted from *Munro v Southern Dairies Ltd* (1955) VLR 332.

'The Tale of the Trickster Tippler' was adapted from *Kelly v Brooks* (1975) NTJ 927.

'The Tale of the Famous Button Seller' was adapted from *Doyle v Jones* (1952) 54 WALR 1.

'The Tale of the Superior Shamrock Whiskey' was adapted from *Kirker Greer & Co Ltd v Mayman* (1901) 1NSWR 73.

'The Tale of a Lost Invitation' was adapted from *Gilles v Pugh* [1842] TASSSupC 24.

'The Tale of the Jealous Doctor' was adapted from *Pugh v Haygath* [1843] TASSupC 1.

'The Tale of the Naughty Comic Books' was adapted from *Transport Publishing Co Pty Ltd v Literature Board of Review* (1956) 99 CLR 111.

'The Tale of the Persistent Customs Officer' was adapted from *Ah On and Ah Con v Williamson and Pickett* (1925) 28 WAR 74: *Williamson v Ah On* (1926) 39 CLR 95.

'The Tale of the Shattered Skiff' was adapted from *Streather v Clarence and Richmond Rivers Steam Navigation Company Pty Ltd* (1887) Knox's Reports 453.

'The Tale of the Short-Changed Surveyor' was adapted from *Austin v Clifton* [1841] WASupC 29.

'The Tale of the Troublesome Tractor' was adapted from *McKenny v Drummond Dvoretsky* (1926) 29 WAR 6: *Sykes v Drummond Dvoretsky* (1925) 27 WAR 126.

'The Tale of the Burning Bus' was adapted from *Choat v Cohn* (1948) SASR 21; 'Casabianca' (1826) Felicia Hemans; other articles from Trove.

'A Tale of Boys and Sugar' was adapted from *Paul v Buttenshaw* (1877) 1 QLR (Beor) (Pt 2) 4; Newspaper articles retrieved from Trove; Queensland Parliamentary Debates, 29 October 1880.

'The Tale of the Bag of Money' was adapted from *Willey v Synan* (1935) 54 CLR 175; *Willey v Synan* (1937) 57 CLR 201.

'The Tale of the Ditch' was adapted from *Stevens v Wylie* (1959) PGSC 25.

About Upswell

Upswell Publishing was established in
2021 by Terri-ann White as a not-for-profit
press. A perceived gap in the market for
distinctive literary works in fiction, poetry
and narrative non-fiction was the motivation.
In her years as a bookseller, writer and then
publisher, Terri-ann has maintained a watch
on literary books and the way they insinuate
themselves into a cultural space and are
then located within our literary and cultural
inheritance. She is interested in making books
to last: books with the potential to still be
noticed, and noted, after decades and thus
be ripe to influence new literary histories.

About this typeface

Book designer Becky Chilcott chose
Foundry Origin not only as a strong,
carefully considered, and dependable
typeface, but also to honour her late
friend and mentor, type designer Freda
Sack, who oversaw the project. Designed
by Freda's long-standing colleague,
Stuart de Rozario, much like Upswell
Publishing, Foundry Origin was created
out of the desire to say something new.